FORM AND CONTENT IN CHILDREN'S HUMAN FIGURE DRAWINGS

KAREN VIBEKE MORTENSEN

Form and Content in Children's Human Figure Drawings

Development, Sex Differences, and Body Experience

New York University Press   New York and London

Library of Congress Cataloging-in-Publication Data
Mortensen, Karen Vibeke, 1936–
    Form and content in children's figure drawings : development, sex
differences, and body experience / Karen Vibeke Mortensen.
        p.   cm.
    Revision of the author's dissertation, originally published:
Children's human figure drawings. 1984.
    Includes bibliographical references and index.
    ISBN 0-8147-5456-2 (alk. paper)
    1. Children's drawings—Psychological aspects.   2. Sex differences
(Psychology) in children.   3. Personality assessment in children.
I. Mortensen, Karen Vibeke, 1936–   Children's human figure
drawings. II. Title.
BF723.D7M69   1990
155.4—dc20   90-37231
                    CIP

New York University Press books are printed on acid-free paper,
and their binding materials are chosen for strength and durability.

Book design by Ken Venezio

Contents

Preface

Children's drawings have probably always attracted interest because of their immediate emotional appeal; but only for about a century they have been subjected to systematic, scientific studies.

Among the numerous subjects children draw, the human figure has always held a prominent place, and the same is true in the research on children's drawings. It has always been sensed more or less intuitively that children in their drawings of human beings give important messages both about themselves and about their experience of other persons. But the understanding and interpretation of these messages have varied over time.

The present book has its roots both in the immediate fascination of children's drawings and in the scientific tradition, hoping to combine the best aspects of both in a fruitful way. Without fascination the work becomes tedious and dull; on the other hand, there are plenty of examples showing that without the necessary scientific discipline, explanations and interpretations can run wild, following their authors' personal preferences and prejudices.

This book concentrates entirely on the drawings of human beings. It has its starting point in the different and sometimes conflicting interpretations of children's human figure drawings, and in the obvious sex differences, which seemed neither well described nor understood. More specifically, it builds on my doctoral dissertation "Children's Human Figure Drawings," which was published in 1984 by Dansk Psykologisk Forlag in Copenhagen. It is based on the empirical studies of 540 human figure drawings made by 180 Danish children, 5 through 13 years of age. These drawings were described in as detailed and precise a way as possible. The detailed description is not by itself very valuable, however, if not related to sufficiently broad and encompassing psychological theories. The theoretical foundation has often been inadequate in studies on drawings. It is understandable when it is seen how many and different theories are necessary to do justice to the drawings. The drawing of a human figure is a most complicated enterprise, involving such different aspects of the drawer's personality as his concept formation, sexual identity and body experience, his perceptual, motoric, cognitive, and emotional skills.

The combination of the precise descriptions and the wide theoretical range resulted in a dissertation which was burdened by much detailed documentation and, probably, not very tempting to more than a narrow group of professionals. It was my wish to be able to write a book which was kinder to the reader and yet could convey the message clearly enough. This has now been made possible. The present book concentrates on the main results of the study, including the theoretical parts, while the methodological elements and some less central findings have been left out. Those interested in the scoring manual for the drawings and in the detailed results are referred to the original dissertation, which contains this information. The text of the present book is slightly abbreviated and the literature updated.

I am grateful to chief psychologist Alice Theilgaard, Rigshospitalet in Copenhagen, and Professor Leo Goldberger, New York University, for their support of this book. Among the staff of New York University Press, I want to thank senior editor Kitty Moore and editors Jason Renker and Despina P. Gimbel, who have helped me with the preparation of the manuscript and have patiently undertaken the long-distance communication across the sea.

KAREN VIBEKE MORTENSEN

COPENHAGEN

Introduction

The background of the present book lies in my many years of work as a clinical psychologist, in which, among other tools, I have used drawings of a human figure for assessment of children. In this work I was struck by the seemingly paradoxical fact that the exact same subject—the human figure—was used by psychologists for two quite different purposes:

1. as a measure of the drawer's intellectual function (the Goodenough/Harris Draw-A-Man Test) (1963) and
2. as a projective test, revealing the drawer's personality, with special weight on drives and defence mechanisms.

The usefulness of each of these applications of drawings was advanced with equal conviction by the proponents of each. As it was, I was not content with either of the systems. The method for the use of drawings as a measure of intelligence is carefully described and easy to apply; but it is apparent that drawings contain a lot of information which is simply lost by this use of them alone. And often it was precisely the apparently superfluous and irrelevant traits that seemed to constitute the most fascinating and immediately interesting aspects of the drawings.

In the projective use of drawings, many of the more individual aspects of the figures are included in the assessment; however, this method suffers from other shortcomings, first and foremost from a lack of knowledge of normal children's drawings. This may sound surprising in view of the great amount of knowledge about normal children's drawings which forms the basis for the use of drawings as an intelligence test. But these studies have selected limited aspects of the total drawings, which are different from the aspects used in the projective test. The risk exists, therefore, that traits which normally occur in children's drawings are considered signs of pathology. This risk of erroneous judgment is particularly great because most of the studies on drawing as a projective tool are made on adults, and inferences cannot as a matter of course be drawn as to the drawings of children. On the whole, this use of drawings suffers from a considerable uncertainty with regard to both reliability and validity.

Not only have earlier researchers on drawings had different goals, but the methods applied have also differed. In the studies of drawings as an intelligence test, large collections of drawings from normal children have been collected, statistical methods have been employed, and age norms, averages, and standard deviations have been established. The interest has centered on general traits.

In the studies of drawings as a personality test, emphasis has been on the detailed study of single drawings and on strictly individual traits. Drawings have mainly been collected from patients, and the goal has been the understanding of the single individual with little reference to norms.

Also the applied theories have varied. In the systematic studies of large numbers of drawings, the use of more general theories has on the whole been surprisingly scarce, but when used, they have been drawn from general or developmental psychology. Drawings have been related to language or concept formation, or to such general theories as Gestalt theory or organismic theory. In the studies of drawings as a projective technique, the choice has almost exclusively been psychoanalytic theory, both in the early Freudian and in later, more ego-oriented versions. The two approaches have often contrasted sharply with each other, and surprisingly rarely have attempts been made to try to bridge the gap between them.

These differences are, of course, not accidental, but are the consequences of a difference in the rationales behind the two applications of drawings. When used as a measure of intellectual maturity, drawing is seen as a mainly cognitively determined activity, reflecting the conceptual development of the child. The ultimate goal of drawing development becomes the lifelike depiction of the human beings which the child visually perceives around him. The closer the child comes to this ideal, the more highly will his drawing be evaluated.

When used as a projective test, drawing is seen as a reflection of the child's personality, of his subjective experience of what it feels like from the inside to be a human being. In this way drawing is seen as determined as much by kinesthetic and other bodily sensations as by vision, and such aspects as body image, body concept, and self-concept become central. The visually correct drawing is no longer considered the ideal, but this does not mean that normative considerations are not implicit. Instead of "realism," however, such dimensions as normality/pathology become relevant.

Another aspect of human figure drawings which attracted my interest and which seemed to be connected to the question of what drawings actually express, was their very outspoken sex differences. These sex differences have never been satisfactorily described, let alone explained.

Both the different diagnostic uses of drawings and the sex differences point to a basic question concerning drawings. The drawing of a human being is a subject which can be approached from two angles: (1) from the outside, so that the drawing expresses the drawer's (mainly visual) perception of what other persons in his surroundings look like, or (2) from the inside, so that the drawing is seen as determined by the drawer's inner experience of what it feels like to be a human being. This question is not necessarily limited to the drawings of human figures, as all subjects may be regarded as symbolic representations of the drawer's inner self; but human figure drawings present the problem most unavoidably and lend themselves more easily to investigations of the question. So, during the work with the drawings, this fundamental question gradually became more and more important. From the beginning, I was convinced that it is a question of both/and rather than either/or; but in the psychological use of drawings, as described, the tendency has been to separate the two aspects completely.

In order to attempt to answer these questions, I designed an empirical study of development and sex differences in normal Danish children's drawings of human figures. The study was designed as follows:

DESIGN OF THE STUDY

Ten normal children of each sex at each age level from 5 through 13 years of age each made three drawings of a human figure, a figure of either sex and a drawing of themselves. This gave a total of 180 children (90 boys and 90 girls) and 540 drawings. The drawings were obtained from children in schools and kindergartens in a suburb of Copenhagen. The sample of children was not intended to be representative of Danish children in general. Please also note that, for stylistic convenience, I refer to a child of unspecified sex throughout this book by the generic "he," although the reader should understand that "he or she" is meant.

The drawings were scored according to a very comprehensive scoring system devised by myself. The system comprises both content and formal variables and both the variables from the use of drawings as an intelligence test and those from the use of them as a projective test. In addition, other traits were included, particularly those that were found to show sex differences. Actually, it was attempted to score the drawings as completely as possible. A total of 268 variables were included. At the same time, great care was taken to objectify the scoring as much as possible. The reliability of the scoring was examined and found to be satisfactory. The data were computerized and significant age- and sex-differences described. The chi^2-test was used as a screening instrument, with the 5% level used as the limit of significance. The course of development was examined separately for the sexes. In the study of sex differences all age groups were combined, as the material was regarded as too small to allow the comparison of sex differences for the single age groups. Those interested in a more detailed description of methods and results are referred to the original dissertation (Mortensen 1984) which also contains a detailed scoring manual and tables of results.

THE PRESENT BOOK

The original study suffered from the necessity of giving the detailed documentation of the results. This resulted in a work burdened by many tables and difficult to read for those who are interested in the ideas more than in the exact evidence for them.

In the present book, I have tried to avoid this danger by omitting these details, hoping that the readers will trust that they have been adequately controlled. The scoring manual has been omitted, as well as all the tables of results, appendices, etc. The text has generally been tightened and a few chapters left out. At the same time, as a few years have passed since the publication of the original study, the literature has been updated.

This book contains three main parts, the first of which treats the earlier literature on human figure drawings. It consists of four chapters. Chapter 1 describes studies of drawing development related to chronological age. Chapter 2 describes drawing development in relation to mental age, including the most frequently used drawing test of intelligence, Goodenough's (1926) Draw-A-Man test, its revision by Harris (1963), and further studies on both versions. Chapter 3 treats some of the fundamental questions arising from the use of drawings as a projective tool. The research in this field is extensive, and no attempt has been made to include it all. The purpose has been to outline some of the principles behind this use of drawing and some of the main problems connected with it. Finally, the last chapter in this part treats earlier studies of sex differences in human figure drawings.

The second part of the book, consisting of two chapters, describes the results of the Danish study. Chapter 5 contains the description of drawing development, which is described both quantitatively and qualitatively. While relatively homogeneous in the beginning, the drawing development of the two sexes was found to differ so much already from the age of 7 that it was necessary to take this into consideration. A general description for both sexes was found not very meaningful and was therefore abandoned. So, although the sex differences are treated separately in the following chapter, it was necessary also to take them into account here. The Danish results are compared to the results found by Goodenough (1926) and Harris (1963), and good overall agreement is found between their results and the Danish ones.

Chapter 6 contains the results from the study of the sex differences. They were found to manifest themselves in all aspects of drawings. In contrast to what has often been described, they are not a group of more or less disconnected details, but make up a coherent and meaningful pattern. It has been customary to distinguish between quantitative and qualitative sex differences in drawings, but this distinction was found impossible to maintain.

The last part of the book also consists of four chapters. Here, the attempt is made at relating the different aspects of figure drawings to different theoretical frames of reference, something which has much too often been grossly neglected. Drawings have often been considered in isolation—as an entertaining and fascinating activity of children—but hardly as a factor which contributes seriously to their development and therefore deserves its place in general and developmental psychology in line with such activities as perception, language development, concept formation, and other necessary tools for survival and success in our societies.

In order to do justice to the various aspects of drawings, it was necessary to reach out into quite different theoretical fields. First, in chapter 7, drawing development is related to general developmental theory. Werner's (1964) organismic theory was chosen as the basic frame of reference, partly because of its scope and partly because of its emphasis on concept formation which is of fundamental importance for the understanding of drawing development. It was found particularly valuable because it connects concept formation with many other person-ality factors and does not see it as a limited intellectual activity. It was also found useful to connect drawing with (other) languages, where particularly the distinction between digital and analogic language was found relevant.

Chapter 8 relates the found sex differences to the results from other studies on sex differences. Differences in intellectual abilities between the sexes have earlier been used as explanations for the differences found in drawings, and their possible influence is discussed. It is concluded that they can only account for a small part of the total pattern of sex differences. It was found necessary also to include theories on children's psychosexual development. Psychoanalytic theories are those which most comprehensively have examined this aspect of child development. Freud-ian theory was not found adequate because of its lack of acknowledge-ment of a primary feminine psychosexual development, whereas Klein-ian theories were found to be in better harmony with the results presented in the drawings. The sex differences are seen as the reflection of basic and fundamental sex differences, connected with differential experiences of one's body.

The importance of body experience in human figure drawings is further elaborated in chapter 9, which describes aspects of the research on body image or body experience.

The book ends with an attempt at integration of this quite comprehensive material. It is certainly fascinating that the simple act of drawing a human figure—which may take less than five minutes—in order to be only partly understood, brings the observer into contact with so many different aspects of our total psychological knowledge.

PART ONE

Earlier Studies of Children's Human Figure Drawings

ONE

Drawing Development Related to Chronological Age

Interest in children's drawings arose as part of the general interest in child psychology which developed during the last decades of the nineteenth century. The first studies of drawings consisted of descriptions of what children actually draw and how they do it at different ages. A great number of such studies appeared during the years 1890–1920. Although they were not confined to the study of drawings of human beings, they all included this theme, and all agreed on the importance of it. Some of the older studies (e.g., Maitland 1895; Lukens 1896; Ballard 1913; Luquet 1913) found that human beings were the most frequently drawn subjects by children.

The earliest research on drawings resulted in descriptions of drawing development related to the children's age. The most notable early works of this kind are from the beginning of the century, e.g., by Kerschensteiner (1905) and Rouma (1913), but also later authors have contributed, e.g., Lowenfeld (1947). These descriptions are broad and general, and have resulted in the establishment of stages of drawing development. The number of these stages may vary from one author to the next, but the descriptions of drawing development itself show great similarities. There seems to be general agreement on the following three main phases:

1. A scribbling stage, characterized by no attempts at representation.
2. A schematic stage with representational content, but with drawings that may be described as more symbolic than naturalistic. Drawings at this stage represent human prototypes more than individual persons.
3. A more naturalistic stage, characterized by a gradual increase in the number of lifelike details, proportions, and forms. This stage culminates before puberty, which is a critical age, when drawing development often stops completely.

Later studies introduced more detailed analyses of the drawings and statistical treatment of the data, aiming at the establishment of age norms. This method was used by, e.g., Goodenough (1926). This approach has the advantage of greater precision, the possibility of the establishment of age norms and of making comparisons between groups, but there is the danger of ending up with a mere listing of details and no overall synthesis of the results. By this method the descriptions of the qualitative differences between the stages, which were pointed out in the broader and more general studies, may be lost.

In the following, a general overview of the accumulated knowledge about the development of human figure drawings is summarized.

DEVELOPMENT DESCRIBED IN STAGES

The Scribbling Stage

Most children start drawing during the second year of life. The earliest beginnings consist mostly of unsystematically scattered lines spread all over the paper. At this stage the pencil is gripped by the fist, and the point is held vertically towards the paper. Little by little the child draws still longer lines, and the pencil is lifted less frequently from the paper. From what Lowenfeld (1947) describes as "disordered scribbles" the child goes on to "controlled scribbles," which at first consist of curved diagonal lines, and which later develop into circular and spiraling lines. These may grow into voluminous and elaborate pictures covering large areas. At first the child's motoric development only allows him to move his whole arm, but gradually it becomes possible to differentiate the movements, so that only the lower arm and at last only the hand is moved.

Kellogg (1959) has particularly studied the scribbling stage and describes 20 basic scribbles which she finds are being used more or less by

FIGURE 1 Controlled scribbles in curved, diagonal lines (Boy, 16 months old).

all children. Although the scribble is spontaneous, she emphasizes that it is not incidental, and neither is it placed haphazardly on the paper. Children were found to have their own preferences for the placement of the scribbling on the paper, some preferring to cover the whole area, others perhaps only half of the page. The diagonal was found to be one of the most popular forms, as was the variation where the child covers two-thirds of the paper. The scribble is not planned by the child, but develops during the work and not until it is finished does the child stop to observe—and admire—his work.

Around the age of 3 the child discovers that he is able to draw a specific form, e.g., a circle or a square. Kellogg mentions 6 such diagrams, namely the Greek cross, the rectangle, the circle, the ellipse, the triangle, the diagonal cross and areas with nonspecific form. The pleasure of the movement and the filling of the paper is now supplemented by the pleasure of being able to create a specific form, and during this period the children may be seen exercising their newly discovered skills over and over again.

Around 3–5 years of age the children begin to combine their forms into patterns, e.g., to encircle their squares or put squares around their

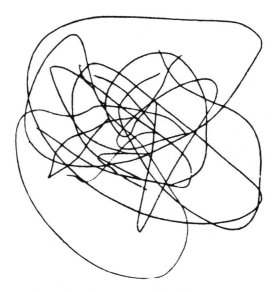

FIGURE 2   Round scribbles (Boy, 20 months old).

circles. Also here every single child may have his favorites, and every child develops his own characteristic and often easily recognizable style.

Using Jungian theory as her frame of reference, Kellogg stresses particularly the appearance of the Mandala, which in its most uncomplicated form is a circle cut by a cross. It is regarded as a universally used symbol. Children begin drawing Mandalas around 3 years of age and develop them into suns where the cross is extended beyond the circle and the middle cross finally disappears, and into human beings where the circle becomes the head of the figure. Arms and legs are often fastened to the head in a similar way to the radiants of the sun to the sun itself.

Kellogg does not mean that children, at this early stage, aim at a representation of the human being that actually resembles one, but rather that they endeavor to place something on the paper in such a way that it "looks right" and satisfies the child's sense of balance, rhythm, and proportion. Particularly the attainment of balance is regarded as a very essential goal for the child; often big hats or voluminous masses of hair and curls serve the purpose of balancing off the long legs.

While Kellogg centers her interest on the formal qualities of the drawings, particularly the structure, Grözinger (1971) attempts to interpret the meaning of scribbles.

He regards scribbles as mainly motorically determined and finds that the child is particularly interested in the rhythmic element. Drawing at the earliest stages is to him mainly a kind of movement on paper, and he relates the elementary scribbles to the elementary states and forms of movement that are known to the child. Spirals or repeated circles are seen as a kind of representation of the child's experience of floating, an experienced state or quality which has to do with being on a horizontal plane and perhaps with its roots all the way back to the fetal stage. In the drawing of the cross he sees the child's representation of the upright position, of standing, and in the zigzag line the experience of the rhythmic forward movement, of walking. Later the box pattern, the square, appears, which represents the child's experience of room (space). Grözinger maintains that whenever circular lines appear, these have to do first and foremost with the child's inner space, and that straight lines have to do with movement and direction of movement. All acute or right angles signify an inhibition or stopping of the movement, caused by some obstacle, e.g., the plane on which we walk, the wall, etc. The tadpole-man is regarded as the result of a synthesis between the spiral and the vertical intersecting line, i.e., the combination of the child's "inner space" and the experience of the upright position.

Just as the rhythm of the pulse and the breath influence the rhythm of the child's drawing, so do other bodily factors play a part. Grözinger distinguishes between the function of the right and left hands and suggests that the right hand (in right-handed children) which does the heaviest work and is connected with the left half of the brain where also the speech center is located, is the hand which is connected with the more conscious part of the child's personality, while the left hand is "the sensitive (feeling, emotional) hand." In left-handed children it is the opposite.

In the same way that a certain tension may exist between the two hands, he also talks about the tension between the child's representation of what he sees and his representation of his bodily sensations and feelings.

The Schematic Stage

All who have studied children's drawings agree on the developmental importance of the transition from the scribbling stage to the stage when the child is able to give his drawings a representational content. Although the transition is gradual and can in itself be subdivided into steps and stages, there is no doubt that the change from the scribbling stage to the schematic stage and its precursors is not only a quantitative, but also a qualitative step. It is also this stage which has given rise to the greatest number of—and the most conflicting—theories about the nature of children's drawing.

Rouma (1913) emphasizes that when the child starts naming his drawings, he is often inspired by eager parents or other relatives who ask him what he is drawing, or who directly call on him to draw certain things. At that time the child may be influenced to call his drawing almost anything. By thus putting a label to his drawing, the child copies the surrounding adults or children, but he does not so far recognize any relationship—not to say similarity—between his drawing and the object which gives it its name. The child may over a short period give his drawing many different names in the same way that a stick may have many functions in his play.

It is regarded as a new developmental step when the child names his work *before* instead of *after* the process of drawing. Sometimes the child during the process names one detail after the other—"here is the nose, the eyes, the arms, etc." The drawing is here a mechanical tool helping the child to hold on to a concept and be more specific about its details. Rouma also sees in this manner of approach a possible imitation of adults; the child imitates the outer manner, but does not understand the representative function of his drawing. The drawing is some sort of language, which accompanies the spoken language in a way similar to gestures and facial expressions.

But at some point in his development the child begins to see pictures in ambiguous lines, e.g., he interprets the pattern of the wallpaper or of his clothes as faces, animals, or the like. In an analogous fashion, one day he sees a similarity between some lines he has made on a paper and the form of some object. The child is often excited by his discovery, which may have the quality of an "aha-experience," and may for a long time continue in his attempts to draw the same thing over and over.

Rouma describes as a very important point in the intellectual development of the child when he is able to compare a concrete object with an abstract representation and experiences so great a similarity between them that he can identify the two things with each other. In all the normal children he observed, this step was taken before 3 years of age, but it may take place later in retarded or abnormal children. The child may go one step further, after having experienced the similarity between drawing and object, by attempting to add further details to the drawing. Thus he passes from the passive recognition to the active creation of similarity. The whole development takes place gradually, and in between real attempts at representation the child may still for a long time draw scribbles with no attempt at creating representation.

In the first phase of the representational stage, there may still be no visible similarity between the lines and the object with regard to either form, direction, positioning, or proportions. But the number of lines diminish gradually, and every line gets its meaning, represents an idea. In the beginning it is particularly the form and direction of the objects which are caught, i.e., the child draws the human being as an elongated, vertical figure. Lowenfeld (1947) emphasizes that in the beginning the establishment of a relationship between drawing and object is the most important thing for the child, while the quality of the work is of second-ary importance.

Eventually the child reaches the so-called tadpole stage where the human figure is usually drawn as a circle to which are fastened one or two long lines as legs. Sometimes two horizontal lines are added as arms to the circle or to the vertical lines. Generally, the arms are omitted in the beginning, and the child is more likely to add details to the head such as eyes, mouth, nose, or hair, although the details are often not correctly placed initially, and may even be placed outside of the figure. More details may be added, but the body is rarely drawn. This stage is what Lowenfeld names the preschematic stage. Lack of stability is a characteristic feature; the representation of an object may vary from one day to the next. The child has not yet worked out any fixed schemata for various objects, and if the different parts are separated from the whole gestalt, they are not recognizable, e.g., a head is just a circle, which—out of context—may just as well represent the sun, a flower, or a balloon.

With some children, the body is suddenly added as a whole, with others certain details appear first, such as a row of buttons, a round belly, a belt, or a navel, but without the outline of the body itself being drawn. Around the age of 5, the child usually has found a certain mode of representation of the human being, where the major body parts are all included, and enters thus the schematic stage proper.

FIGURE 3 Preschematic drawing (Girl, 5 years old).

At this stage, every single body part is represented by a symbol which cannot as easily as before be exchanged with something else without the whole being disturbed. This does not mean, however, that they are represented naturalistically; the body may be round, triangular, or square, the hands may be round circles or one-dimensional sticks, etc. Both Kerschensteiner (1905) and Lowenfeld (1947) have emphasized that the drawing at this stage is not an imitation of a visually experienced form. Kerschensteiner writes that the child's drawing at this stage "does not strictly speaking deserve the name of drawing, if by drawing is understood a more or less graphical expression of the lines, planes and space relationships of the object, it is rather just a writing down of that which the child knows about an object" (1905, 15–16). To him the drawing is not a naturalistic representation of what the child sees, but rather some symbolic expression, a writing down of the conceptual characteristics of the objects. Lowenfeld emphasizes that the concept which the drawing expresses is due to a combination of many factors: the child's thinking, his experience of his own feelings, and his development of perceptual sensitivity. The schema is consequently very individualized and may be regarded as a reflection of the individual development.

FIGURE 4 Schematic drawing (Girl, 6 years old).

The drawings are usually stable and fixed unless special factors motivate the child toward something else. Lowenfeld distinguishes between "pure schemata" and drawings through which the child intends to communicate something more specific, e.g., he may draw a person performing some activity which has importance for himself. In that case the otherwise well-established schemata may change. The child may for example want to represent some kind of movement such as running or throwing, some strong sensory experience such as the feeling of cold or wetness, or some strong emotional experience.

Because of the relative stability of the drawings, deviations from the schemata are important. Kerschensteiner noticed that children know little about how to characterize individually the persons or objects they draw, but if they indicate differences it is done through the addition of certain extra attributes such as a pipe, a tall hat, or an umbrella. Lowenfeld describes three kinds of deviations from the pure schemata: (1) exaggeration of important parts, (2) omission or neglect of unimportant parts, and (3) change of symbol (e.g., alteration of form) of emotionally important parts. These deviations need not be conscious to the child and often are not.

Growing Naturalism

Also the transition from the schematic stage toward greater naturalism takes place gradually. Children's drawings change little by little through the addition of more and more lifelike forms and proportions, while the more unnaturalistic forms disappear. One and the same drawing may contain purely schematic traits together with traits that are drawn with greater regard to form. According to Kerschensteiner (1905), the child at this stage is not content with the mere writing down of the conceptual content, but also wants to characterize the formal relationships, the integration between the various parts.

Children at the schematic stage are not able to draw a model. They hardly look at it and seem much more influenced by their inner concepts of the objects than by their perception of them; but during the next stage their ability to observe improves greatly. By observation is meant not only the act of seeing, but also an analysis of the observations which breaks down the visual impressions. As the single parts are heavily influenced by the whole context, this analysis is a difficult process, which is only mastered without errors by few adults; but children begin to be aware of the necessity of active observation and to practice it more or less consciously.

These different mental sets have been related to differential use of the two hemispheres of the brain (e.g., Edwards 1979). During childhood the brain is less lateralized than later, but Edwards states that when a clearer lateralization occurs, around the age of 10, children can come

FIGURE 5 Beginning realism (Boy, 10 years old).

into conflict concerning the best method to draw. The left hemisphere works in a logical, analytic way and is involved in categorization, naming, and symbolization processes. The schematic way of drawing, where certain fixed symbols represent certain objects almost in the same way as certain letter combinations represent certain words, is therefore heavily influenced by the function of the left hemisphere. In contrast, the right hemisphere works more intuitively, nonverbally, concretely, with relations instead of categories, and is space-oriented instead of time-oriented. It is maintained that in order to learn to observe actively, it is necessary to work primarily with the right hemispheric function in order to prevent the quick categorization and classification process which ends up in the use of predetermined symbols. So, the drawer must learn to inhibit the left hemisphere and concentrate on the use of the right.

The function of the hemispheres is hardly as simple as here described, but it seems safe to maintain that the different ways of drawing require different mental sets by the drawer, and that children—or adults, for that matter—vary in their ability to use the different sets and to change between them. It is equally certain that in our culture, where so much weight is placed on analytic, classificatory, and verbal abilities, the use of the space-oriented, nonverbal, and intuitive way of relating to the world is underestimated and little trained. This may be one reason why few people are able to enter the later stages of drawing without help.

At this stage, children also begin to be interested in the representation of sexual characteristics and to differentiate between men and women in their drawings. They also often try to characterize specific kinds of persons, e.g., a sailor, a spaceman, or a princess and do so through the use of typical details. Lowenfeld (1947) emphasizes that the interest in the representation of details to a certain extent may happen at the expense of the whole, which may lose life and movement and make a somewhat rigid impression. The earlier tendency to change size and form of important parts disappears partly and is replaced by an abundance of details.

The children begin to experiment with the drawing of the body in differing positions, and profile drawings become more common. Many transitional forms are found between pure profile drawings and drawings seen from the front. One of the most difficult details to draw correctly is the eye.

The representation of three-dimensionality is, according to Kerschensteiner (1905), one of the last things to be mastered by the child, and a stage which is not reached by all children. He saw it most often in boys and not until after 11 years of age, and thought it probable that it could not be reached without teaching. Three-dimensionality may be shown, for example, through the use of perspective, of shading, of foreshortening, or by overlapping of body parts.

When approaching puberty, the child reaches a critical stage in his drawing development. He loses his spontaneity, while the observing and reflective attitude which is developed toward the environment is also

FIGURE 6   Profile drawing (Boy, 12 years old).

turned toward himself. The child can no longer unreflectively enjoy the drawing process, but the result of the work becomes more important. Many children develop such a degree of self-criticism that their drawing activity stops completely.

The drawing of a person now often reflects the children's preoccupation with their own bodies and their development. Many exaggerate sexual traits in their drawings, while others carefully avoid any representation of sexual details, due to fear or shame with regard to the bodily changes which are experienced so intensely.

At this stage Lowenfeld (1947) distinguishes between two characteristic developmental lines. Some adolescents are particularly visually disposed, i.e., taking their starting point from the surroundings, while others, whom Lowenfeld calls primarily haptic, so to speak start from the inside and first and foremost notice their own bodily sensations and subjective experiences of an emotional nature. The primarily visual children represent their experience of the world as spectators while the haptic ones to a greater degree are involved as partakers in the processes they describe in their work. The groups are not considered to be sharply separated, it is rather the case that most children can change their set depending on the situation; but the individual child may prefer or feel it easier to react in one or the other way.

For the visually disposed child the human figure will be part of the environment in line with other things, and he will consequently take an interest in representing it as naturalistically as possible, using his ability to observe and analyze as earlier described. The visual child, according to Lowenfeld, mainly takes his starting point in the whole, which is then analyzed into its components, which are then again synthesized into a whole. Technically, this means that the visual person will begin by sketching the whole and later build in the details.

The haptic person, in contrast, approaches his theme so to speak from the inside and has, therefore, no whole to start with, but chooses more selectively, concentrating on sensory impressions and kinesthetic experiences which to him are more important than the purely visual impressions. As the sensory impressions received from senses other than the eye are often isolated and partial, it means that the haptic person concentrates on the details that he finds important, and if he is going to create a whole, this happens more gradually, through a successive accumulation of details. Often, however, a great number of details will be omitted, if they have no sensual or emotional meaning to the drawer, and the same is true of the whole, which is not always regarded as essential. The human figure is here used as a tool to interpret the drawer's own emotions. As different parts of the body may have different emotional meanings, this leads the haptic drawer to return to the methods of characterization which were used at earlier developmental stages, i.e., exaggeration of size or change of form to emphasize essentials.

These two attitudes point clearly toward different schools in the art of painting, the visual one toward the naturalistic and impressionistic schools, the haptic one toward the more expressive schools.

It is universally agreed that while the sequence of the stages seems fixed, the rate of progression through them may vary as may the point where the individual drawer's development stops. There is also consensus that progression and regression may vary for each individual child.

DEVELOPMENT DESCRIBED IN AGE NORMS

The establishment of age norms for human figure drawings was introduced by Goodenough (1926) and further developed by Harris (1963). They both related drawing development to mental age instead of to chronological age, however, so their work is treated in the following chapter. Koppitz (1968) relies to a great degree on their work and also uses the same methodological approach, analyzing the drawings for a number of variables which are then treated statistically.

Koppitz sets up a list of 30 "developmental items," defined as items that appear relatively rarely with small children, but more and more frequently with older children until at a certain age they appear in the drawings of all or almost all children. Many of these developmental items are taken directly from Goodenough's (1926) work.

Koppitz (1968) describes the drawings of children 5–12 years old. She divides the developmental items into four groups, according to the frequency with which they appear:

1. *Expected items,* appearing in 86%–100% of the drawings of children at a certain age. These are items that are so frequent that their absence is more significant than their presence.
2. *Common items,* appearing in 51%–85% of the drawings of children at a certain age level.
3. *Not unusual items,* present in 16%–50% of the drawings of the children at a certain age.
4. *Exceptional items,* appearing in no more than 15% of the drawings of children at a certain age.

Koppitz suggests that omission of expected items is due to either immaturity, mental retardation, or regression caused by emotional problems. Exceptional items are only expected to appear in children with a mental maturity above average. More items appear with increasing age, but only up to the age of 10. After that age it is concluded that no significant changes occur.

These 30 items fall, according to Koppitz, into two groups, one consisting of items that are basic and essential, and which seem to be due almost exclusively to age and maturity, and another, consisting of less essential items, which are due both to age and to the child's social and cultural experiences. Traits which are found to be typically "masculine" or "feminine" are regarded as belonging to the latter group.

Among the earlier investigators, it was particularly Kerschensteiner (1905) who noticed sex differences in drawing performance; their existence was further confirmed by both Goodenough (1926) and Harris (1963) (among others). Koppitz found it necessary to describe the development separately for the two sexes, maintaining that girls develop more quickly up to the age of 8 or 9, but that boys around 9 years of age catch up with them and even surpass them, both with regard to quality of drawing and number of details included. Her list of expected items contains, however, a greater number of these for the girls at all ages, even the oldest; this incongruity is not explained.

Koppitz believes that the developmental items primarily depend on age and maturity and that they are not much influenced by (1) instructions and drawing medium, (2) learning, or (3) artistic abilities.

At the age of 5½–6½ boys do a little better with crayons than with pencils, however, while the medium makes no difference with girls. She concludes that this difference is due to the fact that the motoric abilities of the boys develop later than those of the girls, and it is easier for them to use crayons.

The influence of learning was only examined in young children. A group which had attended a kindergarten for a year was compared with a group which had not had this experience. There were small differences between the groups, although the group in kindergarten had a tendency to draw two-dimensional arms and legs and more clothes than the group that had not had any training. Koppitz thinks that these items are learned specifically, but concludes nonetheless that the basic developmental items primarily depend on maturation and that they are not influenced by learning. This conclusion may be true for the age-group examined, but the relationship between maturation and learning may well be expected to vary at different ages, the role of learning increasing with rising age. Several other studies have shown that training programs designed to produce changes in body image have resulted in changes in human figure drawings (David 1975; McCarthy 1973; Potts 1970; de Chiara 1982). Also sensorimotor training programs have produced positive changes (Matthews 1971; Sunal 1976).

Koppitz states correctly that it is difficult to find a valid measure of artistic abilities. She thinks that they at any rate must have some connection with a good visuo-motor perception and a good fine motor coordination, abilities which, among other things, are measured in the performance part of the WISC (Wechsler Intelligence Scale for Children). She therefore compared children whose performance IQ was more than 10 points higher than their verbal IQ with children whose verbal IQ was more than 10 points higher than their performance score. She found no differences between the groups with regard to their human figure drawings and concludes therefore that her research supports the hypothesis that the developmental items are not influenced by the child's "performance ability." The change of terminology is notable, as there is no more talk about artistic abilities, but apart from that the method chosen to validate children's drawing abilities is rather crude. A good visuo-motor perception and a good motoric coordination are probably necessary conditions for being a good drawer, but hardly sufficient, and for example the motoric abilities measured by the WISC are not necessarily identical with those that make a good drawer.

THEORETICAL CONSIDERATIONS

The attempts at relating drawing development to more general theories of child development are sparse. The most explicit connection with theory is found in Kellogg's (1959) work, which is related to Jung's theories, but it covers a very limited part of drawing development. A closer inspection shows not only the existence of underlying theories, however, but also of quite conflicting viewpoints regarding the factors that influence drawing development and their relative weight.

To say that drawing development is a function of age is, of course, no more than a practical, descriptive shortcut. Age is no explanatory, let alone causal factor. The differences in drawings from children at various ages must be due to differences in their physical and psychic organization and function which can be more closely analyzed.

There seems to be general agreement that the motoric element is of major importance in the earliest phases of drawing development, and that the sheer pleasure of rhythmical movement is a strongly motivating factor for the small child; but the relative importance of this factor seems to diminish with age, while other factors have increasing influence. The limitations of the child's motoric development also set limits to his early drawing activities, however.

Also visual perception is important from the very beginning, but at the earliest stage it seems to be the child's perception of his own work which is of major importance as a reinforcing factor rather than the visual perception of the objects around him, which the child does not yet try to represent at all.

There are, however, differences in the theories regarding some of the determining factors even at the earliest stages. Kellogg (1959), for example, emphasized the importance of certain structures or dispositions as common to all human beings, thanks to our inborn organization, some archetypal patterns which will find expression in similar formal structures in the drawings of all children. Grözinger (1971), on the other hand, relates drawing development to the child's early bodily experiences which he finds symbolically expressed on the paper. The bodily states of being passively held and of moving actively, and the experience of the difference between soft, organic matter and hard, inorganic objects are for him the (universally human) experiences that determine the content and form of early drawings. As these experiences are so very basic and common to all children, no matter what their living conditions, the differences between the two theories might be regarded as of only theoretical interest, but it must necessarily make a difference for the later drawing development to what extent bodily and sensual experiences will enter as intervening factors and to what extent the development is predetermined by inborn, internal structure.

Grözinger also raises the question of the relative weight of visual and of motoric-haptic perception and suggests that these factors may play different roles for different children according to their physical and psychological makeup. This viewpoint is shared by Lowenfeld (1947), who, however, does not describe the conflict as occurring until prepuberty.

The whole idea that bodily experience and haptic sensations should influence drawing development is, however, a relatively recent idea, probably influenced by later psychoanalytic studies of drawing. While the earlier studies of course acknowledged the role played by perception,

perception was mainly defined as visual perception of the outer world, while the influence of other sense modalities was ignored.

One of the main points of conflict is not the relative influence of various forms of perception, however, but rather the relative weight that should be given to perception versus cognition, to sensual impression versus intellectual conceptualization.

Kerschensteiner (1905) was cited earlier for his very well-known statement that the drawing (at the schematic stage) is a writing-down of what the child *knows* about an object, a phrase which has been extensively cited and has caused much confusion and misunderstanding. The idea was originally formulated by Ricci (1887) and is not only used by Kerschensteiner, but has also, according to Moustgård (1962), found its way into the writings of such an influential writer as Piaget (1951). It can thus not just be discarded as an old-fashioned viewpoint but has to do with a very rational outlook on children's drawings, which still exists (see also later the theories of Goodnow [1977]). According to this view, the ideal drawing development follows an unbroken line toward the lifelike and visually true representation of the outer world. Drawing is seen mainly as the expression of the child's conceptualization of the outer world. What is emphasized is the mastery of visual analysis and of the correct depiction of such aspects as space, perspective, movement, etc. Drawings that do not achieve these goals are seen as falling short of an ideal and as more or less defective. When Kerschensteiner for example found that girls more rarely than boys reached the later stages in drawing development, this was attributed to a lack of certain abilities in girls (e.g., the ability to synthesize). Although not explicitly stated, it is quite obvious that this was related to certain cognitive and intellectual shortcomings in the girls compared to the boys. The idea that drawings might have other functions and purposes was not stated and probably not conceived at all. This outlook on drawings is naturally connected with an attitude toward art favoring naturalism and an academic tradition that emphasizes drawing skill and perception of visually correct representation and that gives great weight to aesthetic qualities.

Rouma (1913) compared drawing development to language development and linked it thus also with concept development. There is no doubt that these theories have been very influential in the further development of the use of drawing as a measure of intellectual function.

The intellectual theories have been criticized most severely by perceptual psychologists (e.g., Arnheim 1954; Moustgård 1962, 1964) who state that they rest on a misconception of what perception is. In perception, no isomorphic relationship exists between stimulus and perception (Von Fieandt and Moustgård 1977).

Moustgård (1962) describes that when a child for example sees a box, he not only sees the front of it, although the front may be the only visible part, but he will immediately perceive a box with extension in space. In his drawing he will draw a box on the paper, possibly with several sides, not because he sees a square and knows it to be a box, but because he immediately perceives a box with several sides and draws it as well as he can. The perspectively correct drawing of the box would require a perceptual analysis of the visual pattern which children are not yet able to make and which for most people requires considerable training and concentration on the observation process itself.

It may, of course, be argued that in order for the child to see a box and not just a square he must through earlier experience have learned it to be so, and that the perception thus rests on the child's knowledge. It is undoubtedly true, but these experiences seem to be so early and fundamental that they are completely integrated in the child's perception. At the time of drawing, no cognitive process is necessary to perceive the box as such.

Moustgård (1964) stresses further the fact that we perceive things more unchanged in regard to size, form, placement, and color than they are when observed by more "objective" media, as for example a camera, or when they are observed under special conditions. The analytically trained drawer will be able to break down his visual impressions so as to draw a correct perspective, but for the unsophisticated drawer a plate is round or a table square no matter how elliptic or foreshortened the retinal image is. With Gibson (1950) we can distinguish between "the visual world"—the immediate perception of things around us—and "the visual field"—the surroundings when we look at them with the analyzing set.

In these considerations Moustgård is in agreement with Gestalt psychology, as for example represented by Arnheim (1954) who also emphasized that regarding children's drawings as abstract concepts presupposes an intellectual process which is impossible at this early stage, when the mind is still thoroughly dependent on sensory experiences. The application of knowledge can be seen for example in the drawing of the correct number of fingers when the child resorts to counting.

Arnheim also maintains that the eye does not register the complete set of individual details contained in the retinal image; perception starts from generalities, not from particulars. Children draw generalities and undistorted shapes (e.g., undistorted by perspective) precisely because they draw what they see.

But, unquestionably, children see more than they draw. The reason why their pictures are still so undifferentiated, Arnheim finds in the process of representation and in the drawing medium used. A pencil creates objects by circumscribing their shape. Pictures always deviate grossly from the things they represent both in size and dimensionality (being two-dimensional instead of three-dimensional). The young child spontaneously discovers and accepts the fact that a visual object on paper can stand for an enormously different one in nature, provided it is its structural equivalent in the given medium. The psychological reason for this, according to Arnheim, is the fact that in human thinking perceiving is not based on piecemeal identity, but on the correspondence of essential structural features.

Arnheim emphasizes also that the principle of simplicity favors the drawing of a circle as the simplest visual pattern. Perception tends spontaneously toward roundness when the stimulus gives it leeway to do so. The tendency toward simple shapes in visual and motor behavior is likely to play a leading part in the process. At the stage of the circle, shape is not differentiated at all. The circle does not stand for "roundness," but only for the more general quality of "thingness," i.e., for the compactness of a solid object which is distinguished from the nondescript ground. The law of differentiation says that a perceptual feature will be rendered in the simplest possible way as long as it is not yet differentiated. The circle is the simplest possible shape available in the pictorial medium, standing for any shape at all and for none in particular. Also in adult abstract model-description, the circle is often used as a symbol to represent a unit with no shape or whose shape is irrelevant.

Although acknowledging what has been learned from perceptual psychology, Goodnow (1977) again returns to the role of cognition in drawing, which she describes as mainly problem-solving behavior. The problem is the transformation of three-dimensional objects onto a two-dimensional plane, a task which is by its very nature impossible, but the drawer can attempt to solve it in different ways.

She characterizes drawings as "visible thinking" and describes some of the main principles governing them. They are for example: (1) economical use of units (the same graphic unit will be used over and over again for different purposes), (2) conservatism (a tendency to change only one part at a time), (3) certain principles of organization, and (4) the determining influence of the sequence in which a drawing is made.

One of the organizing principles is the tendency—at least in small children—to avoid overlapping of lines and to let each part of the figure have its own space. She describes how children invent all kinds of ingenious methods to avoid overlapping of for example arms and long hair, including the omission of arms, and she is skeptical about the attribution of emotional significance to such details which in her eyes may be determined mainly by the technical problems of the drawing. Goodnow's observations are no doubt relevant; technical limitations and special work patterns do influence the final result. But what she seems to miss is the immediate spontaneity of children's drawings, which are not created in a laborious atmosphere of thinking and problem solving. At times children will stop and wonder about the solution to a technical problem and may even ask for help, but that is not the typical process. Besides, her theories can only explain limited aspects of the final product, and they also leave unexplained, for example, the whole question of why the child chooses his different motives. Neither do they explain why different children prefer different patterns of approach, personal modes of problem-solving behavior. Such preferences are difficult to explain except as consequences of the children's personalities. Some children may, for example, always choose a systematic approach, resulting in drawings with all details included, while others with equal regularity will draw their figures in a more haphazard order and thus tend to omit important parts. And one child may be anxious to give each body part its own space, while another lets parts overlap freely. Moreover, the idea of problem-solving behavior does not exclude the possibility that different body parts may have special meanings for different children.

Further discussion of the relationship between perception and cognition belongs to the broader context of a more general theory of child development and will be taken up later. What can be said so far is that concept formation, cognitive processes, and problem solving certainly play a part in children's drawings. But it seems necessary to warn against theories of drawing that too one-sidedly emphasize the role played by purely cognitive processes in young children at the expense of immediate sensory impressions and perceptual experience. And what must particularly be regarded with skepticism is any theory that regards children's concepts as determined solely—or even mostly—by their experience with "objective realities" in the outer world, without taking into account the role played by the child's "inner realities," such as emotions, needs, bodily experiences, and fantasies.

Another basic question that is raised is the relative roles of maturation and learning for drawing development. Those who have mainly worked with very young children obviously tend to stress the influence of maturational factors, while those who have worked with older children tend to emphasize the importance and even the necessity of learning specific skills in order to reach the latest stages of development. The great homogeneity of early drawing development lends support to the hypothesis that maturational factors are decisive at this stage, and so does the dominance of the motoric element. At the other end of the scale, it seems possible that specific training is necessary for even the most gifted child (or adult) in order to obtain, for example, the ability of visual analysis which is a prerequisite for the drawing of visually "correct" pictures. It seems well documented that the conscious perception of the outer world as a direct model of the drawing only occurs in older children and seems to presuppose a certain maturational level.

Actual experimental work on the role of learning has been scarce. The studies on training have indicated that at least a slight short-term effect can be seen when kindergarten children are taught to include specific body parts in their drawings, but much more systematic studies are needed of both the short- and long-term effects of training of children of various ages in order to determine exactly what can be learned at what ages—and by whom. So far only the broad generalization seems justified that the role of maturation is relatively great in the small child and that the role of learning gradually increases with age. It might also be suspected—as in other areas where training is needed—that learning would tend to increase individual differences, with the more talented children being able to profit relatively more by training than the less talented, another hypothesis that needs further testing.

TWO

Drawing Development Related to Mental Age

Already in the early studies of drawing development, it was observed that while the sequence of development was stable from child to child, the rate of development varied with the intellectual abilities of the children. Feeble-minded children went slowly through the developmental stages, and their development tended to stop early, while intellectually gifted children progressed quickly and continued their development longer. This led to a closer investigation of the relationship between drawing development and mental age, and to the idea of using drawing development as a measure of the child's intellectual functioning.

As early as 1921, Cyril Burt used the drawing of a man as one of a number of "Mental and Scholastic Tests," but found that the drawing showed a smaller correlation with the child's intellectual or educational abilities than tests of reading, writing, spelling, or arithmetic. On the other hand, he regarded drawings as having the advantage of being less dependent on learned skills in manipulating abstract symbols such as words or numbers.

Another early attempt at using drawing as a measure of intelligence was made in France by Fay (1923), who let the children draw "A lady takes a walk and it rains." The drawing, which was limited to a maximum of 5 minutes, was scored according to the number of details. The test was later revised by Rey (1946), but has not been much used outside French-speaking countries.

THE GOODENOUGH TEST AND THE HARRIS REVISION

By far the most important work in this field is the Draw-A-Man (DAM) test developed by Florence Goodenough (1926). She tried through her instruction to ensure that the child performed at his very best and therefore used no time limit. The test has been used in very many countries and subjected to much research.

Goodenough had originally hoped to let the children decide on their own subject, but this, of course, confronts the tester with an impossible job, trying to compare the quality of subjects with varying degrees of difficulty. She chose a man as the subject for several reasons. It is a universal one known to all children, with minimal variation from culture to culture, in contrast, for example, to a house. It had to be so simple in outline that even small children dared approach it and yet so differentiated that it would challenge older children. Finally, it was found that this subject usually appealed to children, being beforehand one of their favorite ones. The choice must be characterized as lucky, although in certain cultures attempts have been made at developing a corresponding test with a different subject, in India for example the drawing of a cow (Desai 1958) and in the United States, where the drawing of a horse was claimed to be a more relevant task for children of the Pueblo-Indians (DuBois 1939). When a man was preferred to a woman it was due to the greater uniformity in the clothing of men.

In the evaluation of the drawings, three main aspects were considered:

1. Number of details included, such as head, facial features, hands, fingers, etc.
2. Correct proportions between the various body parts, e.g., between head and body or between legs and feet.
3. Motoric coordination as seen for example in the fluency of the lines and the integration of various parts.

In order for an item to be included in the test, it should appear more frequently with increasing age, and this increase should be rather regular and quick. As a criterion of differentiation, Goodenough (1926) chose the condition that a trait differentiated between children of same age but in different classes. The value of this criterion was due to the at that time ordinary practice of letting slow learners repeat classes and of promoting quick learners. Each drawing was evaluated with regard to 51 items, the sum of scores was related to the age of the child, and an IQ calculated.

Goodenough was very thorough in her preparation of the test, and this care is probably one of the main reasons why the test was used for almost 40 years without any attempt at revision. In 1963, however, a revision was made by D. B. Harris under the title *Children's Drawings as Measures of Intellectual Maturity*.

The revision had several purposes, the most important of which was an examination of the validity of the norms from 1926.

Another purpose was to try to extend the test so that it could be used with older children and adolescents. Goodenough's original sample consisted of drawings from children 4–10 years old, but her test was extrapolated to be used with children 3–13 years old, which is in itself questionable. Furthermore, it was found difficult to find new criteria for evaluating the drawings of children above 11–12 years of age. After this age not many new details are added—rather a certain reduction may be found—and it seems difficult to find measurable improvements in other aspects of the drawings. It is thus difficult to do justice to the most intelligent of the older children. Goodenough mentioned herself that the norms seemed to be too easy at the low end of the scale and too difficult at the upper end, so it must be concluded that the test is relatively invalid for the older children.

A third purpose was to include more criteria in the test to improve its reliability and validity, a fourth to try to find alternative forms of the test, and a fifth finally to develop a basis for a possible projective use of the scale. In consideration of Harris's otherwise negative evaluation of the use of drawing as a projective test, this purpose seems surprising. It is less surprising that it was not fulfilled.

Partly for technical reasons and partly because of the changed outlook on the concept of intelligence, no IQ is calculated when a drawing is scored according to the revision; the children are instead given a percentile score at each age level.

As expected, changes were found in the age norms; the children did generally better at the time of the revision than when the original test was made. Differences were found, however, between various aspects of the test, some areas showing progress, others no change, and others again regression.

No change was found in such traits as the presence of head, legs, fingers, neck, clothing, more general aspects of proportions, and motoric coordination. Progress was seen in the appearance of arms and body, positioning of arms and legs, correct number of fingers, representation of hands, head, two-dimensionality of arms and legs, ears, details in ear, chin, and forehead. Especially great progress was seen in the drawing of hair, finger details, thumb drawn as distinct from other fingers, no transparencies, body proportions, and coordination in the drawing of arms and legs. Regression was found in the projection of the chin, nose, and mouth in two dimensions, and legs in right proportion.

Harris's own explanation of these changes stresses partly a changed art education which allows children to express themselves more freely from an earlier age, and partly a more general change in the attitude toward children which allows them to be freer, more spontaneous and expressive. Also a greater acceptance of the body and its functions may play a part.

The second purpose—to try to extend the test to be valid also for older children—was not satisfactorily fulfilled. The same problem as met with by Goodenough was seen again: the difficulty in finding new criteria with increasing age. No increase in the number of items was found by Harris after the thirteenth year, and the variance after this age diminishes. This result confirms not only Goodenough's earlier experiences, but also those of Rey (1946), Eggers (1931), Levy (1931), and Cohen (1933). It is therefore surprising that age norms are made up to the age of 15. It seems inevitable to conclude that the test should be used with great caution with older children, if at all, and certainly never as the only measure of intelligence.

The attempt at including more items in the test in order to increase its reliability and validity resulted in an extension of the number of items from 51 to 73 and in an improvement of the instructions.

The attempt to find alternative forms of the test resulted in a scoring scale for the drawing of a woman. The correlation between the drawings of a man and a woman for both girls and boys was found to vary between .72 and .80 with a joint correlation of .75. This correlation is, according to Harris, smaller than the one usually found by retesting with the DAM test. It was suggested that the two drawings measure partly different abilities which only partly correlate. That each of the tests measures several abilities is supported by the fact that the drawing of a man alone only shows a split-half reliability of .77. Harris suggests that the children should draw both figures and that the average of the scores be used.

No attempt was made to discuss the interesting question about which different abilities the two drawings are supposed to measure. An explanation including factors other than "abilities" might seem considerably more plausible to an observer who does not as persistently as Harris stick to the conviction that drawing exclusively represents the cognitive aspects of the child's personality. The drawing of a person of each sex contains two emotionally very different tasks. Children's feelings toward their own sex are evidently different from their feelings toward the opposite sex, based on their experiences of themselves, of parents, and of other persons in their environment. Finally, the drawing of a woman is normally presented as a second task, which by itself might influence the quality of the work. It is not mentioned whether children regularly draw their own or the opposite sex better, or whether the sequence of drawings influences the result.

It was shown, however, that girls normally scored higher on the test than boys and so much so that it was found necessary to establish different norms for the two sexes. In the drawing of a man the girls were found to be a half year ahead of the boys, in the drawing of a woman about one year ahead. Incidentally, this is an indirect answer to the question whether own or opposite sex is drawn better.

A further addition to the original test was made by the inclusion of the so-called quality-scales. Through a quick comparison with 12 drawings representing the different age norms, any drawing can be placed somewhere around the level at which it belongs. This method correlates between .76 and .91 with the ordinary scoring method (the point method).

The quality-scales are said to be most reliable with smaller children where the number of details included plays a relatively greater part. With older children, improvements of proportions are of greater importance, which seems more difficult to evaluate without exact measurements. Quality-scales were seen to favor girls even more than a regular scoring of the drawing. This is probably due to the fact that the regularity, symmetry, and order of their drawings may influence the judgment favorably. It is, therefore, also stressed that any evaluation of intellectual maturity based on drawings that are scored according to quality-scales must be regarded with great caution.

The interrater reliability of the DAM test has generally been found satisfactory (e.g., McCarthy 1944; Williams 1935).

COMPARISONS BETWEEN THE TWO FORMS OF THE TEST

The reliability of the revision has been found almost identical with the results for the original Goodenough test (1926) (Dunn 1967; Yater, Barclay, and McGilligan 1969). Dunn concluded that in spite of the greater length and the presumably greater objectivity of the revision, no significant increase was found in rater reliability. However, the original reliability was so high that improvements could hardly be expected.

Vane (1967) tried to evaluate whether the revision of the scoring of the DAM test by Harris was significantly more valid than the original form of the test. She found a higher correlation between Goodenough's original test and Binet IQs of children 5–7 years old (.40–.52) than between the revision and the Binet (.34–.42). She found that the IQs obtained by the Harris form were consistently lower than those obtained by the Binet test, and it is suggested that Harris may have obtained his norms from a population with a fairly high intellectual level. If this is true, a question mark is also placed on the norm differences between the two versions of the test. They may only reflect differences of sampling and not actual changes in drawing performance over time. Vane further criticizes the fact that all children of the same age in years are evaluated according to the same percentile scale. This means that children with 11 months' difference in age, with the same number of points on the test, according to Harris's method of evaluation, will receive the same score, while with Goodenough's method they would receive quite different IQs. Finally, it is stated that the DAM test, scored by either method, may underestimate the intelligence of above-average children. The conclusion is that the revision of the test is less adequate than the original test.

Pikulski (1972) also compared the two forms and the results of both with results from the WISC. As subjects he used 50 boys, 7–11 years old, who were nonachievers in reading. He thought that particularly this group of children might profit from the use of the drawing test because of their difficulties in reading test instructions and test items. The correlation between Goodenough's and Harris's scoring systems was here found to be .87, a result similar to that reported by Harris.

The correlation between the Goodenough test and the full-scale WISC was .44, while that between the Harris test and the full-scale WISC was .32, a result corresponding to Vane's (1967). It was therefore recommended to use the original Goodenough test instead of the revision.

It is generally found that the performance part of the WISC shows a higher correlation with the results of the drawing test than the verbal part. This result was confirmed here and was found to be even more pronounced than usual. Of the verbal subtests, only information showed a significant correlation with the Goodenough test (.32), while all the others were insignificant. Of the performance tests, three were significantly related to the Harris scores, and four to the Goodenough scores (all except coding). Object assembly showed the highest correlation (.47 with Goodenough, .51 with Harris); the other correlations ranged between .27 and .39. The abilities measured in these subtests seem to have to do with the ability to note and respond to details, to analyze wholes into parts, and to synthesize parts into wholes.

A general tendency was found in this study for the drawing IQs to be lower than the IQs of the WISC, generally by about 10 points. Pikulski attempted to explain this in two ways, partly as a result of difficulties in perceptual-motor coordination, which seemed to influence both the drawing and reading performance of some of the children, and partly as a result of anxiety and impulsiveness, which made it difficult for them to function in as unstructured a task as the drawing test. In other words, emotional difficulties seemed to contribute to a lower score. It was stressed that the two IQ measures were strikingly different in individual cases and that the scores in the figure drawings might very seriously underestimate the intellectual ability of the child. There were far fewer instances where the drawing scores were higher. When they were, the performance score of the WISC was also higher than the verbal score. It was concluded that in working with groups one may be able to use figure drawing scores to estimate WISC scores, but caution should be exercised when interpreting the results of an individual child. This seems particularly necessary if the child obtains a low score on the drawing test.

UNDERLYING THEORIES AND VALIDATION STUDIES

The basic assumption behind Goodenough's (1926) test was the idea that certain aspects of drawing performance correlate with children's mental age and thus could be used as a measure of intelligence. In the twenties the idea of a "general intelligence" was dominant, and the drawing test was thought to be a measure of this g-factor, which was believed to be relatively uninfluenced by cultural or social factors.

At the time of the revision, the idea of a general intelligence had been replaced by theories of more specific abilities, and the idea of intellectual functions as separated from cultural influences had been largely abandoned.

Harris (1963) consequently redefined the test as a measure of intellectual maturity or, more specifically, of conceptual maturity. By this he means the ability to form concepts of increasingly abstract character. According to Harris, intellectual activity requires:

1. the ability to *perceive* i.e., to discriminate likenesses and differences,
2. the ability to *abstract,* i.e., to classify objects according to such likenesses and differences, and
3. the ability to *generalize,* i.e., to assign an object newly experienced to a concrete class, according to discriminated features, properties, or attributes.

These three functions, taken together, comprise the process of *concept formation,* which is seen as a purely cognitive process.

Harris expresses his main hypothesis as follows: the child's drawing of any object will reveal the discriminations he has made about that object as belonging to a class, i.e., as a *concept.* In particular, it is suggested that his concept of a frequently experienced object such as a human being becomes a useful index to the growing complexity of his concepts generally.

Harris suggests that "very possibly the child's conceptualization of the human person is not greatly different, in process, from his conceptualization of other animate or inanimate objects in his experience. Because the human being is so basically important to him, affectively as well as cognitively, it is probable that the human figure is a better index than, for example, a house or an automobile. The concept of a person as a concrete object undoubtedly undergoes a more elaborate differentiation with age. The human figure, both in its parts and as a whole, must come to include a richer store of associations, or "meaning," than most other complex objects" (Harris 1963, 7).

While no one will probably disagree with Harris's description of the human figure as an object of greater importance to the child, also affectively, and including a richer store of associations or meaning than any other object, it is exactly these aspects which place a very serious question mark on its suitability as a measure of concept formation, understood as a predominantly cognitive function. As expressed by Fisher: ". . . one's body is psychologically closer to self than anything else; and thus the body is a prime target onto which one projects intense feelings. The body seems to be a maze of landmarks and prominences that are charged with meaning" (1986, 39). This whole question will be discussed more thoroughly in later chapters.

Harris (1963) acknowledges that visual perception plays an important part in concept formation and probably increasingly so with increasing age, while the drawings of small children reflect several perceptual modalities, tactile and kinesthetic as well as visual.

The most common attempts at validation of the drawing test have consisted of comparisons between the IQs obtained by it and by other tests of intelligence. Early studies of the original Goodenough test (e.g., Williams 1935; Yepsen 1929; McElwee 1932) showed correlations between .60 and .72 with the Binet. Rottersman (1950) found somewhat lower values both when comparing with the Binet (.36) and with the WISC, where he found a correlation of .38 with the verbal part, of .43 with the performance scale, and of .47 with the full scale. Havighurst and Janke (1944) obtained correlations between this test and the Binet of .50 when comparing the results for 70 normal 10-year-olds. Vane and Kessler (1964) found correlations ranging between .53 and .58 between the DAM and the Binet with kindergarten children.

Pechoux, Kohler, and Girard (1947) found small correlations with Porteus's Maze results, only .25 and .27 for boys and girls, respectively, but the Maze is not considered a very valid measure of intelligence by itself. They found only slightly higher correlations with the Binet, however, .26 for girls and .38 for boys, but they worked with abnormal and delinquent children and adolescents up to the age of 18, which means that both the age and the maladjustment of the children may have contributed to the low correlation.

Hanvik (1953) compared scores on the drawing test with WISC scores for 25 children who were psychiatric patients, aged 5 to 12, and found a rank order correlation of only .18 between the IQs from the two tests. He also found that the drawing test IQs in almost all cases were lower than the IQs obtained by the WISC. These results are in line with other results from children with psychic problems.

Smith (1937) did not give specific correlations in a study of 2,600 children, but stated that "certain significant deviations from Good-enough's IQs were revealed which indicates that the drawing test proba-bly measures somewhat specialized abilities rather than general intelli-gence of the conventional linguistic type." A very similar conclusion was reached by White (1979) 40 years later. White compared results from the drawing test with results from the WISC and the PIAT (Peabody Individual Achievement Test). While the later two tests showed high correlation with each other, the correlation of the drawing test with either of them was only moderate. It was concluded that the drawing test may be tapping abilities not adequately assessed by any of the other measures. This conclusion might of course just as well have been turned the other way round or it might have given room for factors other than "abilities."

Harris (1963) sums up the validity coefficients from comparisons with other tests to range from the twenties into the eighties, depending on the age of the subjects and the measure used as a criterion. He concludes somewhat surprisingly that the test measures intellectual factors better than aesthetic or personality factors—the latter being indeed very little examined in the studies cited.

It seems safe to conclude that there is a positive correlation between what the drawing test and other intelligence tests measure, but it seems just as obvious that the tests do not measure identical functions.

One way to approach the question about which functions the drawing test actually measures could be to compare it with tests of more specific functions. This has been tried relatively rarely. Ansbacher (1952) exam-ined the relationship between the drawing test and subtests from the Thurstone Primary Mental Abilities Test, and with special tests of me-chanical ability, and found the highest correlation with reasoning (.40), space (.38), and perception (.37), while the correlation was smaller with the more mechanical abilities such as tapping (.23) and dotting (.16). His study was made with 10-year-old children. But even the highest correlations of his study are relatively low. Harris (1963) used the same test with kindergarten children and found that the drawing test corre-lated better with quantitative and space tests than with verbal and perceptual tests—somewhat in contrast to Ansbacher's results. It is possible that the drawing test correlates with different functions at dif-ferent ages, a hypothesis that has not been tested further.

Müller (1970) used another approach to determine the validity of the test, more closely inspecting the construction of it. In an attempt to evaluate the split-half reliability he found that for 6-year-olds the Goodenough test actually contains only 26 usable items instead of the 51 of the whole test, and, furthermore, several of these items are interdependent. He found the validity of the test unsatisfactory on account of this analysis of the items. In addition, the internal consistency is only found to have a relatively low value (R = .73) which is, as a matter of fact, almost identical with the value found by Goodenough (1926) herself (.77), but apparently they differ in their opinion of the meaning of this factor, as Müller's conclusion is that the internal validity of the test is unsatisfactory.

He also compared the test with other intelligence measures and found the best correlation with the Binet-Kramer test (Kramer 1959) (.74), while it did not at all correlate significantly with some group tests, among others the Raven matrices (R = .25). He concluded that the DAM test may be useful for the diagnosis of mentally retarded children as a supplementary test, but that it cannot be used to differentiate between more intelligent children.

Finally, he criticized the test for using equivalent steps between the different ages, with four additional points per year, as he found that the addition of new items follows a negatively accelerating curve. In particular, many new items are added to the drawings from 5 to 6 years of age. This problem can of course be avoided through the use of the revision of the test, which applies percentile scores instead of a mental age concept.

Schaefer and Sternfield (1971) compared the validity of the Harris quality scale to that of the Goodenough point scale in assessing the IQs of 40 emotionally disturbed boys, 8–14 years old. No significant differences were seen in the IQs obtained by the two versions of the drawing test, but the correlation of the two scales was no higher than .81. The point scale correlated .35 with the WISC scores, the quality scale only .20, which is not a significant relationship at all. More important than the relative similarity or difference between the two scales is the poor correlation found between the drawing test (in either version) and the WISC, although the mean IQs of the tests were very similar. This means that in many individual cases the drawing test is very invalid (if the WISC is taken as a valid measure of intelligence).

Harris (1963) describes what he calls some indirect evidence of the validity of the test by examining the influence of the examiner and of artistic abilities. He found no difference in the results of the test whether the instructions were given by a complete stranger or by the children's usual classroom teacher. He cites a study by Phatak (1959) concerned with the relationship between the artistic merit of the drawings and the score obtained by the Goodenough test, showing that very few items on the test differentiated significantly between drawings of high artistic merit and drawings without such qualities. Each group of drawings was found to be better than the other in only three items. This result supports earlier observations by Goodenough herself about the lack of importance of artistic qualities for her test.

THE INFLUENCE OF EMOTIONAL OR PERSONALITY FACTORS ON THE DRAWING TEST

In several of the studies it was suggested that emotional states and other personality variables may have influenced the results obtained in the drawing test. A number of works have attempted to focus specifically on this aspect. Some have worked with more temporary affective states, e.g., Reichenberg-Hackett (1953) who found that experimentally induced positive feelings increased the score of the drawers.

Minor variations between normal children with regard to personal-social adjustment or popularity do not seem to affect the score. Thus, Palmer (1953) found no connection between the discrepancies between the Goodenough and the Binet scores and the children's personal-social adjustment as measured by the California Test of Personality. Neither did Fowler (1953) find any correlation between Goodenough-Binet discrepancies and the sociometric measures of the child.

Most studies have been concerned with children with more permanent behavior disorders or with various groups of handicapped children. Among the first category is Hinrichs (1935) who compared delinquent and nondelinquent children on the Goodenough test and found a tendency for his delinquent boys to obtain a lower IQ score on the drawing test than on the Binet. He also found—among other things—more "incongruities" in their drawings and more stereotyped drawings with fewer indications of activity. However, his groups were generally older (9–18 years old) than the groups with which the drawing test is reliable, which of course complicates the interpretation of the results.

Brill (1937) also found that a group of maladjusted boys scored lower on the DAM test than on the Binet, while the opposite was more often true of a well-adjusted group.

Springer (1941) tried to use the Goodenough scale as a qualitative aid in the diagnosis of specific behavior disorders, trying to find items that differentiated between well-adjusted and maladjusted boys, and found that 15 of the 51 items did so. The pattern of the differences was the same as that found between normal and retarded children, in spite of the fact that the two groups were equated for their scores on the drawing test.

As an example of studies on handicapped children Berrien (1935) should be mentioned, who tried to use the test to measure specific diagnostic differences between groups of postencephalitic children, "psychopathic" children, and some borderline mental defectives. The postencephalitic children were found to show some of the characteristics noted by Goodenough as possible indicators of neurotic and psychotic states, such as reversals of sex characteristics and combinations of mature and immature traits in the same drawing.

Bender (1940) found relatively lower scores in the drawing test than in the Binet test in a group of children suffering from postencephalitic behavior disorders, and the same result was found with schizophrenic children by Des Lauriers and Halpern (1947). In both studies the result is explained by disturbances of the children's body image. Hanvik (1953), in a study similar to Bender's, found such a low correlation as .18 between the WISC IQ and the drawing test IQ, with the drawing test significantly lower on the average. Johnson and Wawrzaszek (1961) and Nielsen (1961) both worked with physically handicapped children and obtained quite similar results. In the latter case it is suggested that the brain injury of the spastic children examined may have resulted in visuomotor disturbances which may have caused the drawing retardation. Also deaf children are seen to obtain a lower score on the drawing test than on other tests (Peterson and Williams 1930; Shirley and Goodenough 1932; Springer 1938). This is noteworthy as these children might have been expected to profit from a nonverbal test.

In a later work, Bender (1967) found that in children with organic impairment, the drawing of a man is usually two years or more below the mental age of the Stanford-Binet test. She interprets this as the result of a specific imperceptivity for body image. Johnson and Myklebust

(1967) found that the mean IQ on the Goodenough drawing test was 84, whereas the mean on the Wechsler scale was 103 in a group of learning-disabled children. They conclude that the moderate correlation which is generally found between the DAM IQs and the IQs in individually administered intelligence tests is significantly reduced in a population of learning-disabled children. Like Bender they considered body image immaturity or disturbances to be the intervening variable to explain the differences. McAninch (1966) directly cautions against the use of the IQ obtained through the drawing test when dealing with a learning disabled child.

Also Colligan (1967) found that children with learning inhibitions scored lower on the Quality scale of the drawing test than children without such inhibitions. He found fewer characteristics of maturity, fewer details, and less body fluidity and lifelikeness. These traits were attributed to differences in self-concepts rather than to body image immaturity.

Hartman (1972) reached the conclusion that when the drawing test is used together with a WISC and a Bender test, and when the variation due to intelligence and visuo-motor coordination is taken into account, the drawing test adds no further information and can thus be regarded as superfluous.

CONCLUDING REMARKS

The drawing test can be evaluated from different starting points. Its underlying assumptions can be questioned, or its basic theories can be accepted, and it can then be estimated whether the test functions satisfactorily so to speak on its own premises. This will be done first, and the critical evaluation of the underlying ideas will follow afterward.

Even if the general validity of the test is accepted, it is obvious that its validity for the upper and lower age limits of the scale can be seriously disputed. For very young children, the estimation of their intelligence comes to rest on very few items, which gives a high degree of inaccuracy. For older children the problem seems still greater. For one thing, it was found difficult to find new items to include in the test. But what should also be taken into consideration is the often considerable change in drawing style which takes place around puberty. The children gradually attach less importance to details, change to a more sketchy and more varied manner of drawing, and become more self-critical. All these factors may affect the result of the drawing test considerably. In spite of the fact that this insecurity was already acknowledged by Goodenough (1926) and was confirmed by many others, also by Harris himself (1963), the test is nevertheless not only used in the original age range, but even extended beyond it. This seems highly criticizable.

Another questionable aspect of the test concerns the age norms. Goodenough's (1926) norms are more than 60 years old and cannot without reexamination be regarded as still valid. It is a well-known fact that the drawing norms are sensitive to cultural changes, as are norms in other intelligence tests. It is doubtful, however, whether the norms found by Harris (1963) reflect actual changes of norms or whether they are only—or partly—due to differences of sampling. The lower correspondence which is generally found between the revised test and other tests of intelligence compared to the correspondence found with Goodenough's test, supports the suspicion of sampling differences playing a part.

As the original test thus still may be more valid, and as it is also shorter and easier to use, the conclusion might be that the old form of the test is to be preferred. But this version of the test has the disadvantage of relying on the old concept of intelligence quotient. Besides, the sex difference in performance is not taken into account.

The basic premises on which the drawing test rests need, however, to be reexamined. The use of drawing as a measure of intelligence or intellectual maturity tells perhaps more about Western culture than about children's drawings. It reflects the keen overconcern of our culture with the cognitive aspects of personality and a corresponding neglect of other aspects such as sensual perceptivity, body awareness, imagination, and affectivity. The eagerness with which the test has been accepted and used shows the great interest in easy and "handy" instruments to evaluate intellectual function in children. This enthusiasm has seemingly led to a certain blindness toward some of the obvious shortcomings of the drawing test as a measure of intelligence and to a negligence toward some other equally important aspects of drawings.

Even a naive acceptance of the concept of intelligence as that which is measured by traditional intelligence tests such as the Binet and the WISC shows that performance in the drawing test is influenced by factors other than purely intellectual ones. Although there are positive correlations between the other tests and the drawing test, the correspondence is always far from complete, and often the correlation quotients are rather low. The fact that the performance part of the WISC corresponds better to the drawing test than the verbal part seems to be in opposition to Harris's idea of drawing as mainly reflecting concept formation, which should be expected to play a greater role in the verbal part of the WISC. Harris's (1963) own findings that drawing at kindergarten age corresponds better with quantitative and space tests than with verbal and perceptual ones point in the same direction.

Also the great sex difference found in the drawing test points against drawing as being purely cognitively determined. Outspoken sex differences in other intelligence tests usually lead to their exclusion from a test battery even in composite tests. When only a single test is used as here, such a big sex difference seems to disqualify the test even more. Not even the use of different norms for the two sexes justifies the use of it. Unless it is accepted that girls are generally more intelligent than boys—which it is not—it shows clearly a strong influence by factors other than purely intellectual ones.

Equally convincing evidence comes from the very many studies of various groups of children who are found to perform more poorly in the drawing test than in other forms of intelligence tests. It is seen quite universally that children with any kind of handicap or deviation from "normality" are handicapped in the drawing test. This is true of children with either physical or psychic handicaps and even of those with such a minor form of deviation as reading disabilities. The lowered performance has been explained by the interplay of different factors, sometimes by visuo-motor disturbances, sometimes by more central disturbances of, for example, body image or self-concept.

Research on the drawing test, which was relatively extensive following the revision of the test, has diminished considerably. The research which does take place concentrates mainly on other aspects of drawings. More detailed study of the essential problem—which factors influence the drawing of a person—has therefore not advanced much during recent years.

It seems necessary to conclude that although there is a positive correlation between intellectual function and drawing performance, this correspondence is far from complete. If the test is used at all, its results should be regarded with great caution, especially if they are found to lie below average or below what would be expected for a given child. Also special warnings should be raised regarding the use of the test with children with any kind of handicap, great or small, physiological or psychological—which is certainly a serious objection to a psychological test.

Although some doubt was cast on the hypothesis that drawing reflects concept formation, this may still be predominantly true. It may be that the child's drawing of the human being reflects the child's concept of a person. What must be seriously questioned, however, is the degree to which the child's concepts are purely cognitively determined. It may even be the case that some concepts are influenced by, for example, affective factors to a higher degree than other or more neutral ones, and that particularly the concept of a person is subjected to the influence of very many factors in the child's total personality.

THREE

Drawing as a Projective Technique

As mentioned, the exactly identical subject—the drawing of a human figure—has formed the basis of interpretations of extremely different aspects of the drawer's personality. The use of it to give an assessment of the drawer's mental age and stage of concept development was described in the preceding chapter. But the same subject has been used to describe the drawer's total personality, with special weight on psychosexual development and identification, on sexual and aggressive impulses, and on anxiety and defence mechanisms.

The starting points for the two different applications of drawings have also been as diametrically opposed as possible. The use of drawings as a measure of intellectual functioning had its basis in the studies of normal development, in drawings by normal children and by large groups, and emphasis was on the common and general traits of the drawings. The use of drawings as a personality test developed out of clinical work and the study of psychopathology, from work with adult patients and with single individuals, and emphasis was on the strictly personal and individual traits in the drawings. These different backgrounds have naturally led to emphasis on quite different aspects of the drawings. The projective use of drawings has actually had two starting points: psychoanalysis and graphology or the study of expressive movements. The first trend dominated in the United States and has come to form the most widespread basis for the projective use of drawings. The study of graphology and expressive movements started in Germany, but has been less influential.

THE DEVELOPMENT OF PROJECTIVE DRAWING TESTS

Already Goodenough (1926) was aware that some of the drawings in her material differed from what might be expected as normal and described four types of deviations:

1. the "verbalist" type, i.e., drawings with many details, but few ideas,
2. the "individual response" type, drawings with traits that seem incomprehensible to those other than the drawer himself,
3. drawings showing evidence of flight of ideas, and
4. drawings characterized by an uneven mental development, as indicated by unusual combinations of primitive and mature characteristics.

Goodenough found that the children who made such drawings to a greater extent than others could be characterized as having "psychopathic" tendencies or the opposite, but she saw only a few of them, and did not follow up on this line in her work.

In the late twenties, Lewis (1928) attempted systematic personality descriptions on the basis of drawings which he regarded as more valuable than dreams. The most well-known attempts at creating systematic projective tests on the basis of the drawing of a human figure are, however, Buck's House-Tree-Person (HTP) Test (1948) and Machover's Draw-A-Person (DAP) Test (1949). Of the two, Machover's test seems to have been most widely used and to have inspired more research, partly because of the provocative statements and hypotheses that she has set forth. As the tests on the whole rest on the same theoretical foundation, I have chosen Machover's test for a more detailed description.

As the rationale for her choice of the human figure as the subject, Machover stated the intimate relationship between the drawing of a person and the person himself. Faced with this task, the drawer is forced to enter into a process of selection from among the innumerable possibilities that exist. This process of selection involves identification through projection and introjection. Everybody has during his development associated various sensations, perceptions, and emotions with various body organs, and this whole "body image" is activated by the task. The drawing thus comes to express the conflicts and needs of the drawer, as these are associated with his body.

According to Machover, our attitudes to our body parts are influenced by several factors:

1. Certain social norms and stereotypes—e.g., certain body types such as the pyknic or the asthenic are associated with certain psychological characteristics.
2. Individual and personal experiences have linked specific emotions and conflicts to certain bodily parts.
3. Special symbolic meanings may be attached to body parts and other details in drawings, e.g., to pipes, cigarettes, buttons, pockets, hair, nose, and feet.

On the basis of all these sources, the drawing is the result of a process of selection and integration by the drawer. Both conscious and unconscious motives are supposed to influence each drawing.

According to Machover, drawings may give both direct and compensated expression to the drawer's basic needs and conflicts, which makes it possible sometimes to see the dominating defence mechanisms.

Machover also appreciated the expressive qualities of drawing and saw particularly the structural or formal elements such as size, quality of line, positioning, symmetry, and shading as more reliable than the content of the drawing such as body parts and clothing.

She stated explicitly that it was not intended to construct a list of "signs" that could be used mechanically to establish differential diagnoses, but that the total configuration and the connection between the various elements of the drawing are more important. Nonetheless, the possible meaning of various details was described, often in such a way that specific meanings rather authoritatively were ascribed to certain ways of drawing. For instance, erasures and shading were described as general indicators of conflict. Machover based her interpretations not only on the drawings, however, but also on associations made by the drawer to his work.

A somewhat unfortunate formulation is the often-quoted phrase that "in some sense, the figure drawn *is* the person, and the paper corresponds to the environment" (1949, 35). It may lead to the mistake that the drawing represents the drawer physically which is clearly not intended. On the other hand, the theoretical foundation of the test is so vaguely formulated that there is wide room for personal interpretations, and many concepts remain poorly defined. This is for example the case with the very important concept of body image.

Machover stated that the method was validated through innumerable clinical examinations and through blind analysis, but, unfortunately, no data at all are given in support. She stated further that although some of her hypotheses lacked experimental validation, they had proven themselves clinically valid.

The test has inspired an extensive body of research. Most of the studies have been made on drawings by adults and cannot be applied to the drawings of children, without due regard to age differences, but the principal problems associated with research in this area are relevant to drawings of persons of all ages. Before entering this discussion, however, the work of Koppitz (1968) should be considered once more, as she has also systematically worked with the use of drawing as a projective test with children. She has tried to integrate clinical insight with traditional scientific method and has regarded drawings as both determined by mental development and by personality traits, with due reference to age, sex, and stage of development.

Koppitz does not, like Machover, use classical psychoanalytic theory as her theoretical frame of reference, but relies instead on Sullivan's Interpersonal Relationship theory. She has thus followed the general trend toward greater emphasis on ego-psychology and conscious processes which was dominant in American psychoanalytic work in the sixties. Instead of unconscious needs, defense mechanisms, and psychosexual development, she emphasized more the child's attitude toward himself and toward the most important persons in his life, and his attitude to current problems and conflicts.

She also questioned the validity of the body-image theory. She did not see the drawing as the expression of the child's basic and lasting personality traits, nor as the representation of his actual (physical?) appearance, but rather as an expression of his present state of mind and his present attitudes which are determined by both development and social and emotional conditions at any given moment.

She stated three general principles for children's drawings of a human being:

1. No matter whom the child draws, the way in which he draws the figure reflects his own self-concept.
2. The person the child draws will be the most important person for the child at the time of the drawing.
3. What the child expresses in his drawing may be one of the following two things: a direct expression of his attitudes and conflicts or a wishdream—or a combination of both.

Koppitz described 30 specific traits in drawings, which she called "emotional indicators." In order to belong to this category, a trait must fulfill the following conditions:

1. It must be clinically valid, i.e., able to differentiate between children with and without emotional problems.
2. It must be found in less than 16% of the children at any given age.
3. It must be neither a function of age nor of maturity.

She operated with three different types of emotional indicators:

1. qualitative aspects such as poor integration, asymmetries, and shading,
2. presence of unexpected traits, and
3. absence of expected traits at certain ages.

Koppitz found that the presence of a single emotional indicator did not necessarily indicate emotional problems in the drawer, but the presence of at least two raised suspicion. Comparing the drawings by a group of children from a child guidance clinic with those by a group of well-adjusted children, she found predominance of emotional indicators in the clinic patients' drawings; they were not found in the work of all the clinic patients, however, so unless these children were referred to the clinic for wrong reasons, apparently the absence of emotional indicators does not exclude the existence of emotional problems.

Koppitz attempted to interpret the meaning of these traits and to relate some of them to the presence of specific symptoms. She contrasted a group of openly aggressive children with an equal number of shy, withdrawn, and depressed children. She also compared children who had psychosomatic complaints with neurotic stealers.

She found no unequivocal connection between the symptom and specific traits in the drawing in the sense of finding one or more traits present in all children in one of the groups (which might hardly have been expected), but she did find certain significant differences between the groups. Shy and depressive children had the tendency more often to draw tiny figures, to omit the mouth, the nose, and the eyes, and to cut off hands, while the aggressive children tended to draw long arms, big hands, teeth, genitals, and transparencies.

Children with psychosomatic complaints showed significantly more often short arms, legs pressed together, omission of nose or mouth, and drawing of clouds, while the children who stole more often shaded hands and/or neck, drew small heads, big hands, or omitted body, arms, or neck.

She also studied the relation between school achievement and emotional indicators and concluded that some of them seemed to be connected particularly with learning problems while others seemed more closely connected with emotional problems. The traits that were found characteristic of children with learning problems placed in special classes, were the following: asymmetric arms or legs, tiny figure, short arms, big hands, hands cut off, poor integration, slanting figure, omission of body, arms, or nose, and the drawing of three or more figures.

However, there was considerable overlapping between the groups; only two-thirds of the children in the special classes had two or more emotional indicators in their drawing, and 19% of the control group had at least two in theirs. Koppitz's conclusion is that one-fifth of the control pupils also might have emotional problems, which is indeed possible. But the conclusion might as well be that the presence of two emotional indicators is not a valid sign of emotional problems, and, conversely, that the lack of such indicators does not preclude problems, unless it is maintained that one-third of the children in the special classes were misplaced. The results may tell something about groups, but not with any high degree of accuracy about the individual child.

Koppitz's study lends itself to criticism in several ways:

1. She has not examined the reliability of the "emotional indicators." As suggested by Swensen (1968), drawings containing certain indices of pathology tend to be unreliable, and as the reliability of a trait is a necessary condition for its validity, the reliability of the "emotional indicators" should have been tested. Actually, their reliability was examined as part of the original Danish study (Mortensen 1984), and it was found to be much lower than that of the developmental traits, thus confirming Swensen's hypothesis. (The chapter describing the occurrence of emotional indicators in the Danish study is omitted in the present book. Those interested in it are referred to the original study.)

2. Second, she compared only extreme groups of children, clinic patients and outstanding pupils. Nonetheless, she claims emotional indicators to be characteristic of emotional problems in general, without knowing to what extent they occur in an average population. Actually, she cannot generalize from her results to unselected groups of children.

3. Finally, her study is yet another example of the "sign approach,"

which will be discussed later in this chapter. In her comparison between groups, she uncritically places children with identical symptoms (e.g., aggression) in the same group without considering the probably very different dynamics behind their apparently similar symptoms.

It is impossible — and unnecessary — to give a detailed overview of the extensive research on drawings as a projective technique, but some of the main conclusions and some of the more central problems encountered will be described in the following. First the concept of body image will be discussed, followed by a comparison of two different ways of using drawings as foundations of personality descriptions: through interpretation of specific details (signs) and through global evaluation.

FIGURE DRAWINGS AND BODY IMAGE

Machover's (1949) somewhat unspecific characterization of the concept of body image and of the connection between the drawer's body image and his drawing has already been mentioned.

It seems as if the question becomes still more complicated when the drawer is a child. Koppitz's (1968) statement that the person, whom the child draws, will be the most important person for him, implies that the child's drawing may not only represent himself, but also other persons. In her experience, children will draw themselves rather realistically, but some are so discontented with themselves that they distort the figure, drawing a clown, a monster or the like, or they draw an idealized figure, e.g., an identification figure such as an actress, a singer, a sports hero, etc. If a young person draws an idealized figure of the other sex, it may also be an idealized partner more than a self-ideal. In some cases the child drew a family member and, in all cases, she found it to be a family member with whom the child had a conflict. A few children chose to draw the examiner, but they were either children with organic brain damage, who were concrete and inspired by the immediate situation, or lonely and unhappy children, who found that nobody cared for them and therefore overresponded to the examiner.

Koppitz is here in agreement with Hammer (1958) who also found that the child might draw (1) an ideal self, (2) himself as he experiences himself, or (3) other important persons.

The whole question about whom the drawing represents and in which way it represents the drawer, if at all, is one of the most difficult questions to answer about figure drawings. In an example, Koppitz (1968) describes a drawing that represents the child's father, but where the drawing is made with a continuous outline. Koppitz interprets this as an attempt by the child to control and integrate his strongly disorganized personality. It might be generalized to mean that mainly the formal aspects characterize the drawer (as suggested also by Machover). But in many other cases, the content of the drawing is included in the personality interpretation as well. If a child draws an adult man and attributes a great many phallic symbols to his drawing, does he then depict his father's psychosexual conflicts (or his experience of his father's potency) or his own insecurity for which he tries to compensate? And is the size of the drawn figure an expression of the child's experience of his father's power and size (psychologically speaking), or is it a reflection of his own self-esteem? The possibility exists that one and the same trait may at one time characterize the drawer and at another his model. This may be true of both content and formal aspects.

Although no physical similarity has been postulated between drawing and drawer, nonetheless some studies have found some connection between the drawer's physical appearance and the drawn figure. For example, Berman and Laffal (1953) found a significant relationship between body type and figure drawn by adult men. Apfeldorf and Smith (1965) matched draw-a-person tests (DAPs) with photos of the drawers and found a significant correlation at the .01 level. Craddick (1963) found similarities between own size and size of figure drawings, and Kotkov and Goodman (1953) found that obese women drew figures covering an unusually large area of the paper. Nathan (1973) found, however, that obese children drew neither unusually small nor large human figure drawings (HFDs). Gross bodily disturbances such as polio, amputations, and other disablements seem generally not to be depicted in HFDs, as shown by a number of studies (e.g., Silverstein and Robinson 1956; Sims 1951; Corah and Corah 1963; Johnson and Wawrzaszek 1961; Centers and Centers 1963; Weininger, Rotenberg, and Henry 1972; Dines 1982). Neither are facial deformities represented in drawings (Fisk 1981).

Others have tried to relate the drawn figures, not to the drawers' physical appearance, but to their self-concept or body image, as measured by other methods. For example, Kamano (1960) compared drawings made by schizophrenics with different aspects of their self-concepts, namely with their actual self, their ideal self, and their least-liked self. The highest correlation was found with their actual self-concept.

Bodwin and Bruch (1960) compared specific traits in the drawn figure with the drawers' self-concept, as judged in an interview, and found a correlation between the DAP scores and the judges' ratings of .61. Delatte and Hendrickson (1982) and Ludwig (1969) found a positive relationship between self-esteem and size of the drawn figure.

Hunt and Feldman (1960) related Machover's (1949) scoring indices to scores on the Secord-Jourard Body Cathexis Scale (1953) and found no relation between the drawings and the subjects' ratings of 25 different body parts. (The Secord-Jourard Body Cathexis Scale is a verbal self-rating scale that measures the degree of feeling of satisfaction or dissatisfaction with the various parts or processes of the body. It is frequently used in studies of body concept and self-concept.)

In a study on children, Silverstein and Robinson (1961) found a negative correlation between the estimated height and weight of a group of children and the estimated height and weight of figures drawn by the same children. This study also tried to compare the drawings with the children's body image instead of with their actual physique.

McHugh (1965) found that a group of children uniformly assigned ages to their figures that were greater than their own ages.

Bennett (1964, 1966) found no relationship between self-concept, as determined by the (Q-sort), and the DAP for sixth-grade children.

It is difficult from these results to conclude whether the DAP reflects a person's body concept or not. It is noteworthy that most of the studies using adult subjects found significant relationships between the DAP and some other measure of body image or self-concept. But generally the studies with children as subjects got negative results. This supports the hypothesis that figure drawings may reflect partly different things for children and adults, and that the relationship between body image and drawing may be more complicated in the case of children.

Perhaps some of the difference is best characterized by saying that while adults in their drawings are oriented toward the present, children are to a greater degree future-oriented. This is shown for example by the fact that they tend to draw their figures older than themselves or to depict ideals. Another factor is of course children's greater dependence on the adults in their surroundings.

In the preceding pages the words "body image," "body concept," and "self-concept" have been used in accordance with the various authors' use of them. They are not synonymous, however. Machover (1949) speaks of body image, while Koppitz (1968) who rejects the body-image hypothesis, describes drawings as reflections of the drawer's self-concept. The latter is clearly a broader term. Body image is related more closely to a person's experience of his physical self and of the basic sexual and aggressive impulses, whereas the self-concept is related to his experience of his whole person, including psychological and social characteristics and interpersonal ways of functioning.

The concept of "body image" has itself changed over time, however. In Machover's (1949) original work, it is a relatively vaguely defined and undifferentiated concept. It has been subjected to intensive research, however, and Fisher, who has been a leading figure in this research, concludes in his latest work (1986) that it no longer makes sense to talk about a simple unitary body image or body schema. The organization of body experience is multidimensional. The research has further shown that modes of body perception may be quite different, even polar opposites, in men and women. The various aspects of body experience may not even correlate with each other. He concludes that it does not mean that body image is not a valid concept, but that it is far more multidimensional than the early models envisioned. He finds it premature to distinguish sharply between the terms "body image," "body concept," "body scheme," "body attitudes," and "body experience." The word body image may have the disadvantage of suggesting a limitation of the concept to the realm of imagery. This is clearly not the way it is used by Fisher, however, and neither is it the use made of the concept here.

It is so far neither clear what aspects of a person's self-concept (if any) drawings may reflect, nor how closely they are connected with body image.

If, for example, the size of a drawn figure is related to the drawer's estimation of his own physical size, the drawing will be a reflection of his body image. But if the size of the drawing shows a connection with his feeling of self-esteem, the relationship is with his self-concept. To complicate matters further, body image and self-concept are, of course, interrelated. Many of our psychological qualities are based on and dependent on physical properties and qualities and are inseparable from them. Fisher (1970), in a discussion of the relationship between the self-concept and body image variables, concludes that although not identical, they are "inextricably interdependent." He cites a few experimental studies that demonstrate this interdependency, e.g., a study by Jourard and Secord (1954), who reported that body cathexis (the degree of satisfaction or dissatisfaction with various parts or processes of the body) was significantly related to feelings about the self. Other experiments have reached similar results.

For the use of drawing as a projective test, however, the relationship between drawings and either body image or self-concept is utterly uninteresting, unless these two concepts again are related to specific traits, attitudes, or behavioral aspects of the personality. Otherwise only circular inferences of no clinical or practical value can be made. That differences in self-concept manifest themselves in differences in behavior is commonly accepted; on the other hand, the self-concept is so encompassing that the postulation of a relationship between drawings and self-concept is not too informative or interesting, unless it can be much more precisely defined.

A relationship between the narrower concept of body image and drawings might lead to more specific information, but the connection between body image and other aspects of personality is less well known. This problem cannot be solved solely through the study of drawings, however, but must include direct studies of the body image. Some promising leads seem to have been found which will be discussed in chapter 9.

Other studies have focused less on the concepts of body image or self-concept as intervening variables, but have related aspects of drawings more directly to aspects of behavior or to specific personality traits. Some of the main results and some of the problems inherent in this research will be described in the following.

SIGN-INTERPRETATION OR GLOBAL EVALUATION OF FIGURE DRAWINGS

In general, "sign-interpretation" is regarded with skepticism by clinicians because it violates one of the basic principles in clinical work, namely the fact that each trait derives its significance from its place and function in the totality and through its connection with other traits. It is common knowledge, also from research on other projective tests, that studies which find connections between specific signs and some personality variables on replication often fail to confirm their earlier results. This may be due to sampling difficulties, to differences of definitions or simply to the fact that the relationship has been incidental. In many cases, the lack of an integrating theory is obvious, and the postulated relationships may appear meaningless.

In two reviews of the research on drawing as a projective technique (1957, 1968), Swensen has summarized the results of a great number of studies, both with regard to content and to formal variables.

In a list of works on content variables, the number of studies with significant and insignificant results are compared, and it is concluded that the empirical evidence supporting a significant relationship between the treatment of a particular body part and some behavioral measure is either conflicting or negative. The only clear exception is the sex of the first drawn person. (For a more thorough discussion of this variable, see chapter 4.) The drawing of different body parts is found to be less reliable than both the quality of the global drawing and formal aspects, which makes the evaluation of their validity more difficult. It is concluded that the evidence summarized supports the notion that global ratings are more valuable than sign-interpretations.

Swensen's (1968) conclusion is perhaps a little too negative. Actually quite a few of the studies show significant results, but in many cases a certain trait is only examined in one or two studies, so the material is too small to draw definite conclusions from it. "Sex drawn first" is treated in 18 studies, while no other trait is found in more than at most 6 studies.

It is, of course, a difficulty if a specific body part is not reliable, but it should not lead to the conclusion that it is not valid, *when present*. It is possible that the same personality trait manifests itself in different ways in different drawings by the same person, or it may be found in direct form in one drawing or in compensated form in another. This principle is directly used in some drawing tests which require the execution of several drawings, e.g., Hammer's Chromatic HTP Test (1958) or Caligor's 8-Card Redrawing Test (Hammer 1958). What it means, of course, is that no automatic scoring is possible, and that the fact that a certain trait is not present in a drawing cannot lead to the conclusion that the personality variable with which it is associated does not exist in the person. This principle is comparable to what is known from other projective tests, e.g., the Rorschach. Certain formal thought disturbances are, e.g., highly suggestive of schizophrenia or at least psychosis, but the lack of such disturbances does not exclude the possibility of a psychotic state.

The formal traits that have been examined include the following: size, positioning, perspective (the direction a figure faces), stance, line quality, shading, erasures, omissions, transparency, distortion, and symmetry. Also here, a summary is made of studies with significant and insignificant results. The most convincing results, according to Swensen, come from the studies of shading, where considerable more studies show insignificant results than significant ones, contradicting the assumption that shading should be an expression of anxiety. Shading is also found in drawings of high quality.

These conclusions are supported with regard to children in a study by Cohen, Money, and Uhlenhuth (1972), who found shading present in 46.5% of drawings by 385 normal schoolchildren, 6 to 13-years-old. They concluded that, since shading was so common, it should be interpreted with caution as a sign of emotional disturbance. The use of shading was found most often in the drawings of older children.

These examples are ideally suited for illustrating some of the principal problems of sign-interpretation. The word "shading" encompasses such different things as the diffuse, heavy, black covering of the whole figure or parts of it and as light, limited, and barely visible sketching in order to emphasize roundings or details, or to create the impression of three-dimensionality. The emotional meaning of these various uses is obviously very different, and an automatic grouping and scoring of them is simply meaningless. This does not exclude the possibility that some ways of using shading may point toward anxiety or emotional problems. Koppitz (1968) regarded the shading of special body parts as emotional indicators (face, body and/or limbs, and hands and/or neck). The use of shading in general she finds normal for young children and not necessarily a sign of psychopathology. But as children get older, shading on the HFDs takes on a considerable diagnostic significance, according to her. The only exception to this rule is shading of the face, which she finds highly significant at all ages and which she considers a valid emotional indicator for all children aged 5 to 12.

Shading of body (or limbs) is not considered a valid emotional indicator until age 8 for boys and 9 for girls. She states that shading of the body reveals body anxiety, but that this is a normal feature in children at the beginning of school age and only becomes significant if it persists beyond the ages mentioned. She found shading of the body significantly more often in the drawings of clinic patients, of children with psychosomatic complaints, and of children who stole, than in the control group.

Shading of the hands was found by Koppitz to be a valid emotional indicator at age 7 for girls and 8 for boys. After those ages it was found most often in the drawings of clinic patients and children who stole, but she also found it in both aggressive and shy children. She concludes that shading of the hands does not seem to be related to any specific activity but rather to anxiety over some real or imagined activities involving the hands.

Her results were supported in a Danish study by Kyng (1973), who tested some of Koppitz's hypotheses on a group of 5-year-old Danish children. Although not on all points in agreement with Koppitz, it was explicitly stated that shading was found to be the most valid sign of emotional disturbances; this was true whether the shading was found in the face, on body or limbs, or outside the figure. Five-year-olds cannot use the more mature forms of shading found in the drawings of adults or older children, but only the heavier, more diffuse forms. So the conclusion may still be that some forms of shading—in some age-groups —are signs of anxiety; but a scoring which does not take into account the various qualities of it, its connection with other aspects of the drawing, and the age of the drawer, is useless. This is, actually, quite in agreement with the intentions behind the original use of the test. Much of the research on "sign-interpretation" seems much too naively to have disregarded this essential—but naturally also very complicating—factor.

The conclusions regarding some of the other formal variables will be mentioned shortly. Swensen (1968) found that quite a few of the studies on the size of drawings were significant, suggesting that the size of drawings reflects self-esteem and probably fantasized self-inflation, but with an inconsistency that is due to the relative lack of reliability of this aspect of drawings.

Distorted drawings were found to differentiate quite clearly between severely disturbed persons and others. Distortion seems to be the trait that most convincingly is a sign of maladjustment. Here, it was defined as body parts drawn out of proportion, parts not connected to the body, and parts drawn in inappropriate areas of the body.

Also omissions were found to be characteristic of severely regressed patients, but they were not found to distinguish between normals and near-normals. Omissions among children were found to be a relatively sensitive indicator among the very young, but to lose this sensitivity as the children grow older and their drawing skills improve. It is concluded, however, that, in general, omissions of significant body parts are fairly dependable indicators of severe pathology. Koppitz's findings also confirm this, but without reservations with regard to the older children.

Handler and Reyher (1965), who reviewed studies on 21 different anxiety indexes, found the following to have consistently given significant results: omissions of important parts of figure, distortion, loss of details, size increase and decrease, head simplification, trunk simplification, and line discontinuity.

They found that shading, hair shading, erasures, and reinforcements as often as not give opposite results. They suggested that these measures may be poor measures of anxiety, because the anxiety-producing characteristics of the drawing task create a wish in most subjects to finish the drawing as quickly as possible. This may lead to a diminishing of erasures, shading, etc., as this takes time. Thus the presence of, for example, shading may be a sign of ego-strength and ability to cope with the anxiety of the situation instead of fleeing from it. In contrast, the abovementioned traits (omissions, etc.) are almost all traits that would follow from an attempt to go as quickly through the situation as possible. Hammer (1959) also notes that some erasure with subsequent improvement is a sign of adaptiveness and flexibility.

Handler (1967) suggested that shading, erasures, reinforcement, and emphasis line are probably more sensitive to external stress than to intrapsychic stress. This finding raises the important question of what is meant by anxiety. Drawings are often validated against quite superficial measures of anxiety, such as paper and pencil tests, and different studies use different methods which may not be directly comparable, and which may measure anxiety at very different levels and of different kinds. This criticism could be raised against much of the research on the sign-interpretation of drawings. People also differ in their coping mechanisms toward anxiety. Even given a comparable amount of anxiety (whatever is meant by that), one person may react to it by trying to avoid the situation and thus, for example, make omissions in his drawings, while another may try to work hard on his drawing in order to try to master his anxiety in that way and perhaps add shading, etc. This will lead to contradictory results which will be statistically insignificant.

There is general agreement that global evaluations of drawings are more reliable than sign-interpretations and therefore also have the possibility of being more valid. But the use of global evaluations also has its pitfalls. For example, the question has been raised whether the drawer's artistic abilities may not play a part in the rating. Whitmyre (1953) and Sherman (1958a, 1958b) both found significant relationships between psychologists' ratings of adjustment and artists' ratings of artistic qualities in a group of drawings. As the adjustment of the drawers was not evaluated by other means, however, the coincidence may, of course, be justified.

Nichols and Strümpfer (1962), in a factor-analytic study of figure drawings, found a very large factor accounting for most of the variance among the drawing scores. They called it "quality of drawing" and in the beginning did not know whether it was identical with "aesthetic quality." However, a comparison between artists' and psychologists' ratings of the same drawings showed very low correlations. The psychologists gave high scorings to drawings that looked like a person, and the quality of drawing thus seemed to reflect most of all the technical skill of the drawer. The artists, on the other hand, were mostly concerned with such factors as balance, symmetry, freedom of expression, and aesthetic appeal. They also found that the overall quality of drawing had little relationship to the psychological adjustment. They recommended that future studies control the overall quality of drawing. The study also points to the difficulty of knowing what is meant by "quality of drawing." Here it seems to be defined as technical skill to achieve a lifelike drawing, but in other connections, and if not carefully defined, it might as well be synonymous with the qualities which here are called "aesthetic."

Swensen (1968) concluded that the research has repeatedly demonstrated that better adjusted subjects produce drawings of higher quality, but also that the higher the quality of the drawing, the more conflict indicators it contains. Drawings of good quality contain more of the difficult details which may be omitted in drawings of poorer quality. Drawings of good quality therefore contain more frequent erasures, shading, and a wider variety of kinds of lines. There is a positive correlation between the quality of a drawing and the number of conflict indicators that are present in it. These conclusions seem inconsistent with his earlier findings, however, that shading and erasures are not valid as signs of emotional conflicts. It would seem more logical to stick to the first results and maintain that the validity of, for example, shading and erasures *is* dubious—then no conflict exists between the quality of the drawing and the presence of such traits. The more valid signs of emotional conflict, such as omissions and distortions, do not characterize drawings of high quality—quite the contrary.

The importance of a global assessment is also emphasized by Roback (1968) in an overall review of 18 years' research on the DAP, in many ways similar to Swensen's. He also fails to find support for most of the specific hypotheses and states that, in the clinical setting, interpretations of figure drawings are usually impressionistic and based upon a global assessment of the data. He also stresses the importance of the overall quality of the drawings.

The difficulties in the establishment of specific criteria would lead one to expect the existence of differences between raters in their ability to evaluate drawings, and this is exactly what has been found. Guinan and Hurley (1965) found, for example, that experienced raters were better than inexperienced ones in a matching experiment.

But also other personality factors may play a part. Murray and Deabler (1958) found great individual differences between experienced raters. In their study, in which many drawings were rated and in which there was opportunity to learn from experience, raters were found to vary considerably in their ability to learn. Such individual differences in rating ability were also confirmed by Schmidt and McGowan (1959) who, however, did not find any differences connected with degree of training. They also distinguished between raters who had a basically cognitive and a basically affective attitude, but did not find that this factor had any effect.

That more deep-seated personality factors in the raters may be influential was suggested in a study by Hammer and Piotrowsky (1953). They found that differences between raters in their scoring of "hostility" in children's drawings could be explained as a result of the raters' own "hostility," which they found positively correlated to the degree of hostility rated in the drawings.

CONCLUDING REMARKS

The main purpose of discussing the use of drawing as a projective test was not to assess the value of this use of drawing, but to point to the attempts that have been made to connect drawings with basic impulses, drives, and emotions of the drawer's personality. This is done in order to avoid the danger of regarding drawing only as an attempt at a more or less successful reflection or visual copying of the outer realities, based only on the drawer's (visual) perception and more or less well-functioning intellectual capacities. Impulses, attitudes to one's own body, and emotional factors are found to play an important role in the drawings of adults—and they may be even more influential in the drawings of children, who are closer to their impulses and feelings and have not yet built such stable defenses and solid intellectual barriers against them as adults.

In the projective use of drawings, attention is directed toward the drawer's experience of his inner psychic realities. Figure drawings are seen both as a reflection of the drawer's object relations, i.e., his inner representations of the persons in his surroundings, and as a reflection of his perception of himself. Although the development of self- and object-representations are probably highly interrelated, they are not identical, and much of the difficulty in the interpretation of figure drawings consists exactly in distinguishing between these.

As the child grows—hopefully—his inner reality approaches the outer reality more and more, and therefore the correspondence between drawings and the outer reality improves. But it will never become total; the personal experience will never reach complete objectivity, so drawings will always keep elements that betray their origin in the private world of the drawer.

If drawings are seen as naturalistic representations of the outer reality, there will always be drawings which fall outside the general and "normal" pattern, and which are only explained with difficulty—if at all. And even such a "normal" phenomenon as sex differences creates troubles. With the other approach, no problem is raised by the recognition of the fact that children (and adults) differ in the degree to which they have perfected their reality testing, and that there are some persons whose inner fantasies are more dominant than they are for others. As a matter of fact, this seems also to be the only approach which makes it possible to bridge the gap between children's drawings and adult art, where the subjective element is suddenly not only accepted as a necessity, but even cultivated.

Even if the standpoint is taken, however, that drawings can only be satisfactorily described if they are seen as partly reflecting the drawer's inner psychic reality, research on the projective use of drawings shows clearly the difficulties in the establishment of the exact relationship between figure drawings and drawer. It may be tentatively concluded that some relationship does exist between the drawing of a figure and the drawer's experience of his own body in a narrower sense, and also between the drawing and his experience of himself in a wider sense, including aspects of his total self-concept. In the case of children, the relationship between self and drawing may be further complicated by the fact that children have not yet differentiated themselves so clearly from parents and other surrounding figures that they have come to experience themselves as completely independent individuals. These authority figures—or future ideals—may enter their drawings, because they are still to a very high degree connected with the child's picture of himself.

The impossibility of a mechanistic sign-interpretation seems amply demonstrated. That it has come to play such a big role in the research at all is in a way deplorable. It is partly due to some unfortunate formulations in the original works on the drawing test, but probably, most of all, to the desperate attempts at making psychological testing an objective method of assessment and thereby to make psychology a respectable science. The general impossibility of sign-interpretations does not, however, exclude the possibility that certain traits in drawings can have the function of "danger signals," when—but only when—age and sex of the drawer are taken into consideration, when the specific qualities of the trait are noted, and when the trait is related to all other traits in the same drawing and preferably also to other drawings by the same person. This excludes, however, absolutely any automatic scoring process.

Research has shown that people differ in their ability to interpret drawings meaningfully. This connects well with the fact that the global evaluation of drawings repeatedly has been shown to be the most valid form. A global evaluation depends on an accurate perception of a number of details, emotional sensitivity, and responsiveness to them, a subtle judgment as well as the ability to chose between relevant and irrelevant aspects, and finally the ability to integrate these impressions into a coherent totality and express it in words. This process lies closer to the field of art than to anything else. This does not mean that learning is impossible, but it should probably take the form of training under supervision as with other projective tests. In addition, every assessor of drawings should, of course, be well acquainted with what is known about drawing development, sex differences, and the relationships between aspects of drawings and personality.

More recently, studies on drawing as a projective technique have almost disappeared, as is the case with studies on drawing as a test of intelligence. Most of the energy devoted to the study of drawings seems to have been led into therapeutic channels instead of diagnostic ones. The field of art therapy has expanded, dominated more by case studies than by empirical attempts at validation. It seems, thus, as if the inconclusive evidence about the relationship between personality factors and drawings has in no way discouraged people, who have gladly progressed to the therapeutic use of drawings, where this relationship is simply taken for granted and is the very basis on which art therapy rests.

FOUR

Sex Differences in Drawings

Sex differences in drawings have rarely been studied in their own right, but they have often been treated more or less parenthetically in studies with other major goals, mostly in studies on drawing development or on drawing as a measure of intellectual functioning, less often in studies of drawing as a personality test.

Here, the more comprehensive studies of sex differences will be described first, followed by studies of single variables. Among the latter, sexual differentiation and the sex of the first drawn figure have been studied far more frequently than any other variables. A few other traits will also be mentioned: profile drawings, age of figure drawn, height of drawing, and movement.

COMPREHENSIVE STUDIES

Even some of the earliest investigators of children's drawings noticed and described sex differences in their material. These differences were found to be of two kinds: quantitative and qualitative.

Quantitative differences consist of different rates of progression through the developmental stages for the two sexes.

Qualitative differences are found when specific traits are present only in the drawings of one sex or—more often—considerably more frequently in the drawings of one sex than in those of the other, without any connection with development.

Kerschensteiner (1905) found that the drawings of the boys in his material quantitatively surpassed those of the girls in nearly all aspects. The girls progressed more slowly, almost none of them reaching the fourth stage of development, characterized by the ability to draw spatial relationships, while quite a few of the boys did so. Generally the girls' drawings were more primitive than those of the boys.

The degree of difference between the sexes was found to vary with the theme of the drawings. In drawings of human beings and animals, the differences were pronounced, but they were less so in drawings of flowers, where the drawings of the girls in the youngest stages were as good as those of the boys. The greatest difference was found in the drawing of a streetcar, where the boys were far superior. Also in drawings of houses and churches and in the depiction of a scene—a snowball fight—the boys were greatly superior. Kerschensteiner tried to explain these differences by a lack of ability in the girls to organize the perceived details into wholes—a form of synthesizing which he considered to be more difficult for the girls.

The only area where the girls surpassed the boys was in decoration. Kerschensteiner found that the sense of rhythm in the decorations was quantitatively stronger and earlier developed in the girls than in the boys. Also the color sense was better developed in the girls.

Kerschensteiner mentions that the boys were taught drawing in their schools, while the girls were not, but he did not ascribe any importance to this fact, as the drawing education mainly consisted of the copying of classical ornaments and no training in free drawing was given.

Somewhat similar observations were made by Burt (1921). He also found that girls had a better sense of color and were better at drawing decorations and patterns, while boys surpassed them in the depiction of proportions, perspective, and sense of form. He found, moreover, that boys, in their drawings, showed more imagination, humor, and originality, while girls often were better at drawing details. Also Partridge (1902) found boys superior to girls in the drawing of a man.

The quantitative results found by Goodenough (1926) seem at least at first glance strikingly different. She found girls noticeably superior in drawing a man at every age, except at age 12, with a tendency for somewhat greater variability in boys. She attributed this difference to a large degree to the method used for standardization of the test. Class position was one of the criteria used, and more girls than boys were promoted, more boys than girls retarded in school. This situation favored the selection of items in which girls might exceed boys. She also suggested that girls, being more docile and of more studious habits than boys, would be more willing to persevere in the work on the drawing and to give careful attention to details.

The qualitative differences that Goodenough found characterizing the drawings of boys and girls, respectively, were the following:

	Number of Drawings	
Masculine Characteristics:	boys	girls
At least head and feet shown in profile and in same direction	58	36
Some accessory characteristic present, such as pipe, cane, umbrella, house, or scenery	21	9
Trousers transparent	12	3
Heel present	53	37
Figure represented as walking or running	20	7
Arms reaching below knee	11	3
Necktie shown	25	14
Feminine Characteristics:		
Nose represented only by two dots	7	28
Feet less than 1/20 body length	4	16
Eyes showing two or more of the following details: brow, lashes, pupil, iris	1	11
Hair very smooth or neatly parted	13	34
"Cupid's bow" mouth	1	7
Cheeks shown	1	7
Trousers flaring at base	6	21

	Number of Drawings	
Masculine Characteristics:	*boys*	*girls*
Head larger than trunk	9	17
Arm length not greater than head length	11	26
Curly hair	2	7
Legs not more than ¼ trunk length	2	12

The results were collected from 100 children of each sex, scoring between 22 and 26 points on the test.

Goodenough suggested that a greater interest in physical activity might be the reason for the boys to exaggerate the size of the feet and the length of the arms and legs. The boys also more often showed the figure in action. She suggested that the tendency to draw a figure in activity might lead to the change from full-face drawings to profile drawings, a change which happened earlier and more often with boys than with girls. In general, boys were found to show a better sense of proportion than girls.

Girls, on the other hand, were found often to exaggerate the size of the head and the trunk and particularly the eyes. On the whole, girls excelled in the number of items and the amount of detail included.

In the Harris revision of the DAM test (1963), a consistent tendency was noted for girls to score higher than boys on the drawing of a man. This tendency was strongest between 10 and 12 years and diminished after this age. In general, girls were found to be approximately one half year ahead of boys at each age. In the drawing of a woman, the advantage of the girls was even greater, roughly equal to one year. In contrast to what was found in the drawing of a man, in the drawing of a woman the results of the two sexes did not approach each other at puberty.

An item analysis was made on the revision of the test. Only the differences between boys and girls satisfying the 5% level of significance in more than half of the age-groups from 5 to 15 were considered relevant. All the differences had to favor the same sex.

On these criteria, the following sex differences were found: in the drawing of a man, girls did better on eye detail and proportion items, on indication of the lips, on giving the line of the jaw, on hair items, and on proportion of the ears and the arms. They solved the problem of clothing or figure transparencies sooner than boys, but did not otherwise tend to do better on clothing items. They also definitely did better on motor coordination items.

Boys, in the drawing of a man, were considerably more likely to get the nose in two dimensions. They excelled on the proportion of the foot and indication of the heel. They were more likely to portray action in the arms.

In the drawing of a woman, girls did better on most facial features and on hair and hair styling. They more often depicted jewelry and neckline and gave "flare" to the skirt. On the whole, they were more likely to score points on clothes and costume, especially at ages above 8 or 9. They also excelled boys on motor coordination items, such as the drawing of body contours and the inclusion of secondary sex characteristics such as breasts, hips, and calf of leg.

Boys again were better at depicting the nose in two dimensions. They were more likely to draw the legs so that a distinct angle was indicated between them; this was often done by separating the feet. Girls more often drew the legs parallel.

The evaluation of the drawing of a woman according to the quality scale instead of to the point scale, was found to give an even greater advantage to the girls. This may be due to the overall impression of neatness and order in the girls' drawings, which may lead the rater to a general overestimation of them.

Harris found that Goodenough had minimized the quantitative sex differences, perhaps because of influence from the European results, where the sex differences found favored the boys. As class position was no longer used in the Harris revision for the standardization, Goodenough's explanation of the girls' better school performance could no longer be valid as a reason for the sex differences. Harris suggests that Goodenough's other hypothesis—that girls show more perseverance, are more docile and careful about details—may be more plausible. He suggested that the differences could also be due to "cultural" factors which give girls greater practice with drawing and other finely coordinated work or engender greater interest in and attention to people and clothing. He added further that it is a fact that girls exceed boys developmentally in social interests and skills and very possibly in certain intellectual abilities. The widening discrepancy between the mean scores

Smoothed Raw Score Means, Man Drawing

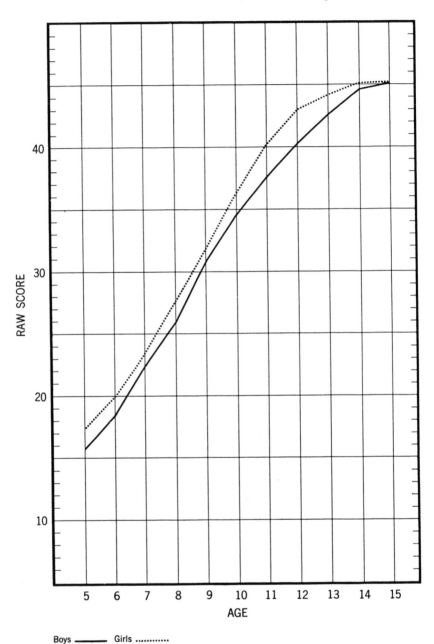

FIGURE 7 Comparison of the development of boys and girls in the drawing of a human figure. (From Harris 1963.)

Smoothed Raw Score Means, Woman Drawing

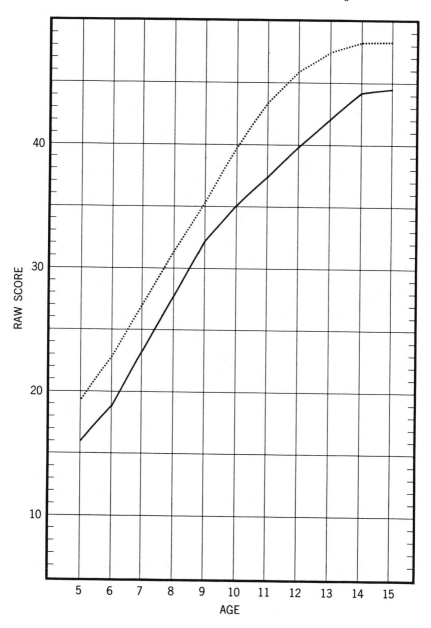

Boys ——— Girls ·············

of boys and girls as they approach puberty is seen as a result of the relatively greater maturity of girls during these years.

Harris mentions that in psychometric tests, the tendency has been to omit the items favoring one sex over the other, but that the analytic study of abilities has constantly found certain sex differences. Without entering into a detailed discussion of general sex differences, he mentions that girls have been found to show a slight, but consistent, acceleration in general development and perhaps in verbal performance. Boys seem to excel in arithmetic performance, particularly reasoning. They also excel in general motor and performance items, notably space orientation, comprehension, and use. Girls do better on fine motor coordination and tests of number and name checking. They show more aesthetic interest from as early as the age of 5 and more interest in painting and modeling. They are often found to show greater awareness of people and personal relationships. No attempt was made by Harris to analyze the connection between the sex differences in drawing and the general sex differences described.

The question was raised—but not answered—as to how the drawing test relates to tests of perceptual and fine motor skills as well as to cognitive and verbal factors. Harris also added that many of the differences here found could be related to dynamic theories of personality organization, and that factors such as culturally reinforced sex differences in libidinal investment of body parts, differences between the sexes in the significance of the body image, and differences in sexual symbolism could all be drawn upon in the discussion of the results. These suggestions are not followed up, however. He attempted to explain the greater sex difference in the drawing of the female figure than in the drawing of the male by a greater identification with sex role for girls than for boys. He found no indication of a rejection of the feminine role in the drawings of the girls, no attempts at masculinization of female figures. He further suggested that girls excel in drawing the human figure because of a greater awareness of and concern with people and personal relationships, but this, of course, does not explain the differential treatment of the two sexes.

Koppitz (1968) found small, but consistent, differences between the sexes in the occurrence of developmental items. She found girls' drawings superior to those of boys in the first grades, but stated that by age 8 or 9 boys not only caught up with girls, but often surpassed them in the quality and details of their drawings. She stated that there was consensus (between Goodenough, Harris, Machover, and herself) about this development. This is not correct, however. As mentioned, Harris found that girls even increased their advantage during prepuberty.

There is also inconsistency between Koppitz's statement that boys catch up with girls as early as age 8 or 9 and the fact that for all her age-groups, including the oldest of 12, girls are expected to include more developmental items in their figures than boys of the same age, which points in the direction of a continued better performance by girls. This inconsistency is not explained.

Koppitz also found some qualitative sex differences in the drawing of her material at all age levels. The "masculine" traits were profile drawing, drawing of knee and ear, while the "feminine" items were hair, pupils, eyebrows, both lips, and clothing. She states that these findings are in accordance with those found by other investigators and have been reported so often that they must be accepted as real differences between the drawings of American boys and girls.

Developmental items were defined by Koppitz as items primarily related to age and maturation and not to school learning. This implies that the *quantitative* sex differences must be primarily biologically determined.

In contrast, Koppitz believes that the *qualitative* sex differences primarily reflect values and attitudes from middle-class Western culture, and that they are not biologically determined. She ascribes the girls' interest in clothes, hair, and facial features to their wish to imitate their mothers whom they see as interested in clothes and makeup. The value the culture places on feminine attire and beauty will tend to strengthen the girls' interest in these features. Boys, on the other hand, are expected to be more independent and outgoing. Profile drawing is often associated with a turning away from others and a striving toward independence. Boys are also encouraged to participate in physical activities which may draw their attention to body movements and to limbs and knees. Finally, because of their shorter hair, their ears are more conspicuous and may therefore appear more often in their drawings.

She concludes that specific "masculine" and "feminine" items on HFDs reflect attitudes in children that have been learned unconsciously in early life from the social and cultural environment they live in. She assumes that the frequency or occurrence of these traits will differ in different cultures with different values. This dependence on cultural values, is, for example, reflected in the drawing of long hair on boys and men during the years when the "long-haired" mode prevailed. She also finds that girls formerly drew figures with many more clothing details than today. She therefore warns against the attribution of too much psychological significance to the presence or absence of clothing and hair items on HFDs, and emphasizes that a child's drawing can only be evaluated if the mode of dress and grooming in his environment is known. She adds that none of the masculine and feminine items were among the Expected items for boys and girls at any age between 5 and 10.

Several hypotheses can be offered to explain the fact that the quantitative sex differences found in the earlier European studies are so much in disagreement with the later American results. There is no reason to doubt the validity of any of the results, which are founded on large samples of drawings and are confirmed by several studies.

For one thing, the studies may not really all be comparable because they have described different subjects of drawings. For example, Kerschensteiner (1905) let his children draw objects and houses, he analyzed the use of perspective, composition, and movement in complex drawings, and the use of decoration. But the fact remains that opposite results are described precisely in the drawing of the human figure, where girls in the earlier studies were found to lag behind the boys in general development, in sense of proportion, and in form level.

Also in the estimation of the developmental level of the human figure itself, however, partly different aspects are emphasized in the various studies. For example, Kerschensteiner stressed form level, proportioning, and movement, while in Goodenough's (1926) and Harris's (1963) studies many facial details and details of clothing weigh heavily in the determination of the developmental level. But even this is hardly sufficient as an explanation for the differences in results. It seems to be a fact that the general developmental level of boys exceeded that of girls in the earlier studies, while the opposite now is the case.

It seems difficult to find a more plausible explanation than the different situation for girls in European societies around the beginning of the century and in the United States some decades later. A very specific difference was the lack of drawing education for girls at the time of the earlier studies, which Kerschensteiner noticed, but regarded as unimportant—perhaps not quite justifiably. A more general and perhaps also more important difference, however, may be the change in opinion regarding the possibilities of girls and the corresponding change in the outlook and treatment of them. The lack of encouragement to use their intellectual and creative abilities earlier may very well have led to an earlier stagnation of development. It is known from many studies of drawings in other cultures that drawing development is slower and stops earlier in children of more "primitive" and less literal societies. From their drawings, it looks as if girls, less than a century ago, made up exactly such a partly underdeveloped subculture in Europe.

Also Machover described in two studies (1953, 1960) the sex differences found in HFDs by children. She only described qualitative differences and did not enter into a discussion of the general developmental differences. In the first article (1953) she compared drawings by about 1,000 children from kindergarten age up to the age of 11. They were Jewish, Negro, and white, but in this connection only the results for the white children will be mentioned. She selected from each group 20–40 random sets of drawings by each age and sex group and states that they were classified according to more than 50 graphic variables.

In her second study (1960), 100 sets of drawings made by white, middle-class children of at least average intelligence were examined at each age level from 5 through 12. They were evenly divided between the sexes. The drawings were studied with regard to 45 variables, covering both content and structural aspects. Unfortunately, however, no documentation of the results is presented in either study, only the author's overall impressions are given.

She claimed that the differences between the sexes were not only as important as age differences, but often also more striking and dramatic. She stated rightly that in spite of the persistent encounter of these differences in daily clinical practice, they have not been taken into serious account in the development and application of projective techniques.

In general, she found that the drawings by the boys showed more signs of conflict than those of the girls. The girls appeared, according to her, more comfortable with regulation and social defenses, incorporating them into their body image early in life. Around the age of 10 and 11, however, she found some disturbance in the girls, and from that age on she described a steady deterioration in self-esteem and efficiency.

In the boys, she found that sexual and aggressive drives displayed in the drawings of the 5- to 6-year-olds were marked by considerable guilt. The drawings were toned down during 7–9 years of age, but trends showed the boys becoming angrier and angrier and directing their anger particularly at women who seemed to be experienced as the "seductive perpetrators" of all the restraint and order. By the age of 11, the aggression came out more fully: heads appeared odd, women were depicted as hostile and menacing, while male figures were drawn as gangsters or pirates, armed with guns and knives. Profile drawings, which she found to enter the boys' drawings at age 8 or 9, were seen as an expression of defensiveness.

The boys, who at ages 5 and 6 drew own sex first, during latency often drew the opposite sex first and ascribed more authority to the female figure and weakened the male. At the age of 5 and 6, boys displayed open aggression through stick figures, heavy line, nostrils, heavy diffuse shading, overemphasized ears, and strong noses, but at latency hid this hostility behind a placating smile.

Girls through latency age were found to exhibit better skill, more orderly integration of their bodies, and to show earlier sexual and social awareness than boys. They made earlier, more positive and more consistent use of clothing defenses, and showed more consistency, less arbitrariness, and better work habits in their drawings. They drew excessively large heads and short arms, but their other proportions were better. Machover suggested that growth and accomplishment drives were shown by emphasis on limbs among the boys, while dependency, display, and social communication were shown by the large head often drawn by girls. The very long legs which girls sometimes drew at prepuberty were often found together with elaborate hair display and were more associated with sexual attractiveness than with the growth and physical prowess with which boys linked them.

Machover found that girls learned to depict weakness through cosmetization and display; she claimed oral dependency features to be found more often in the girls' drawings, but in a disguised form, so that, for example, a dependent, concave mouth might be changed into a "Cupid's bow" mouth. The oral dependency was seen as a consequence of their greater acceptance of regulation by others. She also interpreted the choice of front view drawings by girls as an expression of display and dependency needs. The buckle, often drawn by girls on the front of the figure's body, was interpreted as a transformation of the navel button, again symbolizing dependency on the mother. Disarray of the hair, suggesting sexual excitation, was offered with a crown, a bow, or a fancy hat to top off the display. Similarly, she saw the designs and flowers frequently drawn on the skirt as expressions of sexual preoccupations, perhaps pregnancy fantasies. Although girls were found to show earlier and more persistent sex interest, it was expressed less directly than in the boys' drawings. They would often show it through interest in clothes, e.g., designs on the skirt, flare, sensual lips, and ties on the male. Breasts were seldom indicated before 10 years of age, but bows, pockets, and other substitutes might appear earlier. Girls were generally also found to be more subtle and covert in their aggressions. They used mittened or compressed finger arrangements or left fingers missing altogether.

In summary, she found that latency seemed to be more consistent with the girls' cultural role, while boys made less positive use of that period, and "simmered with resentment," which was found to mount into explosive fantasy at age 11 and later into acted-out rebellion at puberty. She saw this as a reflection of the fact that the world of latency children is mostly dominated by women in the United States. Boys gather strength for a protest which does not show openly until about 11 years of age.

Girls are free to cultivate the male as a potential love object, while boys struggle to free themselves from their libidinal dependency on their mothers and therefore are likely to build up extreme aggression toward women.

In her explanation of the pattern found, Machover described how the girls are prospering because they have their models available during childhood, while the boys do not have such clear male models. They must therefore resort to more stereotyped figures as ideals, such as cowboys, soldiers, spacemen, gangsters, etc. Boys are caught in the conflict between their present role as children, where obedience and compliance are rewarded, and their future role, where dominance, competitiveness, and aggression are expected and rewarded. Their main conflict through childhood is about how to master their aggression.

For girls, the conflict is different. They are rewarded for passivity, docility, and dependency. They are not expected to develop their own powers to achieve or create, but are expected to compete in the sexual area, while their self-respect is not measured by what they can do, but by what they can get. The girl is rewarded for accepting the role of safe security. She learns too well the lesson of being rewarded for obedience, and her own desires and wishes are considered less important. The problems for girls, therefore, show themselves at a later age, in adulthood, when they are expected to make independent decisions and to master their own sexual feelings and impulses, which have till then been disregarded.

Machover's studies are difficult to evaluate. They are an excellent example of both the advantages and disadvantages of the application of strictly clinical theories on a normal population, but they show also methodological weaknesses which are not due to the choice of theory.

The advantages are first and foremost the broad and general approach which links many details together into a coherent and meaningful picture and the very suggestive and provoking interpretations based on intuition and empathy, which take the reader much further than a dry listing of quantitative results can do. It is an approach which may lead to many fruitful hypotheses, and which stimulates feeling and imagination in the reader so as to lead to further investigations.

A serious disadvantage is, however, the very negative tone which prevails in the description of both the drawings and the children drawing them. This problem is well known from other applications of classical psychoanalytical theories on normal populations. The traits described are seen as either direct expressions of conflict or as defensive maneuvers, but not as manifestations of a normal and healthy development. A profile drawing, for example, is seen as an expression of defensiveness in boys, while front view drawings are seen as reflections of display and dependency needs in girls. So what will a normal, healthy child do?

Methodologically, it is a serious defect that no quantitative results are given whatsoever. It is impossible to evaluate to what degree the sex differences described actually exist or how much overlapping can be found. Description and interpretation are mingled unsystematically, and often interpretations are given without any clear description of the observations leading to them. Bold interpretations of specific traits are offered without any attempt at explaining why this interpretation is better than perhaps the exact opposite.

Machover's work is a more in-depth analysis of the possible meaning of sex differences in drawings than any of the earlier studies I have described, partly because the study of sex differences is the central aim of her study, and partly because she attempts to reach a more thorough and dynamic understanding of the results than any of the others. It is, therefore, very regrettable that—as in her other published works on drawing—she completely fails to include any documentation for her claims, which leaves the reader in a position where any serious discussion of the results is made impossible. Besides, the sole reliance on early psychoanalytic theory leads unavoidably to a one-sided view of child development where normal ego development is inadequately described, while too much emphasis is placed on instinctual conflicts.

STUDIES OF SINGLE VARIABLES

Sexual Differentiation

The degree to which children (and adults) differentiate between the sexes in their drawings has been studied among others by Swensen (1955), who suggested that this degree of differentiation indicated the degree to which the drawer had adequately identified himself sexually. He hypothesized that lack of differentiation might be an indication either of a specific sexual impairment or of a more general deficit. He set up a scale consisting of nine steps, extending from little or no sexual differentiation to excellent differentiation.

The scale was first tried on adults, but in a later study (Swensen and Newton 1955) on children from first through eighth grades and on a sample of college students. They found that sexual differentiation improved with age and that girls differentiated better than boys until the age of 13 when the boys caught up. After that age, no difference between the sexes was found regarding sexual differentiation.

The development was found to be slightly different for the sexes: the girls showed a clear improvement in their ability to differentiate between 6 and 8 years and from then on a slower development. The boys also improved rather rapidly between 6 and 8 years, although not as much as the girls, and after a plateau for some years showed another sharp rise from 12 to 13 years of age.

In a later study of adults (Swensen and Sipprelle 1956), no significant differences were found between men and women in their ability to differentiate between the sexes in their figure drawings.

Haworth and Normington (1961) found it difficult to use Swensen's scale for children from other cultures and found also that there tended to be a period when children more adequately portrayed one sex than the other with regard to sexual differentiation. They developed a new scale, in four steps, which they found better for use with children.

They studied the scoring reliability of the scale, the possible effect of intelligence on the results, and the relative emphasis on own or opposite sex, and tried to establish normative data. The scale was tried on 312 children, 7–12 years old, equally divided between the sexes.

The reliability of the scale was found satisfactory, with agreement in 88%–90% of the cases. They found that the ability to differentiate improved as a function of age, with girls consistently scoring higher than boys except at age 11. Higher levels of differentiation were more closely related to developmental age changes than to intellectual ability. In their study of the relative emphasis on own or the other sex at the higher levels of differentiation, they found that girls rather consistently favored the drawing of own sex, while boys showed more fluctuation. At age 9, for instance, more than 50% of the boys favored the opposite sex and only one-third their own. They conclude that it may be more meaningful to consider the sex of the higher-scoring figure than the sex of the first drawn figure or the relative size of figures as a measure of sexual identification. To the extent that aspects of identification may be reflected in all three measures, the data seem to indicate that girls consistently favor their own sex while boys, as a group, show more confusion. This supports Machover's (1953, 1960) results. On the basis of Lynn's (1959) distinction between sex-role preference, sex-role adoption, and sex-role identification, they hypothesize that (1) drawing the self-sex first may be an indication of sex-role preference of own sex and (2) the sexual differentiation scale is a developmental index of sex-role identification.

Cutter (1956) tried to answer the question asked by Swensen (1955) as to whether poor sexual differentiation in drawings was a sign of a specific sexual maladjustment or of a more general deficit. He found that patients with overt sexual deviation (homosexuals and exhibitionists) received the best ratings for sexual differentiation in their drawings. Patients with severe personality disorganization (alcoholics, psychotics in remission, etc.) received the poorest, while neurotics tended to fall in between. He also found that verbal IQ and age were associated with the results. In general, the better the personality integration (as measured by

MMPI scales Mf and F), the better the differentiation in drawings. He concluded that lack of sexual differentiation in drawings is a measure of general psychological deficits associated with the degree of personality integration, rather than with specific sexual deviations.

Levinger (1966) postulated that there would be a connection between general maturational level and sexual differentiation in drawings and found this confirmed in a study of 5- to 7-year-old boys. Scores on the Maturational (global) scales correlated with scores on the sexual discrimination scales at .73. Ratings for maturation of nonhuman object drawings were also significantly related to sexual discrimination at a level of .46.

A closer inspection of the items making up the sexual differentiation scales shows them to consist to a great degree of clothing and hair items. These items are in many studies found to be favored by girls in their drawings, and it is therefore not strange that the results generally show girls to be better at differentiating sexually than boys. The problem then arises of what this better sexual differentiation actually means.

One possibility is that girls actually are more attentive to and interested in the depiction of sex differences and therefore stress the details of their figures which characterize the two sexes. But it may also be the other way round in that girls for some reason are more interested in the drawing of clothes and hair and that this incidentally leads to a clearer characterization of the two sexes. The latter viewpoint gains strong support from the fact that girls are found also to show a clearer age differentiation in their drawings (see p. 173). This has not led to the postulation of a theory about a better age identification in girls than in boys.

Finally, of course, both the interest in sexual differentiation and the interest in clothing and hair may be effects of a common third factor, which has so far not been identified. These questions cannot be answered on the present evidence.

Sex of First Drawn Figure

Machover (1949) regarded the sex of the first drawn figure as an expression of the drawer's sexual identification. She assumed it to be most normal to draw the self-sex figure first and stated that "some degree of sexual inversion was found in the records of all individuals who drew the opposite sex first" (1949, 101). She further stated that the adult woman is more inclined to shift in which sex is drawn first, expressing ambivalence in the preferred role more than the man. In her opinion, the drawing of the opposite sex first for the man can only express feminine identification. Such definite statements have challenged many investigators, and studies have been made both on the drawings of normal adults, of sexually deviating adults, and of children.

Studies of normal adults (e.g., a summary by Brown and Tolor 1957; Gravitz 1966) have consistently shown it to be more common for men than for women to draw their own sex first. These results are often explained as a result of greater confusion of feminine identity and greater dissatisfaction with the feminine role.

A number of studies are reported both on groups with sexual problems, e.g., homosexuals or sex offenders (e.g., Levy 1950; Barker, Mathis, and Powers 1953; Hammer 1954; Whitaker 1961; Grams and Rinder 1958; Armon 1960; Pollitt, Hirsch, and Money 1961; Money and Wang 1966) and on groups with other problems, such as alcohol or drug addicts (e.g., Kurtzberg, Cavior and Lipton 1966; Laird 1962a, 1962b; Wisotsky 1959). On the basis of this research it seems reasonable to agree with Swensen (1968), who concludes that the attempts to relate the sex of the first drawn figure to symptoms of pathology have produced significant results, but that the proportions of abnormal persons drawing the opposite sex first do not deviate sharply enough from the base rate of normals drawing the opposite sex first to warrant using it as a diagnostic sign in individual cases.

In her investigations of children, Machover (1953, 1960) described that girls at the ages of 5 and 6 rather often drew the opposite sex first, at the age of 5 more often than at any other age until 12. During the age of latency, girls identified consistently with their own sex and drew it first, except in 5% of their drawings. At puberty, the confidence of girls was shaken, according to Machover, and their experience of their sex role filled with ambivalence. At the age of 12, 36% of the girls drew a male figure first. The boys in her studies tended to draw their own sex first at 5 and 6, but in latency often drew the opposite sex first, ascribing more authority to women and not having much confidence in their masculinity. At the age of 7, they drew female figures first in one-third of their drawings. At puberty, however, the picture changed, and from about 11 or 12 years of age, the boys tended to gain in self-confidence, which was shown in a greater preference of self-sex drawings first, a tendency which continued into adulthood.

Heinrich and Triebe (1972) summarized 19 studies on children and found a somewhat greater proportion of boys than of girls drawing their own sex first (83% against 78%). The single studies show somewhat varying results, with a majority of them showing a greater preference for own-sex drawings by boys, while a few show self-sex preference to be more common in girls. When grouped by age, no significant differences are found up to the age of 11, except at 7 years, when the boys tend to draw fewer self-sex drawings first. From 11 years of age and on through adolescence, however, the tendency is clear for girls to draw the male figure first more and more often. These results do not quite agree with Machover's findings concerning childhood, but show good correspondence with her results regarding puberty.

A few studies have been concerned with the influence of variables other than age and sex. Hammer and Kaplan (1964), for instance, assessed the reliability for first drawn figure for children from fourth through sixth grade and found that 84% of the boys and 80% of the girls drew their own sex first. On repetition of the test one week later, the subjects who had drawn their own sex first tended to do so again, while those who had drawn the other sex first on the first administration of the test were now equally likely to draw their own sex first. Litt and Margolies (1966) in a replication of this study with a repetition of the test three times, found a substantial amount of variability for the first drawn figure. Starr and Marcuse (1959) noted that 10% of the males and 42% of the females (college undergraduates) varied from the first to the second administration of the test. Since they also found a considerably greater number of males than of females drawing their own sex first, their results may be interpreted as being in accordance with those of Hammer and Kaplan (1964) that drawing of own sex is more reliable than drawing of opposite sex.

These results do not contradict the findings that men and adolescent boys tend to draw their own sex first more often, neither do they tell anything about the consistency with which each sex tends to draw figures of own or opposite sex. In order to know this, a greater number of drawings should be gathered from the same persons.

The influence of the examiner's sex was studied by Holtzman (1952) who found his hypothesis rejected that this factor should influence the sex of the drawn person in adults. Datta and Drake (1968), however, found that, for children 3–6 years old, the sex of the examiner was significantly related to the sex of the drawn figure. It was assumed that at this age a stable, internalized, sexual identity is not yet established, so that children are dependent on cues and "models."

The results of the studies on first drawn sex appear to be relatively clear: among children, the majority draw their own sex first, and no outspoken sex difference is seen regarding the frequency with which own sex is preferred. When approaching puberty, girls shift toward a more frequent choice of a male figure, and among normal adults, a greater percentage of women than of men draw the opposite sex first. Among adults with personality disturbances of various kinds and with sexual problems, a somewhat greater number of persons draw the opposite sex first than among normals.

These results tell in themselves nothing about the meaning or significance that can be attributed to the sex of the first drawn figure, however. Several different hypotheses have been proposed.

The most simple explanation has been offered by Broverman et al. (1970), who suggested that in Western culture, the word "human being" is more or less synonymous with "man," so the greater preponderance of drawings of a man may have cultural and social meaning rather than a personal one.

Machover (1949) clearly interpreted the first drawn figure as a sign of the drawer's sexual identification. Leaning on Freudian theory, she suggested it to be more difficult for girls than for boys to attain a satisfactory sexual identification, partly because of penis envy, and partly because girls have to identify with the same parent who is their first love object, i.e., the mother, and so must overcome a homosexual binding. As earlier described she found girls to have certain advantages during the age of latency, partly due to their greater acceptance of obedience and dependency, and partly due to the fact that most children in the United States live in a world dominated by women. Girls therefore have stable models to identify with, while boys lack their fathers who are often distant figures in the family life. From puberty, however, she described the boys as gaining in confidence, supported by the greater prestige associated with masculinity. The girls, on the contrary, were shaken in their confidence at puberty, both for biological and cultural reasons. Not having learned to trust themselves, they had to seek support in an authority outside of themselves. They did not learn to attain their goals by themselves, but had to fulfill their ambitions through another person.

While Machover's (1953, 1960) own results are claimed to fit in with this theory, they are not in agreement with the results from the other childhood studies, however, where boys were not found to draw their own sex consistently less often than girls. Only the hypotheses regarding the less secure identification of the older girls fit in with the general results.

Lynn (1959), who also accepted the hypothesis of the sex of the drawing as an expression of sexual identification, had a different view of the development of the two sexes. He stressed the fact that both sexes in the beginning identify with their mother; the boy has to make a later shift in his identification while the girl keeps her model. He therefore set forth the hypothesis that the young boy's masculine identification is at first not very strong, while the little girl is relatively firm in her feminine identification. Because, however, the culture tends to reinforce the boy in developing a masculine identification, while it doesn't support the girl in a similar way, with increasing age boys become more and more firmly identified with the masculine role and females relatively less with the feminine role. Boys are likely to be punished or ridiculed if they adopt feminine modes of behavior, while girls, without any negative effects, can adopt aspects of the masculine role. Assuming that this trend is reflected in the drawings, boys at an early age would be expected to draw the female figure first relatively often, while they would later more often draw their own sex first. In practice, Lynn's theory would thus lead to results that are indistinguishable from Machover's expectations. Heinrich and Triebe (1972) favored Lynn's description of the development, although they also had to admit that the assumption that boys in their early childhood are less secure in their role could only be regarded as very slightly verified by their results, if at all.

An alternative hypothesis regarding the meaning of the first drawn person was set forth by Piotrowsky (Hammer 1954), who suggested that the opposite sex figure, in free drawings as well as on the TAT (Thematic Apperception Test) and on the Rorschach human movement responses, expresses personality traits which are not fully acceptable to the individual, while the same-sex figure reflects the more accepted personality traits which are not so likely to cause anxiety or feelings of inferiority.

Piotrowsky then related the choice of the sex of the figure drawn to the degree to which the subject feels free to reveal his inner traits, conflicts, and feelings. This is an interesting viewpoint, but in no way verified by research. Hammer (1954) further quotes Buck for the view that it is just as unjustified to accord an index-of-sexual-identification-status to the sex of the first drawn person as to grant a similar paramount status to any other manifest content item. It is not so much that the subject draws a man or a woman first as it is how he or she draws it, the value that is assigned to its component parts and their relationship, and the value that its content has to the drawer. These considerations seem well worth being taken into account.

Buck further pointed out that the figure drawn may represent a variety of personality characteristics. The drawing may be viewed as a form of self-perception, or as a type of self-aspiration, or as a reflection of a person the drawer likes or dislikes, etc. Other variables that may be influential are momentary preoccupations or other temporary conditions, romantic fantasies, closeness to a parent of the sex depicted, and variations in instructions.

Koppitz (1968) was also skeptical of the theory of the sex of the drawing as a representation of sexual identification and offered the hypothesis that children draw the person who is of greatest concern and importance to them at the time they make the drawing. She found that, in the majority of cases, children would draw themselves, but some would draw ideal images of themselves, while others would go in the opposite direction and distort themselves. Some would draw mothers or fathers or even siblings. She found in her clinical work that a boy who portrays a female figure is emotionally involved with a female in his family, but that he need not identify with her.

Caligor (1951) compared the results from the 8-card redrawing test, a blank card TAT, the MMPI, and a retest of the 8-card test. He found a greater stability of sexual identification in males than in females, in agreement with the cultural patterning. He suggested that the drawing test taps a different level of M-F identification from the other tests, as little agreement was found among the tests. He suggested that the MMPI taps the more conscious aspects of sexual identification, and that the true level of sexual identification may lie deeply buried. He compared the initial figure on the 8-card test to the popular answers of the Rorschach test.

This leads to the question of what is meant by the term "sexual identification." In the earlier literature, it is treated as if it were a simple question of either-or, feminine or masculine. Lynn (1959) opposed the idea of such a simple dichotomy and distinguished between sex-role preference, sex-role adoption, and sex-role identification.

Sex-role preference refers to the desire to adopt the behavior associated with one sex or the other, or the perception of such behavior as preferable or more desirable. It can be measured by simply asking people if they have ever wished to be of the opposite sex.

Sex-role adoption refers to the actual adoption of behavior characteristic of one sex or the other and so refers to one's overt behavior, regardless of preferences.

Sex-role identification is reserved to refer to the actual incorporation of the role of a given sex and to the unconscious reactions characteristic of that role. This concept thus refers to a more basic process and is much more difficult to measure than the other two concepts.

Much research has confirmed that more girls than boys prefer the opposite sex role. For example, Diamond (1954a, 1954b), who had his subjects write stories about a house, a tree, and a person, found that 6% of the male subjects (college students) compared to 57% of the females identified with a person of the opposite sex. With adolescents in the eighth grade, he found that 5% of the boys and 49% of the girls did so. He concluded that girls regard their environment as being predominantly masculine. Whether his results refer to sex-role preference or to actual sexual identification seems, however, not quite clear.

A study of sex-role preferences in children by Brown (1956) showed that boys in the latency period showed an overwhelming preference for the masculine role when asked, while girls often, at least between 5½ and 10½ years, showed a preference for the masculine role or at least were ambivalent about the female role. It was stressed, though, that while many girls might prefer the masculine role, they might still be basically femininely identified. And many boys, who on the surface preferred the masculine role, might in reality have a deeply rooted feminine identification.

The idea of masculine or feminine identification as a single continuum is clearly much too simple and has been replaced by models, where masculinity and femininity are seen as orthogonal, i.e., where both dimensions are found to be present to varying degrees in both males and females. Or, as described by Money and Ehrhardt (1973), in behavior and psychic development, too, there is sexual dimorphism.

The idea of the sex of first drawn figure as an expression of the drawer's sexual identification (or one aspect hereof) is obviously also a simplification and yet another example of the sign-interpretation applied on drawings. The meaning of this trait may be multidetermined and influenced not only by deep-lying personality factors, but also by cultural pressure, and by momentary and situational circumstances. The massive difference between men and women points convincingly to the influence of a cultural pressure; and it may well be that the drawing of the opposite sex for a man has greater significance and a more personal meaning than for a woman, as such a choice will be against and not with the cultural pressure. In the case of children, great caution should be taken not to interpret the meaning of the first drawn sex too heavily in individual cases.

Profile Drawings

Weider and Noller (1950, 1953) studied sex differences in regard to the drawing of profile figures versus figures seen from the front. In their first study of 8- to 10-year-old children, they found that half of the boys drew full-faced figures, while the other half drew profiles, regardless of the sex of the drawn figure. Only 19 girls (out of 80) drew profiles, 61 drawing full-face figures. In their second study, they hypothesized that more intelligent children would draw more profile drawings, but this was not confirmed. The sex difference from their first study was, however, repeated.

Age Assigned to Figure

The main emphasis in the studies of age has been on the question of whether children assigned similar or different ages to figures of the two sexes. McHugh (1963) found a consistent tendency for both boys and girls to draw the male figure older at some ages. The difference became significant for girls at ages 7 and 8, and for boys at age 8.

In a later study (1965), she found that girls, 7–11 years old, attributed progressively older ages to both sex figures with increasing age, and that they consistently assigned an older age to the male figure than to the female. The difference was only significant at age 9, however. The age assigned to the female figure bore a relatively constant relationship to the girls' own ages, being approximately 4 years older. The age assigned to the male figure varied between 6 and 8 years older than the subject's own age. For girls of all ages, the variability of ages assigned was greater for the male figure than for the female.

The age assigned by boys to both sex figures did not increase with increasing age. Although the boys consistently assigned an older age to the male figure than to the female, none of the age differences were significant. The mean age assigned to female figures was approximately 8–10 years older than the boys' own age, to male figures 11–15 years older. For boys of all ages, the variability of ages assigned to male figures was greater than that for female figures. Boys at all ages made both sex figures older than the girls did.

She concluded that age identification by children, as suggested by mean age associated with figures, appeared to be at an older age than their own, usually a teenage for the girls and a teenage or an age in the early twenties for the boys, suggesting that these ages could be ideal ages.

Height of Figure

In the studies of sex differences in height of drawn figure, the differential treatment of male and female figures by both sexes has also been emphasized.

Weider and Noller (1950), in a study of 8- to 10-year-old children, found that 80% of the girls drew their own sex larger, while the boys were almost evenly divided between those who drew their own sex and those who drew the opposite sex larger.

In a later study (1953), the same authors compared two larger groups of children, 7–12 years old, and found comparable results: 69% of the girls drew their own sex larger, 39% of the boys did so.

McHugh (1963), investigating the same question in a group of more than 600 children, 7–11 years old, found that the tendency to draw the self-sex larger was significant for girls at all ages 7–11 and for boys at ages 8 and 11. The differences between the sexes in the tendency to draw the self-sex figure larger was significantly in favor of the girls at ages 9 and 10. She suggested that girls are more consistently identified with own sex than boys. The absolute sizes of the drawings of the two sexes were not compared.

Finally, Cohen, Money, and Uhlenhuth (1972), in a study of 385 children, 6–13 years old, found a tendency for the older children to draw themselves taller than the younger children. In their study the children were not asked to make a drawing of both sexes as in the other studies, but to make one drawing of themselves and a friend, and one of themselves together with the examiner. They found that girls tended to draw themselves taller than boys did. They hypothesized that this might be a reflection of the girls' earlier growth and maturation compared to the boys.

Movement

This variable was examined by McHugh (1963) in drawings by 7- to 11-year-old children. She found no significant sex differences in the distribution of activity assigned to the drawn figures. When data on activity was considered for male and female figures separately, it was found that girls at age 10 made the female figure more static while boys made it more active.

CONCLUDING REMARKS

Sex differences in drawings are obviously many and characteristic, and it is surprising that they have not more often been the main subject of studies.

The existence of quantitative sex differences is amply documented, but they can hardly be said to have been adequately described. Although later authors seem to agree on the girls' superiority over the boys in the drawing of a human being, even contemporary authors do not agree as to the degree to which boys catch up with girls and at what age.

When it comes to qualitative sex differences, both descriptions and attempts at explanations are found to be equally dissatisfying. It is characteristic that the one author (Machover) who uses a solely psycho-analytic frame of reference, is the one who is most negative in her description of the personality development of the children. But none of the authors seem really satisfied with their results. The boys are found to have many conflicts, while the girls—even worse—are found to be too dependent, docile, and obedient. It clearly bothers the authors that girls emphasize hair, clothing, and facial features in their drawings, and they are eager to explain this as a consequence of social and cultural influences. Inherent in all the descriptions is a certain regret about the fact that girls are occupied by such "inferior" aspects and that their drawings do not show them as being as outgoing and independent as the boys.

In the studies of single variables, it is striking how readily single traits in the drawings have been associated with specific personality traits. For example, both sexual differentiation, first drawn sex, and size of self-sex figure have without hesitation been interpreted as expressions of the drawer's sexual identification and acceptance of own-sex role. Much too often, studies on drawings have concentrated on very few aspects of the drawn figure and their authors have courageously drawn bold inferences from them without seeing them in light of the totality. The very fact that these different aspects have all given rise to exactly the same interpretation should raise doubt about its validity. As the overview of the research shows, this doubt is highly justified, both in the case of groups and even more in individual cases. The sign-approach seems as little justified in the interpretation of sex differences as in the estimation of other personality traits. In light of this, it is perhaps not very surprising that the research findings have been contradictory, alternately showing boys and girls as having a better and more stable sexual identification.

PART TWO

Results of the Danish Study

FIVE

Description of Drawing Development

As described in the Introduction, the Danish study included 540 drawings of human beings, made by 90 boys and 90 girls, 5–13 years old, with 10 of either sex at each age level. Each child had made a figure of both sexes and a picture of himself.

All variables were examined statistically for their course of development, and when showing a deviation from what might be expected by chance at the 5% level or better, the development was regarded as significant.

Some traits showed no connection with age. Those which did belonged to one of the following three groups:

1. Traits that increase in frequency with increasing age. Examples are the presence of many body parts, the use of naturalistic shapes, lifelike proportions and sizes, and a number of formal aspects showing improved motoric control. These items are called *developmental items*.
2. Traits that decrease in frequency with increasing age. Many immature and undifferentiated shapes belong here, together with size distortions and asymmetries as well as formal variables showing lack of control. A few traits were found simply to disappear without being replaced by other forms, e.g., the drawings of surrounding objects.
3. Traits that show a more irregular course, e.g., a rise, followed by a decrease. Examples are some transitional forms, lying between the most primitive and the most developed ones. Other traits seem to be favored by children of a certain age, e.g., some clothing details, and then disappear again.

Because of the universal agreement on the existence of sex differences in drawing development (although not on their precise nature), the development of the variables was examined for each sex separately.

For some variables no sex differences were found. Other items showed a parallel development, e.g., an increase with age in both sexes, but with one sex introducing the item earlier than the other and keeping the advantage. An example of this is the drawing of a head only instead of a whole figure, which is introduced much earlier by boys than by girls and used more frequently. In still other cases, a trait showed a significant development in one sex and not in the other.

As sex differences are the focus of a more systematic examination in chapter 6, they are only described here to the extent that is necessary in relation to drawing development. However, the sex differences are so many and varied that a description of drawing development which does not take them into account becomes crude and incomplete.

In the following, a description of development will be given, first quantitatively, then qualitatively.

Afterward, to get some impression of the general level of the drawings of this sample of Danish children, a comparison is made with the results of Goodenough (1926) and Harris (1963). In this comparison, the drawings of boys and girls are combined in accordance with their presentation of data.

QUANTITATIVE DESCRIPTION

The developmental items will first be described, followed by a description of the traits that decrease in number with age. The traits that show more irregular developments will not be described quantitatively, but will in some cases be included in the qualitative description.

Developmental Items

There could be a variety of ways in which to present the developmental items. The method here chosen is to describe the age of their first appearance. In this way the general *rate of development* can be studied, i.e., the number of new items introduced at various ages, and the *sequence of development*, i.e., the sequence in which the various aspects of the drawings are developed.

Other ways of presenting the developmental items might be to describe at what ages they reach their maximal frequency or at what age
they can be expected to appear in the majority of children's drawings.
The reason why neither of these methods is chosen lies in the fact that
quite a few of (particularly the older) children have chosen to draw only
a head or another limited section of the figure, which reduces the number
of whole figures in the older age groups. That the children have been left
free to determine how great a part of the figure they wished to draw
added information in some respects, but in other ways made the collection of information more difficult. It was not found very meaningful to
determine the percentage of children drawing a certain trait when the
total number of figures becomes very small. When the age of first appearance or introduction of a trait is used instead, the focus is m tly on
the younger age groups where the number of whole figures is great

It must also be remembered that the group of children in the Dan h
study was not meant to be representative of Danish children in general
and the results should therefore not be regarded as normative. By no
giving the age at which a certain trait reaches its maximum appearance,
an (unfounded) norm setting is more easily avoided. Of course, the age
of introduction of the various traits should not be regarded as normative, either. But it is in accordance with earlier findings on drawing
development to assume that the sequence in which various traits appear
will be of relatively general validity, while the rate of development and
the level at which development stops vary with the general cultural and
intellectual level of the children.

This study tells nothing about the development of the individual child.
We can follow the introduction of new items in the most advanced
drawers, but we know nothing about whether the child, who is fast at
introducing some new traits at the age of 5, will also be one of the more
advanced drawers at a later age. Neither do we know how the sequence
varies between the children, or to what degree it is identical. These
difficulties are shared with other group studies, however.

It is, of course, to some extent a matter of chance whether a certain
trait appears at the age of 6 or 7 for the first time. But the number of
developmental items is so large that general tendencies and patterns will
come out clearly, regardless of minor variations.

The beginning age of a developmental trait is defined as the age at
which it appears for the first time, on condition that it is either seen in

more than one drawing at that age level or that it is also found in the drawings of the following age group. Thus, if a trait was found in one drawing of a 6-year-old boy for the first time and then again not until in the drawings of some 8-year-olds, it was regarded as starting at the 8-year level. If, however, it appeared in several drawings at the 6-year level or if it also appeared in one or more drawings at the 7-year level, it was regarded as being introduced at the 6-year level. (Those interested in the exact list of developmental items and the age of introduction are referred to the original study [Mortensen 1984].)

The number of items introduced by both sexes at the age of 5 (or earlier) is 42. Besides these common items, the boys introduce 8 other traits, the girls 9, which are found later in the drawings of the other sex. This gives a total number of introduced developmental traits of 50 for the boys, 51 for the girls.

The curve in figure 8 shows the gradual accumulation of developmental items for the two sexes. Here, only those items are included that are significant for both sexes.

At the age of 6, six common items are introduced by both sexes, and besides, both boys and girls introduce 5 new items first. This brings the number of traits up to 61 for the boys, 62 for the girls. But as both sexes now also begin to catch up with the other sex on a number of the traits that are introduced at different ages, these traits must also be added. The boys add 7 traits which were seen already in the 5-year-old girls' drawings, which brings the total number of introduced items up to 68 for the boys. The girls catch up on 5 items, giving a total of 67.

The development continues in the same way, with both sexes adding both common items and items which in the beginning appear exclusively in one of the sexes. Both sexes also continue to catch up on these items.

The course of development clearly shows a negatively accelerating curve. More than half of all the traits are already present in the drawings of the 5-year-olds, and the number of new additions becomes very small after the age of 9. It might be suspected that this is due to the limitations of the sample, and that many traits might still be added at the ages of, e.g., 11 or 12, but that they cannot reach statistical significance because the total number of drawings in which they appear becomes too small. If later ages had been included, they might have reached a statistically measurable level. But this is not the case. It is a fact that very few new items are introduced at the highest ages. The picture shown by the curve is a reflection of the actual development.

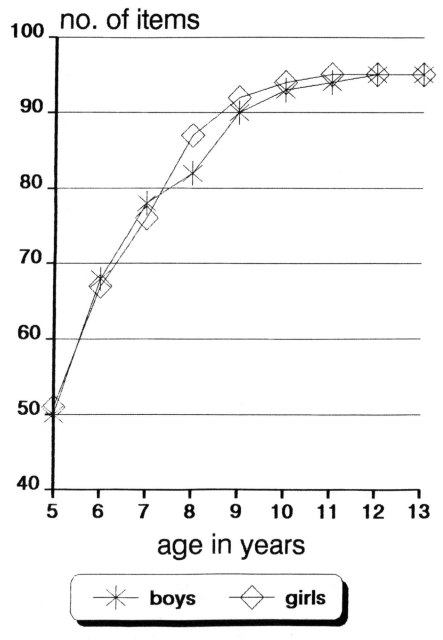

FIGURE 8 The accumulated number of developmental items that show a significant development in both sexes.

Quantitatively, the course of development is almost completely identical for the two sexes until the age of 7. If anything, the boys are slightly ahead of the girls at ages 6 and 7. The development of the girls continues to follow a very regular curve, while that of the boys shows a delay between the ages of 7 and 8; this means that the girls' development is somewhat faster than the boys' at this age. The boys begin to catch up with the girls as early as the following year, but the difference does not disappear completely until at age 12. It is not known whether this sex difference is due to the sampling of children or whether it is a more general difference in the drawing development of Danish children.

At most ages, a number of traits are found that show a significant development in one sex and not in the other. An analysis of these specific traits shows, in most cases, the difference to be due to a more frequent and regular occurrence of the trait in the sex in which the development is found to be statistically significant. It is possible that with a greater number of children included in the study, a greater number of these items would be found to be statistically significant in both sexes.

In a few cases, the traits in question can occur only in figures of one sex, e.g., "female figure in slacks," which naturally favors the girls, who draw twice as many female figures as the boys. Surprisingly enough, however, such traits may occur more often in the drawings of the sex in which they should be expected to appear more rarely. For example, the drawing of a jacket or sweater, which is a detail only scored in male figures, actually occurs more often in the drawings of the girls and shows a significant development there and not in the drawings of the boys, although they draw twice as many male figures. Some of the traits that clearly favor one sex show a statistically significant development in both sexes, e.g., the drawing of a beard or stubble.

Besides, it is not always easy to tell whether a given trait will be favored in drawings of figures of one or the other sex. For example, it could not be known in advance that ears are drawn twice as often in male figures as in females, as was found to be the case. No traits were therefore excluded on the suspicion that they favor one of the sexes.

Figure 9 shows the total number of traits that are significant for only one sex. It is clearly seen that the total number of these traits is considerably greater among the girls than among the boys, encompassing a total of 30, while the boys only include 21. As was the case with the common traits, about half of them are introduced as early as at the age

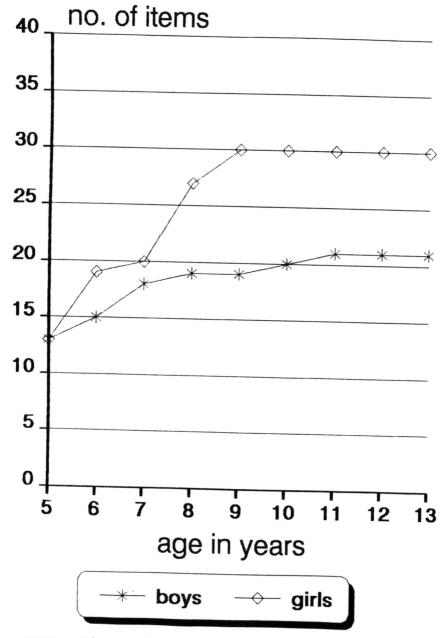

FIGURE 9   The accumulated number of developmental items that show a significant development in only one of the sexes.

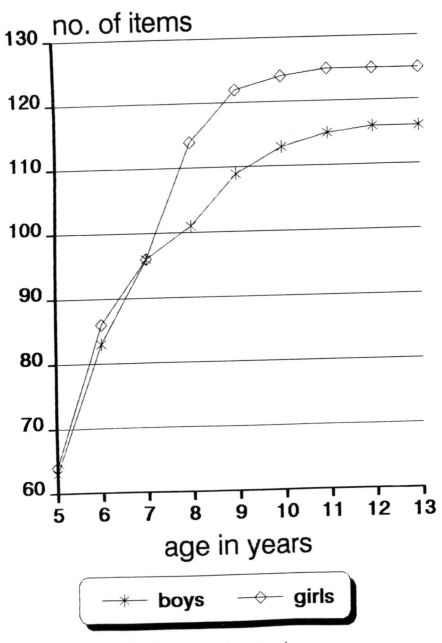

FIGURE 10 The combined results from figures 8 and 9.

of 5 (for the boys a little more than half, for the girls a little less). The curve shows a particular increase in the number of specific traits for the girls between 7 and 8 years of age, the same age when the number of common traits also showed a particularly big rise in the girls. The age between 7 and 8 seems, thus, particularly productive in regard to the introduction of a great many traits, especially in girls.

The introduction of specific traits stops earlier than the introduction of common traits, and it stops earlier among the girls than among the boys. The girls introduce no new specific traits after age 9, the boys not after age 11.

When the total number of developmental traits for both sexes, common and specific, are combined (see figure 10), a clear sex difference appears. The sexes are seen to follow a very identical course until the age of 7, when the girls show a considerable and sudden spurt. On the other hand, the developmental curve for the girls shows a tendency to flatten earlier than that of the boys, and their development stops earlier. Nonetheless, the total number of introduced items is greater in the girls.

Items Appearing with Decreasing Frequency with Age

One way of describing development is to describe the traits that increase in frequency with increasing age—as has just been done. Another way is to describe the disappearance of more primitive forms in the drawings. There is, of course, a certain correspondence between the two forms of development, but it need not be complete.

I considered describing the age of last appearance for the disappearing traits, in analogy with the age of first appearance for the developmental traits, but so few of them disappear completely in all drawings before the age of 13 that this method of description would not have given very meaningful results. They will therefore be described only in general terms. It is also of interest to see if there are any sex differences in development here. They can be revealed through comparisons of the total number of traits present in all drawings by the boys and girls, respectively.

The traits that decrease in frequency with age are the following groups.

1. Omissions of body parts (e.g., no legs drawn).
2. Drawings of body parts in one dimension (e.g., arms in one dimension).

3. Extreme sizes (e.g., drawing of a very small or very big head).
4. Wrong proportions (e.g., body more wide than long).
5. Primitive or transitional shapes that are later replaced by more naturalistic ones (e.g., round or oval head).
6. Asymmetries and irregular attachments to the body (e.g., legs very asymmetric in size).
7. Formal qualities indicating lack of control (e.g., lines very uneven).
8. Items that decrease or disappear without being replaced by other traits (e.g., surrounding objects or scenery).

Omissions. Many of the more important body parts are omitted so rarely that the course of development is not significant. The only sex difference found is the following: arms (on whole figures) and trunk are omitted more often by the boys, indicating a faster development by the girls. Also more whole figures are drawn without clothing by the boys than by the girls.

Body Parts In One Dimension. These are some of the primitive forms that disappear most completely from the drawings, and the ages of disappearance can therefore be compared. Girls tend to stop using these forms a couple of years earlier than boys. The last drawings containing one-dimensional arms, fingers, legs, and feet are found at age 7 in the girls, at age 9 in the boys. The total number of these body parts drawn in one dimension is not greater among the boys than among the girls, however, with the exception of fingers.

On the other hand, the drawing of a one-dimensional nose is found significantly more often among the girls than among the boys, and this trait does not disappear before age 13.

Extreme Size. While the general tendency is toward a decrease in the use of too small or too big body parts, the different patterns which the development follows in the two sexes seems to indicate that the size of body parts is not only determined by a general developmental factor, but is bound up with different attitudes to the body and its various parts by the two sexes. The discussion of this subject is taken up more thoroughly later.

The boys tend more often than the girls to draw eyes that are either too small or too big. They also more often draw a big nose and a big mouth. They more frequently draw big hands, long legs, big feet, and a long neck.

Girls, on the other hand, tend to draw big heads much more often than boys, they draw small noses, small ears, and a short neck. In some cases the result is that the drawings by the girls show a relatively greater number of well-proportioned body parts in regard to size. This is true for the drawing of eyes, mouth, and hands.

No body parts are found to be more well-proportioned significantly more often by the boys than by the girls. So, whatever the reason may be, if a strictly developmental view is taken, the girls must be described as being ahead of the boys in this aspect of development.

Wrong Proportions. The use of wrong proportions continues for most variables through all ages in both sexes. Sex differences are found in the following aspects: girls continue to draw the head more wide than long or equally wide and long, while boys earlier change to the more naturalistic proportion where the head is more long than wide.

That girls tend to draw a thin neck relatively more often than the boys, who more often draw a wide neck, may partly be a consequence of the difference in head proportions, as the width of the neck is compared to that of the head.

Boys tend to draw eyes in more primitive proportions to a greater extent than girls.

Primitive or Transitional Shapes. The drawing of naturalistic shapes is one of the most difficult goals to attain in drawings of a human figure. It presupposes all the other aspects which have been mentioned, such as the use of two dimensions, correct size, and correct proportions, but requires in addition the ability to differentiate the outline according to the irregularities of the human figure. It is therefore not surprising that it is the aspect which comes last in development, and that primitive or transitional forms of the body parts persist through all ages.

Also in this area distinct sex differences occur. The body parts where the primitive forms persist more often among the girls than among the boys are the following: a square head and a head in which the eyes are closer to the outline than to its middle axis, primitive forms of the nose, drawn as either one or two dots or as a single line, and ears without any attempt at shaping. The number of figures seen from the front decreases significantly in both sexes and can thus also be regarded as a more primitive form than the drawing of profile figures. The girls continue to use this form more than the boys. They also draw the arms stretching horizontally out from the body and fingers spread out with a big angle between, while the boys tend to vary the position of the figure more. The drawing of a whole figure instead of, for example, only the head is also a trait which decreases with age, but which persists more in the drawings by the girls. By the age of 13, only one-third of the boys' drawings show a whole figure, while two-thirds of the girls' still do so. By age 11 and 12, only half of the boys' drawings show a whole figure.

The boys tend to draw more primitive (round) eyes more frequently, to draw hair only as a scribble, and to use only minimal clothing. The more primitive forms of the trunk, round or oval, or a transitional form, are also more commonly drawn by the boys, while a triangular form, which is also primitive (but more common in female figures), is more frequent in the case of the girls.

Figures whose age and sex cannot be determined are more often found in drawings by the boys. This is probably due to their drawing of fewer details of clothing and hair.

A trait which is probably also a primitive form, the smiling mouth, decreases in number with age in the drawing of both sexes. It shows no sex difference.

It is hardly possible to regard the differential treatment of the various shapes as solely determined by development, without influence by other factors. If this were the case, the two sexes should to a much greater degree than is the case show identical developments. It is also obvious that many of the drawers who choose not to draw, e.g., profile drawings are as skillful or more so than some of those who draw in profile. There is clearly no unequivocal connection between drawing development and the use of the different forms.

Asymmetries. Gross asymmetries of size or positioning are found relatively rarely and are abandoned early by most children. The boys' drawings seem to contain a somewhat greater number of asymmetries than those of the girls. They more often place the mouth asymmetrically in the face, and they continue to do so through all ages, while it is not found in the girls later than at age 8. Legs connected asymmetrically with the body are also seen more often in the boys' drawings. Perhaps the girls can more easily hide the legs under the dress, while the boys cannot avoid drawing the connection between trunks and legs.

Formal Traits. In both sexes, there is a decreasing tendency to place the figure in positions other than centrally on the paper, but the boys more often than the girls continue to use other positions.

The most frequently used position outside the central square of the paper is the upper middle third and the left third. More boys than girls place their drawings in the lower third and not rarely use the edge of the paper as baseline. This traits, which does not decrease with age, is seen more rarely in the girls.

The use of transparencies also decreases, but their number is twice as large with the boys than with the girls. This may be partly due to the boys' greater use of profile drawings and movement, but, for example, such a trait as the head seen through hair or hat cannot be caused by either of these factors, and it is also found twice as often in the boys. The same is true of arms cut off from the body without this being caused by clothing.

Very insecure lines are found more often with boys, as are poor integration and lack of motoric control.

Disappearing Items. The items which are found to disappear with increasing age are surrounding objects. In total, 32 drawings by boys and 41 by girls contain a number of 45 and 50 objects, respectively. The greatest number of objects are found at age 5 by both sexes; the girls, in particular, also draw quite a few at the ages 7–9. The 5-year-old boys, in many cases, draw several objects in one drawing, but later tend to include only one. Girls at the ages 7–9 also include several objects.

QUALITATIVE DESCRIPTION

First, a description is given of the total pattern of development. Afterward, certain aspects are singled out for a more detailed treatment. They are: the drawing of surrounding objects, the drawing of a head only, genitals and sexual differentiation, indication of age, corrections/erasures, and shading.

Description of the General Developmental Pattern

As the 5-year-olds are the youngest children in the sample, it is impossible to know which of the traits appearing in their drawings have been introduced earlier, perhaps at ages 3 or 4, and which are introduced at age 5. The description of the traits in the drawings of the 5-year-olds is thus a description of the summation of all the traits that have developed earlier and at age 5.

It should explicitly be remembered that the following description is characteristic not of the average drawings of the 5-year-olds, but of the best developed among them.

In these drawings, it is possible to distinguish between drawings of a male and a female figure. All the most important body parts are present: head, eyes, nose, mouth, ears, arms, hands or fingers, legs, feet, body, hair, and neck. Hats and shoes are seen, and figures with at least two pieces of clothing appear.

The following details or less important body parts can also be found: forehead, chin, pupils, eyelashes, eyebrows, nostrils, bridge of nose, wings of nose, details in ears, fringes, long hair, neckline, details on hats, and shoelaces with bows.

The mere presence of a body part, however, indicates nothing of how it is drawn. In the case of the more important body parts, the following qualities are examined: dimensionality (one- or two-dimensional), size, positioning, proportions, and form.

When the drawings of the 5-year-olds are analyzed for these aspects, it is found that all body parts which can be drawn in two dimensions (eyes, nose, mouth, arms, fingers, legs, and feet) do appear in this form. The positioning of the body parts can be described as "reasonable," i.e., not too oblique or misplaced. The legs are not only added to the body at the right place, but can also be found with crotch, i.e., they meet at the upper end and are not just drawn as two parallel, vertical columns at each side of the body. The arms may also be placed at the right place on the body, but are only found in two positions, pointing straight out from the body or even upwards, or pointing downward, but with an angle of no less than 30° between arm and body.

All the main body parts can be found in correct proportions in regard to their relative length and width, and also their size can be defined as well proportioned seen in relation to the drawing as a whole or to bigger parts of it.

It might at this point appear as if at least the most advanced drawings of the 5-year-olds already fulfilled the requirements of a naturalistic representation of the human figure. This picture changes, however, if we

FIGURE 11 Advanced drawing by a 5-year-old (Boy, 5 years old).

look at the form level of the drawings. It is then revealed that the drawers have only reached the most primitive stage in their graphic representation of the various body parts, and no attempts at naturalistic shaping occur. So, not even the most developed drawers go beyond the schematic stage.

The head is drawn as a circle or an oval, and the same is true of the body, which may also be found in a triangular or square form. The eyes are drawn either as circles or dots. Noses are drawn in many different forms, but a single line, perhaps supplied with dots as nostrils, is the most dominating form, which is found in half of the boys' and two thirds of the girls' drawings at the age of 5, but which later is much reduced in number. Also the ears are only drawn round or oblong without any attempt at a naturalistic shape.

The hands may well contain the right number of fingers, but are only drawn with the fingers spread out from the hands or from the end of the arm with great angles between. The feet are either round, square, oval, or stick feet.

The hair is drawn as scribbles or as straight lines extending from the head in the majority of drawings, but in a few figures it is drawn as a clearly circumscribed area. No attempts at representations of specific styles or hairdressing are seen and no structure of the hair.

Clothing is scarce, but hats, shoes, trousers, blouses, skirts, and simple dresses are seen. A neckline can be found, but may at this stage as well represent a mere separation of neck and body as an actual neckline.

The figures are only shown in one position, seen from the front and with the feet turned outward or to the same side, but movement may be indicated.

The formal variables show the following characteristics: transparencies are found, but erasures/corrections only in the drawings of the girls. Almost all figures are described as asymmetric, even grossly so. Only long, unbroken lines are used, shorter lines are introduced later. In the great majority of drawings, lines are described as very insecure. Shading is seen, mostly of the hair, and is irregular and loose, not covering a circumscribed area. The motoric integration is medium to poor, and the drawings show a lack of motoric control or—in a few cases—a medium degree of control. Thus, in regard to form level and formal characteristics, the drawings are quite immature.

With increasing age, the differentiation between the drawings of the two sexes increases, making it still more difficult to characterize the development generally. Instead of struggling to try this or of ending up with an uninteresting mere enumeration of the items introduced by the two sexes year by year, an analysis will be given of the differences in development of the sexes.

The boys are seen to be ahead of the girls in such aspects as the drawing of the figure as only a head, in depiction of movement, and in profile drawing. They are also faster at placing the arms in a way other than straight out from the body and at placing accessory objects in the hands.

A number of the traits where the boys excel have to do with naturalistic shaping of the body, head, and ears, indicating the waist, and placing it correctly. They draw hands/fingers, fingers close together with the thumb separate from the other fingers. They are first to introduce knees, arch of foot, arms narrowing toward the wrist, and projection of the chin.

With regard to details, it is particularly striking that boys seem to give the nose special emphasis and interest. The following items show only a significant development in the drawings of the boys: nose present, well-proportioned nose, bridge of nose, wings of nose, and nose continuous with eyebrows. That they also excel in the drawing of details in ears is probably due to the fact that ears are drawn twice as often in male figures than in female (among both boys and girls) (see p. 157). That they are first in the drawing of a beard/stubble is a natural consequence of the greater number of male figures. They are also first in a few other facial details, namely the drawing of the iris, corners of the mouth, cheeks, and frowns or wrinkles.

In the areas of clothing and hair their advantage is slight. They draw four pieces of clothing, indicate the waist, draw pockets, and long hair.

In the area of formal variables, they are not first with any of the traits that show improvement of development.

Quite different traits are introduced first or show a significant development by the girls than by the boys. Most spectacular is the area of hair and clothing. In the girls, such traits as the following appear: structure in the hair, curls, specific haircuts, jewelry, stockings, special type of shoes, trousers indicated by only a line across the ankle or with details added, drawing of a jacket or sweater, and details on jacket. Girls draw fashionable clothes, pleats or folds in clothes, details in the drawing of the waistline, and female figures in slacks.

Another area where the girls' drawings show a faster development is in regard to the formal variables. They draw lines of medium thickness or thin lines, sketchy strokes, and drawings with a high degree of motoric control. They also use thin and light shading and shading that covers a limited area and is not diffuse. They draw symmetrical figures, sometimes even rigidly so.

In the drawing of details, girls are seen to emphasize the drawing of the eyes, exactly as boys did with the nose. Girls are first in the drawings of eyes that are more wide than high, that narrow toward the nose, that have a naturalistic shape and contain eye-corners. They also draw the correct number of fingers and fingers that are more long than thick.

Some traits that show good proportions and naturalistic shape are also found first or predominantly in the girls, such as the drawing of shoulders, of the crotch, and of the connection of legs with trunk, the trunk being more long than broad and head more long than wide. They are first in the drawing of well-proportioned feet, in naturalistic feet, and in feet seen from the front, both with and without attempts at foreshortening. That they also are first to draw waist and breasts on female figures may be a consequence of the greater number of female figures drawn by the girls.

Finally, the girls excel in such special aspects as clear indication of the figure's age, in arms clinging to body, and hands hidden in pockets or behind the back.

Surrounding Objects

The most frequently drawn object is the house, which is included in seven drawings by boys and five by girls, but it is only found at the ages of 5 and 6. The name of the drawer is found in five drawings by boys and two by girls, while other names and words are written in twelve drawings by boys and seven by girls. All other objects are found in less than five drawings by each sex. They are trees or bushes, flowers, flagpoles, cars, bus stops, animals, furniture, and patterns. One boy and one girl drew a complete scenery, and three drawings by boys spontaneously included other persons.

There is a marked tendency for the younger children to include several objects in one drawing, but often with no obvious connection. Typical is the drawing of a house, a tree, and the drawer's name. If Klein's (1975) theory is accepted of the house as a symbol of the mother and the tree of the father, of course the combination of these objects and the drawer's own name gives good meaning. As the drawing of the house is not seen after the age of 6, even if her interpretation is not accepted, it is natural

FIGURE 12 Drawing of surrounding objects—house, trees, flower, and name (Boy, 5 years old).

to see the house as an expression of the small child's feeling for his home, a symbol of his sense of belonging to his family. Trees and flowers also belong in the younger age-groups and are typically found together with the house.

For the somewhat older children, the drawing of a street or a pavement is more typical, sometimes supplied with a bus stop. This can very likely be seen as a symbolic expression of the wish for freedom to move away on one's own, perhaps combined with a wish for some control, symbolized by the bus stop.

The drawing of names and words increases with age and replaces more and more the drawing of objects. This is probably an example of the general tendency, with increasing age, to replace the concrete representations of drawings with the more abstract representation of words, which for so many children ends with their giving up drawing completely. The words may take the form of some joking remark, often with a macabre or aggressive tone, such as when the 13-year-old writes the date of his death on his self-portrait, when the 10-year-old girl draws a man drinking beer and greatly expressing his enjoyment, or when the 11-year-old girl writes "sal-ammoniac and brandy" on the bottle belonging to the ridiculous tramp she has drawn.

Also names of pop singers or parts of popular songtexts appear, mostly in the drawings of 12- to 13-year-olds. The written words thus seem to express opposite emotional qualities, ridicule and aggression on one side, idealization on the other.

Special kinds of "objects" are the sun and clouds which are limited to

FIGURE 13 Drawing with street and a bus stop (Girl, 9 years old).

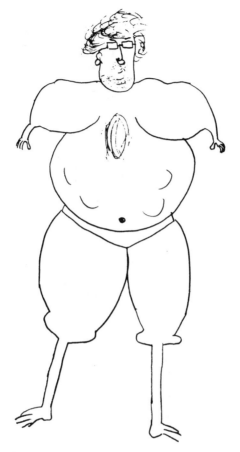

FIGURE 14   Ridiculous figure (Girl, 13 years old).

the age 5–7 for the boys and 5–9 for the girls, with 10 of the 14 examples appearing at the age of 5. Clouds are found in one drawing of each sex and a sun in nine drawings by girls, three by boys. The sun is placed in the corner or somewhere above the person and is in several cases supplied with facial features.

A natural explanation of the relatively frequent occurrence of the sun in the drawings of young children would be the assumption that it symbolizes the parents or one of the parents, or perhaps parental warmth and protection in general. This is supported by the frequent occurrence of facial features on the sun.

FIGURE 15 Idealized figure (Girl, 13 years old).

Koppitz (1968) hypothesized that the drawing of the sun was a possible emotional indicator, but found this not confirmed as it appeared more often in the drawings of well-adjusted children than in those of clinic patients. Suns were found more often in children with high teacher ratings than in those with low. She also associated the drawing of the sun with parental love and support, but also with controlling adult authority, and added that particularly children with psychosomatic complaints tend to include suns in their drawings. They are children whose parents are both loving and quite controlling, and where the children,

FIGURE 16 Drawing of the sun with facial features (Boy, 5 years old).

though feeling ambivalent toward their parents, are only able to express their positive attitudes openly. Koppitz concluded that the drawing of the sun cannot in itself be taken as a good or bad sign.

The drawing of clouds is quite rare, appearing in only two cases. This is one of Koppitz's (1968) emotional indicators, which was found mainly in the drawings of her clinic patients and poorly adjusted pupils. She found clouds especially often in drawings of very anxious children with psychosomatic complaints and not at all in the drawings of overly aggressive children. Clouds are, in her opinion, drawn primarily by children who dare not strike out at others, but who turn their aggression inward, who, so to speak, stand "under a cloud" of pressure from above, especially from their parents.

The specific hypotheses regarding the symbolic meaning of the sun and clouds can, of course, neither be affirmed nor disproved by the present study; but the data confirm that the drawing of the sun is more common than the drawing of clouds.

Drawing of a Head Only

The drawing of a head only or another limited part of the total figure was found to increase with age. This may be due to several reasons. One could be an attempt at avoidance of the task, a way of getting away with

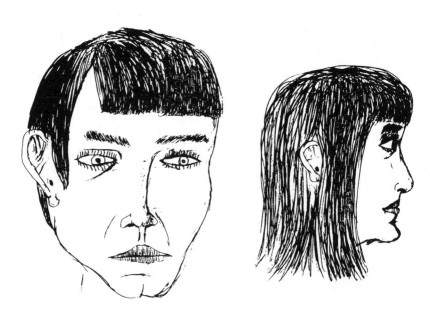

FIGURE 17   Attempts at more personal portraits (Boy, 12 years old).

it with as little effort and involvement as possible, and an avoidance of the difficulties of the drawing of body and limbs. As self-criticism grows with age, the greater frequency of portraits with increasing age might be seen as a support for this hypothesis, so much more as the tendency to draw heads only is most pronounced in the self-portraits, while the less menacing task of drawing a male or female figure in general often results in the drawing of a whole figure.

A closer inspection of the heads does not seem to support this hypothesis, however. Many of them, particularly in the older age-groups, are quite elaborate with many details and seem rather to reflect a heightened interest in the face and its expressions. Quite a few of them look like attempts at personal portraits.

The development may thus be a result of a combination of several factors, an avoidance of the task of depicting oneself, a growing self-criticism with regard to one's ability to draw, combined with the greater interest in psychological characterization and individuality which is typical of adolescence. The possible meaning of the greater frequency of whole figures in the girls' drawings will be taken up later.

Genitals and Sexual Differentiation

Denmark has the reputation for being a country with a relatively free attitude toward sexuality and consequently relatively great openness also toward children with regard to sexual information, which is regularly given in the schools. This freedom has manifested itself—among other things—in the abolition of prohibition against pornography, in the full legalization of abortion, and in a lack of moral condemnation of single motherhood which is probably greater than in most other societies. It would be natural to expect that this freedom toward sexuality might manifest itself also in the drawings of children and result in a more frequent depiction of genitals. The drawing of naked figures has been no rare task in art education in schools and kindergartens, and children might therefore be expected to know that adults would accept the drawing of naked figures.

In contrast stands the experience of Koppitz (1968), who found the drawing of genitals to be a clear emotional indicator. She saw them rarely represented in figure drawings, but when they occurred, it was invariably in the drawings of clinic patients who were extremely dis-

turbed and overtly aggressive. She concluded that the presence of genitals, or symbols for them, must be considered a sign of serious psychopathology, involving acute body anxiety and poor impulse control.

"Genitals" is in the present study used as a heading which also
includes such items as the navel and hair on chest as well as inner organs,
which may be found in transparent drawings. The drawing of breasts on
dressed female figures is, on the other hand, not included as this is seen
as an ordinary developmental trait. In total, seven drawings by boys
contain 12 items under the heading of "genitals," and ten drawings by
girls contain 13 items.

The drawings fall clearly into two clusters; seven of them are found
at the ages of 5–6, while the remaining ten do not appear until from age
10 and onward. This fits in well with psychoanalytic theory, according
to which the sexual interest should be greatest and most clearly manifested during the Oedipal phase and in adolescence and preadolescence,
while it should be given less open expression during latency age.

Twelve of the examples consist of the drawing of the navel, three of
hair on chest, and five of naked breasts or nipples (on either male or
female figures). Genitals proper are only seen in three drawings by boys
and in one drawing by a girl. The three drawings by boys are all made

FIGURE 18 Drawings with genitals (Boy, 11 years old).

by the same 11-year-old boy and contain so many deviant traits that they point strongly in the direction of a severely disturbed personality.

The drawing of the navel seems to have a different meaning from the drawing of genitals proper; it is not supposed to be associated with aggression, but rather with dependency (Machover 1949). This shows good connection with the fact that it is frequently drawn by younger children.

The results of this study do not show that the relatively great sexual freedom of Danish society has in any way affected children's drawings in the direction of a greater tendency to draw genitals or—as perhaps some might fear—to a preoccupation with the subject. On the contrary, the results tend to support Koppitz's (1968) observation that the representation of genitals in drawings occur in children with considerable disturbances of personality (at least under drawing conditions such as these). It might be added that this result coincides well with my general impression from clinical work.

Also the drawing of other sexual characteristics, e.g., in clothing, is worth studying. The drawings were collected at the peak of the unisex period, when many men wore their hair long, and most women wore slacks or jeans. The drawing of a female figure in slacks, however, is found in only 5 drawings by the boys (out of 90 possible) and in 22 by girls (out of 180 possible). This is a surprisingly small number. These drawings are found predominantly from the age of 11, i.e., from the age when attempts at a naturalistic representation occur. For the small child's inner vision, a woman is clearly a person who wears a dress, no matter what the actual persons around him wear. Boys tend to be even more conservative than girls, although the sex difference does not reach statistical significance.

Not only do women wear dresses, they are even relatively often drawn in a long gown, in 17 drawings by boys and 18 by girls, mostly in the age-group 6–10 years. The tendency is also here for the boys to draw a long gown relatively more often than the girls, considering their smaller number of female figures, although this difference is not significant either. Again, the boys to an even greater degree than the girls seem to emphasize the more traditional signs of femininity in the dress. In other aspects of clothing, the girls seem more eager to draw details that emphasize femininity, such as patterns, flowers on clothes, bows, jewelry, and hair styling.

The drawings were also scored for the appearance of special types, e.g., a princess, a soldier, etc., but the findings were not included as no significant results were found in regard to either development or sex differences. It may be mentioned, however, that the most commonly drawn type was the princess/bride, which appeared in three drawings by boys and six by girls, mostly at the ages of 6–8. This is clearly the princess of the fairy tales, often in a happy combination with the brides in the show windows of the shops. It seems to be the symbolic prototype of the Oedipal fantasy and has nothing to do with the ordinary living queen, whom most children are disappointed to see in reality because she corresponds so poorly to their magnificent fantasies.

Both boys and girls draw quite a few persons with long hair (51 by boys, 89 by girls), but the greater majority of them are female figures. The boys have drawn 14 male figures with long hair, the girls only 2. In the same way as boys were found to be more conservative than girls in their drawing of the female figure, girls are thus seen to be more conservative in the drawing of males. It is difficult to say what the reason is for this. It may simply be a greater attention to own sex and a greater knowledge about what is current fashion for one's own than for the opposite sex. But it may also be due to a certain opposition against

FIGURE 19 Drawing of a princess/bride (Girl, 8 years old).

changes of the traditional sex stereotypes, an opposition which is naturally strongest on behalf of the other sex.

While the tie really seems to have disappeared completely out of the
drawings of both sexes, the tall hat still survives although it is very rarely
seen in reality. Hats are found in 46 drawings by boys and 43 by girls.

FIGURE 20   Man with a tall hat (Boy, 5 years old).

Some of these, particularly among the older children, are ladies' hats or other naturalistic representations of various headdresses, but the largest number of hats is found among the youngest children and consists of tall hats, which must probably also be regarded more as a symbolic representation of adulthood and authority than anything else.

In spite of quite drastic changes in clothing and hair style at the time when the drawings were made, it must be concluded that the drawings of the children seem relatively little influenced by them, but appear rather conservative. This is particularly true of the younger children and in drawers of the opposite sex. This seems to support the idea that (smaller) children's drawings are more or less symbolic prototypes rather than naturalistic representations of the outer world.

Indication of Age

Almost twice as many drawings by the girls as by the boys can be estimated as to age, probably due to girls' more frequent use of hair and clothing details. Very few children of either sex have drawn a child younger than themselves; in both sexes there is a growing tendency with age to draw a figure of approximately the same age as the drawer, but this tendency is much more outspoken in the girls. Precisely half of the figures whose age can be estimated belong here, whereas only one-seventh of the boys' figures do so. The boys prefer to draw an adult figure and more and more so with increasing age. The girls draw many fewer adults, and the majority of those who do are found at age 8. The figure drawn as a child older than the drawer is found increasingly with increasing age in both sexes, in about one-third of the drawings. The children of the present study seem thus to a large degree to confirm the tendency described in the literature of being future-oriented in their age-assignments, the boys more so than the girls.

The more frequent appearance of adult figures in the drawings by boys may have several reasons. Boys may to a greater degree than girls have positive expectations of the adult role and the authority that follows from it—or, as the other side of the matter—they may be more in opposition to and more preoccupied by the present adult authorities. For girls, the role as a child of their own age or slightly older may be as attractive as the adult role. But the difference may again also be primarily due to the girls' greater detailing of clothes and hair, where the boys, who are less attentive to these aspects, merely place a symbolic tall hat on the head of their figure and in this way characterize it as an adult.

Corrections/Erasures

The use of corrections/erasures increases clearly with age. In the drawings of the boys, not one is found at age 5, but the number of them increases rapidly until, at ages 12 and 13, all drawings contain them. For the girls, the development is very similar. Only one-quarter of the total number of drawings by the boys and less than one-fifth of the girls' are without any corrections. Being so common, corrections/erasures should definitely not be regarded as signs of emotional disturbances in general, but rather as positive signs of greater self-criticism and a growing sense of realism. The total amount of corrections is rather similar for boys and girls, but the distribution on the various body parts differs somewhat. The possible significance is treated in connection with sex differences in general.

Shading

The use of shading is found in all age-groups and increases with age among girls, while the development in the boys is more irregular. Two-thirds of the drawings of both boys and girls contain some form of shading. This amount is even greater than that found by Cohen, Money, and Uhlenhuth (1972) and supports their conclusion that, being so common, shading cannot in general be regarded as a sign of emotional disturbance. By far the greater number of shadings are found on the hair (a little more than one-third), and this seems simply to be a normal way of characterizing hair. The shading of details of clothes is the next most commonly used form and increases with age, particularly among the girls. This form of shading must be regarded mainly as a way of giving emphasis to details or creating variation in the drawing. Shading of eyebrows is relatively common by the girls, but is seen more rarely by the boys.

The specific forms of shading which were suggested by Koppitz (1968) to be emotional indicators (shading of face, of body and/or limbs, and of hands and/or neck) were also found in the present material. Shading of the face was seen in 2 drawings by boys, 4 by girls; shading of the

FIGURE 21   Shading of eyebrows and as pattern on clothes (Girl, 12 years old).

neck in 7 and 2 drawings, respectively. Shading of arms and hands is somewhat more common among the boys, where it occurs in 21 drawings, while it is only found in 6 by the girls. Shading of the upper part of the body is found in 22 drawings by boys, of the lower part in 21 drawings (mainly the same). Among the girls, the same numbers are 13 and 7, respectively. Finally, the shading of legs and/or feet is found in 20 drawings by boys, 17 by girls.

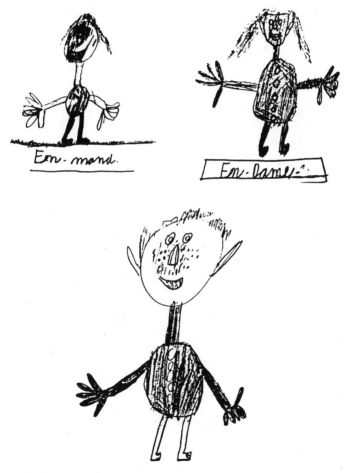

FIGURE 22 Heavy shading on three drawings by the same child, suggesting anxiety (Boy, 9 years old).

One of the criteria of the emotional indicators was the fact that they should not be present in more than at most 15% of the drawings of the children. The use of shading in the Danish study is so rare that this criterion is fulfilled.

There is a concentration of drawings with shading among 9-year-old boys. They are scored for three times as many shadings as any other age-group among the boys. The shadings are not evenly distributed, but concentrated in the drawings of six boys, who have used shading consistently and profusely. One boy has shaded every body part on all three figures, including the face on two of them, while the face on the third is disfigured by a lot of freckles and spots, a trait that Koppitz regards as equivalent of shading. Two other boys have shaded everything except

FIGURE 23   Other examples of heavy shading on drawings by two 9-year-old boys.

the face on all three figures. Two have shaded everything except the face on two of their figures and many details on the last, and one has shaded one drawing heavily and the other two on a great many details. It may be added that these drawings immediately struck me as probably having been made by children with an unusually high degree of anxiety. As will be seen shortly (in the comparison with the Goodenough/Harris results [1963]) the general level of drawing development of the 9-year-old boys is lower than could be expected, so these drawings are both immature and show possible signs of emotional problems.

It looks, therefore, as if the shading of these specific body parts is a rare trait, which, at least under drawing conditions such as these, has a high reliability, which may be connected with a generally lowered drawing performance, and which therefore with a relatively high degree of probability is connected with emotional problems. This would be in accordance with earlier results, e.g., those by Kyng (1973). The same cannot be said indiscriminately about any form of shading, however, which in many cases, on the contrary, rather seems to be a sign of development.

COMPARISON BETWEEN THE DANISH RESULTS AND
THE GOODENOUGH/HARRIS RESULTS

The Danish material is not representative of Danish children in general, and a comparison between it and the American norms can therefore not lead to any conclusions regarding drawing norms in Denmark; nonetheless, it is of interest to see where this Danish material is placed in comparison to the American material.

The results from the two American studies were already compared by Harris (1963), who combined the curves on the same graphs; the Danish results have been added as a third curve. (Those interested in the exact percentages for the Danish drawings are referred to the original study [Mortensen 1984].)

In all cases, when the drawing of a whole figure has been necessary for the scoring of an item, the percentages were seen in relation to the number of whole figures only.

Figure 24 shows that there is almost complete coincidence between all three on the following nine items: presence of head, eyes, nose, mouth, legs and trunk, clothing I and IV, and profile II.

The two American studies differ from each other on a number of

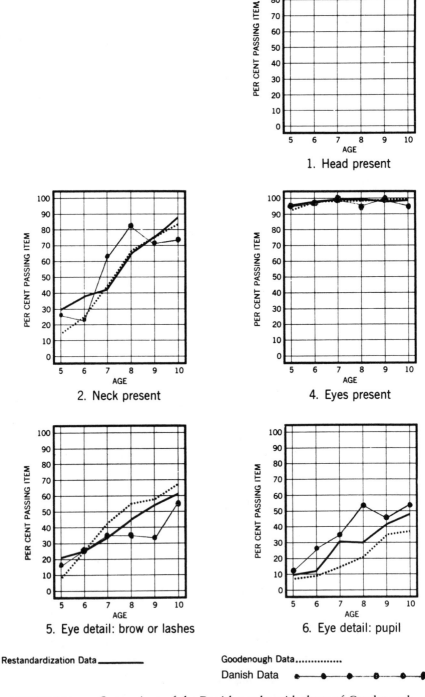

FIGURE 24a–g Comparison of the Danish results with those of Goodenough and of Harris. (The original comparison is from Harris 1963.)

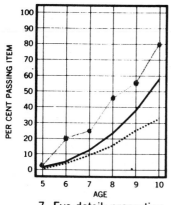

7. Eye detail: proportion

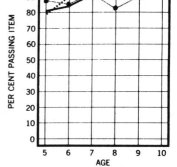

9. Nose present

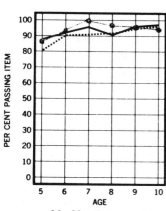

11. Mouth present

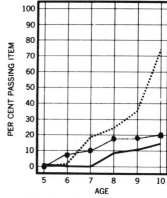

13. Nose and lips, two dimen.

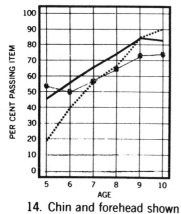

14. Chin and forehead shown

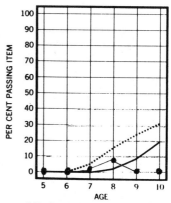

15. Projection of chin shown

Restandardization Data _____

Goodenough Data ....

Danish Data •——•——•——•——•——•

FIGURE 24b

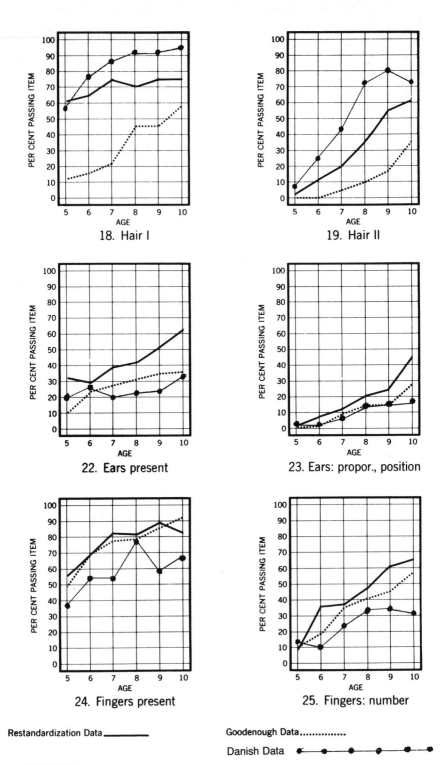

18. Hair I

19. Hair II

22. Ears present

23. Ears: propor., position

24. Fingers present

25. Fingers: number

Restandardization Data _____

Goodenough Data ....

Danish Data ●——●——●——●——●——●

FIGURE 24c

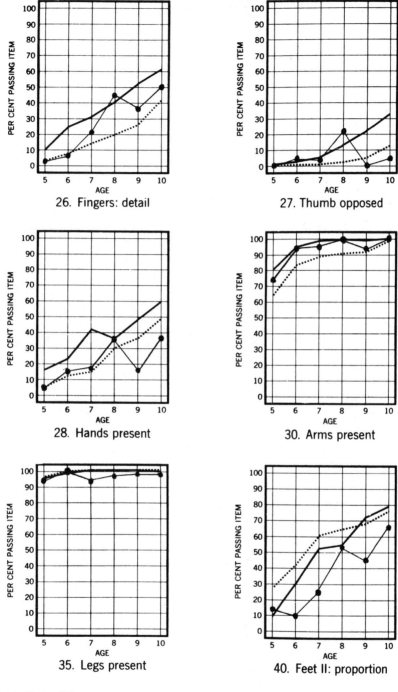

26. Fingers: detail

27. Thumb opposed

28. Hands present

30. Arms present

35. Legs present

40. Feet II: proportion

Restandardization Data _____

Goodenough Data ....

Danish Data ●——●——●——●——●——●

FIGURE 24d

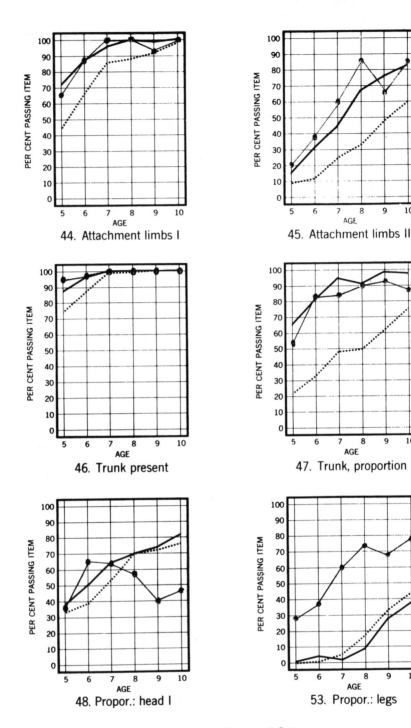

44. Attachment limbs I

45. Attachment limbs II

46. Trunk present

47. Trunk, proportion

48. Propor.: head I

53. Propor.: legs

Restandardization Data _____

Goodenough Data ....

Danish Data

FIGURE 24e

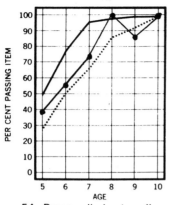

54. Propor.: limbs, two dimen.

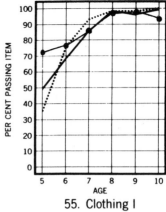

55. Clothing I

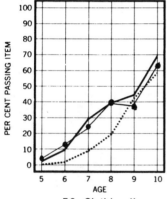

56. Clothing II

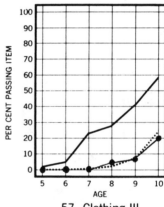

57. Clothing III

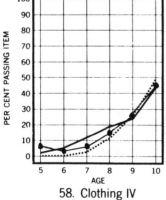

58. Clothing IV

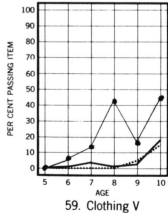

59. Clothing V

Restandardization Data ————————

Goodenough Data ....

Danish Data ●———●———●———●———●———●

FIGURE 24f

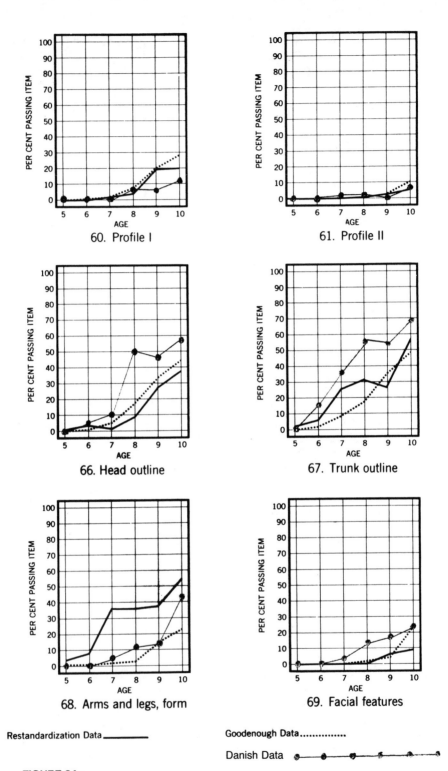

60. Profile I

61. Profile II

66. Head outline

67. Trunk outline

68. Arms and legs, form

69. Facial features

Restandardization Data _____

Goodenough Data ....

Danish Data

FIGURE 24g

items, and in some cases the Danish results are closer to Goodenough's (1926) results, in other cases to Harris's (1963). They are closer to Goodenough's original data on the following seven variables: ears present, proportion and position of ears, number of fingers, presence of hands, limbs in two dimensions, clothing III, and form of arms and legs.

They are closer to Harris's results on the following 14 items: eyebrows or eyelashes, pupils, proportions of eyes, nose and lips in two dimensions, projection of chin, hair I and II, arms present, proportion of feet, attachment of limbs I and II, proportions of trunk, clothing II, and trunk outline.

In some cases, the Danish results lie above both of the others, in some below, and in still others they are intermediate or partly above and partly below. They are consistently above on the following nine items: pupils, proportions of the eye, hair I and II, proportions of legs, clothing V, outline of head, outline of trunk, and facial features.

Clothing V is a complete costume without incongruities. It is difficult to score reliably, and it is my impression that the Danish scoring has been more lenient than intended originally by Goodenough. These results must therefore be regarded with reservation, particularly as the other clothing items follow the American results very nicely. Also the scorings of head and trunk outline are based on subjective evaluations, and the same doubt may be raised as to their reliability.

In the following five items the Danish results are generally lower than for both of the American ones: presence of ears, proportions and positions of ears, presence of fingers, correct number of fingers, and proportions of feet II.

The difference in the presence of ears is most probably due to the fact that the Danish material contains an equal number of male and female figures while the American results are calculated only on the basis of the drawings of a man. As shown in the present study, male figures are drawn with ears about twice as often as female figures. I might have chosen to include only the Danish drawings of male figures in the comparisons, but this would have reduced the number of drawings at each age level to 30. I preferred to include all the drawings to get more material for comparison. The Danish curves are somewhat more irregular than the American ones, due to the still more limited number of drawings included. A special irregularity is found at the age of 9, where the Danish curves show a decline in about half of the tables. This is due to the particularly low results in the drawings by the 9-year-old boys.

The main impression from the comparison is that of a surprising overall similarity between the results. The Danish results are generally closer to those of Harris than to those of Goodenough. If the difference between the two American studies is real and not only due to sampling differences, this is what might be expected, as the Danish and Harris studies are closer in time, and therefore made by children who at least in some respects have more similar backgrounds. Their educational level is probably rather similar. The overall level of the Danish material and that of Harris seems quite similar, when corrections are made for the items where the Danish scoring may be doubtful.

But, of course, the greater similarity between these two studies can in no way be used to support the validity of Harris's results. It is not known whether the Danish group of children is below or above average, neither is it known what effect the geographical/cultural differences between the two groups of children have. The results can, however, be taken as a confirmation of the generality of children's drawing development in the Western cultures.

COMPARISON OF THE DEVELOPMENTAL LEVEL OF THE THREE DRAWINGS BY EACH CHILD

In most studies of drawing development, the children have made only one figure drawing each. An exception is the study by Harris (1963) who collected drawings of both a male and female figure. He found that the results were somewhat different for the figures of either sex, and that the advantage of girls over boys was greater in the drawing of a female than of a male figure. It was, therefore, also of interest in the Danish study to compare the developmental level of the drawings of own and opposite sex (and of the self-drawings).

Furthermore, the fact that the children were asked to make three drawings in immediate succession may by itself have influenced the results. It was, therefore, necessary also to make comparisons between drawings 1, 2, and 3. Different hypotheses may be suggested regarding the influence of these factors. The quality may be expected to decrease from the first to the last drawing, due to loss of interest or motivation, or to fatigue. Conversely, it might be expected that drawing number 3 would be of the highest quality because it was a self-drawing. Similarly, the drawing of own sex might be expected to be of higher quality than the drawing of opposite sex.

Not much information can be gained from the literature. Schubert (1969) had 22 men draw a person of each sex three times, with a week between trials, and found a clearly significant trend toward poorer quality on repeated testing. The reactions of the subjects gave the impression that they were not taking the third test as seriously as the first two, and he concludes that the quality of the drawings is a function of motivation. The results are not quite comparable to the present investigation as the subjects were adults and not children, and as the situation was a real retest situation and not a comparison between different drawings made in one session.

Richey (1965) hypothesized that greater effort and attention would be given to the self-sex figure than to the opposite-sex figure. The drawings of 10-year-old boys and girls were scored according to a modification of the Goodenough DAM-scale (1926). Both boys and girls were found to score significantly higher on self-sex drawings. She also found that girls scored higher than boys on the drawings of both sexes, a finding consistent with Goodenough's own results. As, however, most of the subjects drew their own sex first, the results may also simply mean that the first drawings were of higher quality than the second, a possibility that Richey does not take into consideration.

Gellert (1968) had children 5–12 years old depict themselves and an age-mate of the opposite sex. They were restricted to drawing both figures in bathing suits, however, so no inferences could be made from the investment in clothing. It was hypothesized that the self-sex drawings would be more articulated, detailed, and accurate. In contrast to Richey, Gellert found no significant differences with regard to total items score, symmetry of figure, or body proportion. When age was taken into account, however, younger children of both sexes were found more frequently to earn higher total items scores on self-drawing while older children generally scored higher on opposite-sex figures. This difference was statistically significant. Comparison of the relative mouth- and eye-emphasis provided partial support for the hypothesis that the self-representation would be the more elaborate of the two figures. Among both sexes, a significantly larger group drew the self-sex figure larger than the other-sex figure. It was suggested that the size of the figure is at least partly a projection of the relative value of the person represented.

In the present study, it was found impracticable to compare the drawings on all the developmental traits, due to the large number of them. Besides, only those traits were found relevant which showed a significant development in the drawings of both sexes. Items present in almost all drawings, or, conversely, present in only very few, would not add much information and were therefore also excluded. The same applied to traits which appeared only in the drawings of either female or male figures or which were known to favor one sex. Also all formal qualities were excluded because of their lesser scoring reliability than for the content variables. This left a total of 52 developmental items on which the drawings were compared. In this comparison, only the drawings of whole figures were used, totaling 425. The mean and variance of the number of developmental items were calculated for drawings no. 1, 2, and 3 for all age-groups and for each sex separately.

Comparisons between Drawings No. 1, 2, and 3

In the Danish study, the mean number of developmental items was found to be almost identical for the three drawings through the ages 5– 10 for both boys and girls. From the age of 11, a tendency was found for the first drawing to lie highest and for the third to lie at the bottom, with drawing no. 2 showing a more unclear pattern. This might look as if the older children have less patience with the full task than the younger children or perhaps feel more provoked by the drawings of themselves and therefore try to avoid that part of the work through lesser engagement.

Another explanation is also possible, however. So many of the older children drew a head only or another limited part of the figure in drawing no. 3 that it was found to be a developmental trait. It was therefore suggested that the children who still draw the third drawing as a whole figure are the most immature children whose drawings generally are of a lower quality than those of their age-mates who draw only a head. This might explain the tendency toward a lower quality in drawing no. 3. An answer to this question was approached through a comparison of the quality of these children's drawings no. 1 and 2 with the same drawings by the children who drew their third drawing as a head. It was only relevant to make this comparison for the 11- to 13-year-olds.

This hypothesis was supported. For all the examined age-groups, drawings no. 1 and 2 were clearly of a higher quality (as here defined) when the third drawing was only a head or other part of the figure, than when the third drawing was a whole figure. The means of drawing no. 3

did not differ much from the means of drawings no. 1 and 2 by the same drawers. This indicates that the apparently lowered quality of drawing no. 3 in the older age-groups was not due to a general decline of quality from drawing no. 1 to drawing no. 3, but to a selection of the drawers who still drew drawing no. 3 as a whole figure. The more mature and better developed drawers disappeared from the sample. It seems thus justified to conclude that no noticeable difference in quality could be seen from first to third drawing.

Incidentally, this serves to justify calling the drawing of only the head a developmental trait, since it is found to occur in the children with the most well-developed drawings. It supports also the idea that the drawing of the head is not only caused by the negative motivation of avoiding a difficult task, but that it may be motivated by a positive interest in seeking new challenges in the depiction of the face and in the attempt at mastering a more personal and psychological characterization of the drawn figure.

The variance showed a slight rise during the ages 5–7, which is a natural consequence of the increase in the number of items with increasing age. The variance then became relatively stable until the age of 11; from then on great variations were seen, but they were probably due to the smaller number of drawings included. No general difference was found in the variance between drawings no. 1, 2, and 3. On the whole, the drawings of the boys showed a somewhat greater variance than those of the girls, both in the drawing of male and female figures.

A comparison between boys' and girls' drawings no. 1, 2, and 3 showed the girls' to lie slightly, but consistently, above those of the boys; this is in accordance with the earlier findings.

Comparisons between the Figures of Either Sex

In these comparisons only drawings no. 1 and 2 were included to avoid possible complications through the use of the self-drawing. This left 152 male and 152 female figures (only whole figures).

When the drawings of own and opposite sex were compared for the two sexes separately, they were found to be almost identical in regard to number of included developmental items, particularly among the girls. With the boys a slight tendency could be seen to draw own sex better than the opposite, except at age 9 when the drawings of own sex are at a particularly low level and of a poorer quality than the drawings of the other sex. There is greater variance, however, in the drawings of the opposite sex than in the drawings of own sex among the boys, and variance is particularly great at age 9, so the result is due to a mixture of drawings of very good and not so good quality. Among the girls, the same-sex drawings showed the greatest variance, which means that the female figures drawn by both sexes show the greater variance.

When the drawings of male and female figures were compared between the sexes, the sex differences stood out most clearly. At the ages of 5 and 6, no sex differences were seen in the drawing of either male or female figures, nor at the age of 7 for the drawing of male figures. However, in the drawings of female figures, the girls from the age of 7 showed a consistent superiority, lasting until the age of 13. In the drawing of male figures, they did better at the ages of 8–10, after which age the difference seemed less clear. It became very noticeable here that the poor quality of the 9-year-old boys' drawings was mainly concentrated on their male figures while their drawings of female figures were relatively better.

It seems justified to conclude that no general tendency could be found for children to draw own or opposite sex consistently better than the other. Similarly, the self-sex drawing showed no clear difference in developmental level from drawings no. 1 or 2, as here measured.

The girls showed a higher level in both the drawing of male and female figures than the boys, but in the drawing of the male figure this was limited to the ages 8–10, while in the drawing of the female figure they showed a consistent superiority from age 7 through 13. These results are in agreement with the results of Harris (1963), who also compared the drawings in regard to a selected number of traits. He also found a general superiority of the girls over the boys, but a greater superiority in the drawing of the female figure than of the male. The fact that Goodenough (1926) found less striking sex differences than Harris is understandable because she only let the children draw a male figure where the difference between the sexes is less outspoken.

RELIABILITY OF DEVELOPMENTAL TRAITS

In the study of reliability, only the children were included who had made all three drawings as a whole figure, giving a total of 115 children (345 drawings), and only the 52 developmental traits earlier mentioned were used.

The highest reliability is obtained by the traits which occur in all three drawings by the same child, the lowest by those found in only one. In order to eliminate the influence of the difference in base rate as much as possible (i.e., the difference in the frequency with which the different traits are used), the percentage of children who use a given trait in one, two, or three drawings is not related to the total number of 115 children, but only to the number of children who use the trait at all. Otherwise, a trait which was used very rarely would necessarily show a very low reliability. Some of the traits occur very rarely or never in all three drawings, while other items appear in all three drawings of more than 80% of the children who use them.

The developmental traits with the highest reliability, as here defined, were the following: presence of neck, presence of chin, nose, mouth, arms, legs and feet in 2 dimensions, nose more long than wide, eyes more long than high, and arms attached to the trunk at the right place. These ten traits are all found in all three drawings of more than 60% of the children who use them. All of these traits are very common ones which occur in most drawings, with the exception of the drawing of eyes more long than high. This item is not used by more than a little over half of the children, 62 of the 115, but when it is used, it is found in all three drawings of 88% of the children. This is the highest reliability found among all the traits.

It must be remembered that this is not a complete study of the reliability of all the developmental traits, as only 52 of them were selected for this part of the study. Some of them were omitted here because they occurred either in almost all drawings or in very few. This means that some of the developmental traits with the highest reliability are omitted here, as well as some of those with the lowest (presumably). The traits that were omitted because of their frequency were, for example, the presence of the main body parts and the main facial features, so the reliability of these items is very high. Among the items included in this part of the study, the presence of neck and chin were also found to have a high reliability. Besides, it is obviously the drawing of body parts in two dimensions which is most reliable, as well as a few of the traits showing good proportions.

The traits with the lowest reliability (those found in only one drawing by at least 60% of the children using them) are the following: ears more long than wide, line of jaw indicated, special facial features drawn, corners of mouth, arms narrowing toward wrist, naturalistic shaping of head, arch of foot, pattern in clothes of any kind, pleats or folds in clothes, and accessory objects.

They are seen to be refinements of the shaping of the figure or rather special and unessential details. Most of these traits are found to occur relatively late in the development, while the traits with the highest reliability were fundamental traits occurring early. Traits that are introduced early tend to be well established and stable, while later traits are less reliable.

OVERVIEW OF THE RESULTS

The picture of drawing development is made up of a combination of many parts, and it may be felt necessary to draw out the more general patterns from this somewhat confusing totality. The present description is more comprehensive than most of the previous studies of drawing development, including aspects which have rarely been described.

Quantitatively, the general development is found to follow a negatively accelerating curve, with about half of the total number of items present in the best developed drawings already at age 5. During the following years quite a few new items are also introduced, but after 10 years of age, very few new traits are added. This pattern corresponds well to what has been found in earlier works on drawing development, and also the age at which the introduction of new items stops is similar to earlier studies. This overall agreement is confirmed by the comparison between the Danish results and those of Goodenough (1926) and Harris (1963), with the Danish results lying closer to Harris's.

The introduction of new items follows a certain sequence, starting with the major body parts and major facial features. This is followed by the change from one to two dimensions, by gradual improvement in size and proportions, and finally by improvements in form level and aspects of motoric control. Particularly from the age of 7, many minor details of clothing, face, and hair are added. Variations in posture, movement, and profile drawings are also later achievements, as is the drawing of only a head or other section of the figure instead of the whole person. There are, of course, overlappings between the improvements in the various aspects of the drawings.

It was noted that at least the younger children's drawings seem very slightly affected by recent changes in sex roles and clothing habits. The small children are seen to be conservative in their depiction of sex differences and seem to follow fixed, internal schemata rather than to depict their actual surroundings. With increasing age, a greater influence by outer realities can be found in the drawings, probably due to the older children's greater ability to observe what people around them actually look like. Both sexes seem to be more traditional on behalf of the other sex than of their own.

In spite of a relatively free attitude to sexuality, the drawing of naked figures and the depiction of genitals occurs very rarely and only among the drawings of the youngest and the oldest children, while they are conspicuously absent in the drawings of latency children. The quality of the drawings which include genitals, at least among the older children, gives rise to the suspicion that drawing of genitals is connected with anxiety and emotional problems rather than the expression of a "natural" and uncomplicated attitude to sexuality.

Some of the other traits, which in the drawings of adults often are regarded as signs of emotional conflicts or anxiety, are found so commonly in the drawings of children that it would not be reasonable to consider them as conflict-indicators here. This is true of corrections/erasures which actually increase in number with age and which seem rather to indicate a growing and age-appropriate self-criticism. Shading is another trait which too often has been scored indiscriminately, without necessary regard to its positioning and quality. Heavy black shading of the most important body parts may, in all probability, be a sign of conflict, but light shading of details should rather also be regarded as a sign of development.

The point at which earlier and later studies have been found to vary most between them, is in regard to the relative advantage of the two sexes. The earlier studies generally found boys to be ahead of girls, while later studies equally regularly found girls to be ahead of boys (at least during latency age). The age at which boys were found to catch up with girls—if at all—varies between the studies.

The superiority of boys in the earlier studies, which to some degree seems to be real, may be at least partly due to differences in treatment of the sexes, with boys receiving both more art education and more encouragement toward intellectual achievements in general. It has generally been found that a rise in educational level is followed by a rise in drawing development.

But apart from these possible real differences, most of the variations between the studies seem to be connected with the fact that they have not emphasized the total number of variables, but have focused on different aspects of the drawings. The emphasis has also too narrowly been on the quantitative differences without due regard to the total pattern of both qualitative and quantitative differences. Items such as profile drawing and movement, which were emphasized in, for example, the study by Kerschensteiner (1905), and in which boys excelled, are spectacular and highly estimated when the visually correct depiction of the surroundings is seen as the goal of drawing development. As may be remembered, girls were only found to be better in decoration in his study, and their ability to draw clothes and hair details seems not to have received the same attention or sympathy. On the other hand, in the studies by Goodenough (1926) and Harris (1963), both the better motoric control of girls and their emphasis on a number of details are given high credit, while such traits as profile drawing and movement only count as few items and therefore play a relatively minor role.

The results of the Danish study show clearly the effect of the use of different aspects of the drawings. When only those items are included which show a significant development in both sexes, the girls show a slight superiority at ages 8–11. This tendency for girls to be slightly ahead of boys in many of the common developmental traits is further confirmed by the study of traits which decrease in frequency with age. Girls also tend to leave more immature stages earlier than boys in many aspects of drawings. This pattern confirms thus the results from the later studies on drawing development of a certain developmental superiority in girls.

When the items are included which show a significant development in only one sex, this sex difference becomes even more pronounced. Girls add many more specific items than boys, particularly from age 8. A description that merely takes into account the quantitative aspects of drawing development must thus come to the conclusion that girls do better than boys. But such a description must be regarded as too mechanistic. When more qualitative viewpoints are introduced, it may be maintained that traits such as the drawing of a profile, of a head only, and of movement may be considered to be equally as important as the introduction of a great many details in clothing and hair, although they do not count as so many single items. When both qualitative and quantitative aspects are taken into account, it becomes actually meaningless to describe drawing development for the two sexes as a sort of competition about "who does best." A much more fruitful way of looking at it would be to regard the drawing development of the two sexes as two parallel, but qualitatively different courses of development.

Finally, it is important to remember that the drawing of a human figure is not necessarily representative of drawing development in general. It may be a topic that favors girls in some respects, boys in other, and—as will be discussed later—it may be a topic that has a special appeal to girls. Other subjects, for example technical objects, may be expected to favor boys more.

It was necessary to limit the number of variables in the comparison between the three drawings of each child and between male and female drawings. Therefore, the same criticism can be raised against this part of the study as is raised against earlier studies, namely, that the selection of items and the use of only quantitative description may favor one of the sexes. This does seem to be the case, since the girls' drawings generally show a higher level than the boys' in this part of the study. With this reservation in mind, it seems justified to conclude that no systematic difference in quality (defined as developmental level) was found between drawings no. 1, 2, and 3. An apparent decline of quality in drawing no. 3 in the drawing of a whole figure by the children from age 11 to 13 seemed to be due to a selection of drawers, with the more mature drawers shifting to the drawing of a head only in the self-drawing.

The drawings of female figures showed greater variance than the drawings of male figures (for both sexes). This was probably due to the greater number of clothing and hair details in the female figures which are some of the traits with a relatively low reliability.

The drawing of own and opposite sex showed no outspoken difference in regard to the variables here chosen, except possibly for a slight tendency among the boys to draw own sex better. Neither do the self-drawings show any difference in developmental level from drawings no. 1 and 2. The general superiority of the girls was not distributed evenly on the drawings of male and female figures, but was considerably greater in the drawings of the female figure, a result which is consistent with that of Harris (1963). Again, this is most probably due to the greater number of details on the female figure, which are employed particularly by the girls.

The study on reliability (which was also made on the selected number of variables) showed that the traits that had the highest reliability were the more fundamental and early introduced traits such as the presence of essential body parts, two-dimensionality, and some traits showing good proportioning. A number of minor details and refinements in the shaping of the figure, which are introduced later, were found to be more unstable.

SIX

Sex Differences

All variables were compared with regard to sex differences. With a few exceptions, only those results are described where the differences found were significant at the level of 5% or better. When nonsignificant results are described, it is explicitly mentioned. As mentioned before, the total groups of boys and girls were compared with regard to sex differences as the number of children was not big enough to allow a comparison year by year.

Some overlapping with the results described under drawing development is unavoidable. As pointed out earlier, development and sex differences are closely interrelated. Many of the developmental traits were found to show sex differences and were introduced at different ages for boys and girls, but other sex differences showed no clear connection with age and could, therefore, not be described in connection with drawing development. A coherent account of all the sex differences is necessary to give a full overview of their extent. As far as possible, however, overlapping descriptions or discussions have been avoided.

DESCRIPTION OF RESULTS

Sexual Differentiation

The actual number of male and female figures drawn by each sex was determined through the design of the study. The only variable of interest in this connection is therefore the number of drawings, the sex of which could not be recognized by the raters. Boys more often than girls drew figures whose sex was not recognizable. While all drawings by girls could be recognized as to sex after the age of 7, boys continued to make drawings with ambiguous sex through all ages, inclusive of age 13. The greater frequency of portraits by the boys is part of the reason for this, but not the whole explanation.

Sex of First Drawn Figure

In the cases where the sex of a child's drawing was not immediately recognizable at the time of drawing, the teacher asked him about it and wrote it on the back of the drawing. It is, therefore, also possible to describe in how many cases the children drew own or opposite sex first. Although the sex difference found is not significant, these results are reported because this variable has been the subject of such a great number of studies. The boys have drawn own sex first in 73 cases (of 90 possible), the girls in 68.

Part of Figure Drawn

Girls more often than boys drew a whole figure, while boys more often drew only a head. This variation was not introduced in the drawings of girls until the age of 11, while in the drawings of boys heads only appeared as early as the age of 5; but also for the boys the frequency rose with age, and particularly many heads were drawn at the ages of 11–13.

The drawing of a head instead of a whole figure has not been the subject of study before and is not mentioned among earlier noted sex differences, probably because in most studies the children are simply asked to draw a whole figure.

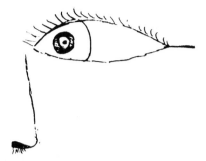

FIGURE 25   Extreme example of only a part of the figure drawn (Boy, 10 years old).

Presence/Omission of Major Body Parts

Although a closer inspection of the material reveals a tendency for the girls to include many of the major body parts earlier and more completely in their drawings than the boys, this difference reaches significance only in the case of arms, ears, and clothing. The presence of clothing is included here, although clothing, strictly speaking, is not, of course, a body part. These are all developmental traits and the sex differences here may, thus, reflect a difference in the rate of growth for the two sexes.

When a certain age is passed, differing from item to item and between the sexes, the presence of these body parts must usually be taken for granted, and their omission becomes of greater interest than their presence. It may reflect an emotional and/or intellectual disturbance. In the higher age-groups, sex differences in the presence of body parts may thus have a different meaning from those of younger age groups and not just be a reflection of a difference in rate of development.

When only whole figures were compared, "no arms" were found in the drawings of 19 boys and 5 girls. Four of the figures without arms were found at age 5 for girls and 15 at the ages 5–7 for boys. The sex difference for the ages 5–7 is significant. This is a clear difference in rate of development, favoring the girls.

More girls than boys omitted the ears from their drawings. As this might be due to the fact that girls drew twice as many pictures of female figures where the hair might conceal the ears, the percentage of male and female figures drawn with ears by both sexes was examined. Boys were

FIGURE 26 Ears present on male figure, omitted on female by the same drawer (Boy, 11 years old).

then found to draw 44% of their male figures with ears and 18% of their females, girls 41% of their male figures, 17% of their females. Thus, both boys and girls gave male figures ears more than twice as often as female figures, and no significant sex difference appeared when the different number of male and female figures in the drawings of the two sexes was taken into account.

"No indication of clothes" was seen in drawings by boys more often than by girls, and even when whole figures only were compared, the sex difference was still highly significant. "At least 4 pieces of clothing" was much more often found in the drawings by the girls. Also the drawing of a complete dress and of fashionable clothes was more frequent by the girls.

In summary, while the sex difference in the drawing of the arms seems to reflect a maturational lag for the boys, in the depiction of clothing the boys never catch up with the girls. Girls continually emphasize the drawing of clothes more than boys, they more often draw four pieces of clothing, a complete dress, or fashionable clothes. This seems to be not only a quantitative, but also a qualitative difference. The difference in the frequency of the drawing of ears was found to disappear when the results were corrected for the different number of male and female figures drawn by boys and girls.

Size of Body Parts

Sex differences in regard to size of body parts were found in the following areas: head, eyes, nose, mouth, ears, hands and fingers, legs, feet, and neck.

FIGURE 27 Drawing of a big head by a girl, a relatively small head by a boy (Girl, 12 years old, boy, 10 years old).

Girls more often than boys drew a big head. For both sexes, there was a tendency toward the drawing of relatively smaller heads with increasing age, but big heads were seen in the drawings of both sexes through all ages.

Well-proportioned eyes compared to size of head were found most often in the drawings of girls. Boys more often drew either too big or too small eyes, but neither of these differences reached statistical significance.

More girls than boys drew a small nose while more boys than girls drew a big nose. An almost equal number of both sexes drew well-proportioned noses. Neither the drawing of a small nor of a big nose seemed to be connected with age.

FIGURE 28 Typical examples of facial features drawn by boys. Note, e.g., the protruding ears, big mouths, and big noses with details (Two boys, 12 years old).

A well-proportioned mouth was found more often in the drawings of girls than of boys, while a big mouth was drawn more often by boys. This variable did not seem to have a clear connection with age either.

Small ears were drawn more often by girls.

Well-proportioned hands were most frequent in drawings by girls, big hands in the drawings by boys. There was also a tendency for girls more often to draw small hands, but not significantly so.

Long legs were seen more often in the drawings by boys, and they also more often drew big feet. In both sexes, there seemed to be a tendency with increasing age to draw big feet less often, most markedly by the girls.

A short neck compared to size of head or a well-proportioned neck was drawn more often by girls than by boys, while a long neck was preferred by more boys than girls. A thin neck, compared to size of head, was more common by girls than by boys while a wide neck was more frequent by boys. The drawing of a well-proportioned neck showed no difference. The drawing of a thin neck by girls may be connected with their tendency to draw bigger and squarer heads, which makes the neck look thinner in comparison.

In summary, with regard to size of body parts, girls tend to emphasize the head in their figures, while boys tend to empasize the extremities, i.e., hands and fingers, legs, feet, and neck. In the drawing of facial features, girls tend toward the drawing of relatively small facial features (nose, mouth, and ears), while the boys tend to draw them bigger. As these features, like the neck, are also compared to the size of the head, these differences may be relative and not absolute. As will be seen later, the differences in size are accompanied by preferences for different forms by the two sexes.

The picture which emerges is thus of a relatively compact figure for the girls, with a big head and a big body (compared to the extremities), small facial features, and relatively small limbs, while the boys tend to stretch the figure through an extension of the limbs, hands, neck, and feet, and to draw relatively bigger facial features. These differences show no clear connection with age, but seem to be mainly qualitative sex differences.

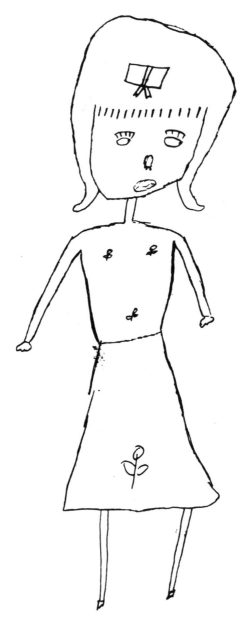

FIGURE 29 Typical example of drawing by a girl, with relatively big head and body, small facial features (compared to the size of the head) and small limbs (Girl, 7 years old).

Form of Body Parts

All body parts were drawn in different forms, varying from the more simple, e.g., a circular head or body, to more naturalistic forms, often with several intermediate steps. Sex differences in the use of form were found in the drawing of the following body parts: head, eyes, nose, ears, arms, feet, body, neck, and hair.

The drawing in one or two dimensions is included under the description of form. Drawing in one dimension is a less mature form which is later replaced by drawing in two dimensions. Sex differences were here found in the drawing of the nose, and of hands and fingers.

The drawing of the simplest form of head, a round head, showed no significant difference when all age-groups were considered together. But when only the age-groups 11–13 years were compared, it was found that the older girls significantly more often than the boys continued to use this form. The more mature form, where a naturalistic depiction of the shape of the head was attempted, was, by contrast, found more often in the boys and they started earlier to use this form. Quite a few girls seemed to prefer the drawing of a somewhat square head (with rounded corners), a form which also showed a clear sex difference. Triangular heads were sometimes seen in the drawings by boys, but this form was rather rare. In the choice of form of head, both developmental trends and qualitative sex differences seem to play a part.

A few other variables were chosen to belong under the heading of "form of head," namely "outline of head" and the drawing of forehead, jaw, chin, and projection of chin. The most primitive form of outline of head, the head drawn as a closed circle, was more frequent by boys than by girls while the more mature form, head closed by hair without transparency, was used more often by girls. There is a clear development with age, with the girls changing earlier than the boys to the more mature form. After the age of 8, there is a sharp drop in the use of the closed circle for the girls, a similar drop occurring for the boys between 11 and 12 years of age. Among the other traits mentioned above, only the drawing of the forehead and the projection of the chin showed measurable sex differences. The forehead was drawn more often by girls while the projection of the chin was more frequent with the boys.

Round eyes were found most frequently with boys, attempts at naturalistic shaping of eyes by the girls. This seems to be a developmental

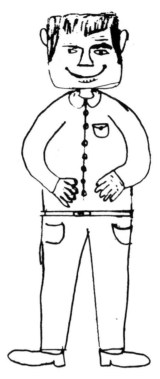

FIGURE 30 Example of a "square head" in the drawings by girls (Girl, 12 years old).

difference, the girls changing rather suddenly from the round to the more naturalistic form between 7 and 8 years of age, while boys made a similar shift two years later, between 9 and 10 years of age. Eyes narrowing toward the nose were also drawn more often by girls than by boys. The development of this trait follows the same patterns as those for the drawing of naturalistic eyes, and there may be some overlapping in the scoring of these two variables.

The nose is difficult to draw, and few children attempted a naturalistic depiction of it. The drawing of only one or two dots was a form which was not used by any boys in this sample, while 22 drawings by girls contained it. The nose drawn as a single line was also used more often by the girls while, in contrast, the nose drawn with a sharp angle was seen more than twice as often in the drawings by boys. The girls, consequently, more often than the boys, drew the nose in only one dimension. The nose drawn as dots showed no age development, but there was a decrease in the drawing of the nose as a single line, which disappeared completely after age 11 for the boys. This seems to be at least partly a developmental trait, favoring the boys.

The simplest form of ears, round or oval, was drawn more often by girls than by boys while attempts at shaping the ear more naturalistically were seen more often with the boys. This seems to be at least partly developmentally determined, most clearly so by the boys.

Arms narrowing toward the wrist was drawn more often by girls than by boys. The trait increased with development.

The only form of feet which showed a significant sex difference was the drawing of pointed feet, which was found most frequently in the girls.

A greater number of boys than of girls drew a round trunk or a transitional form between the round and a more shaped trunk. When these two most primitive forms were combined, the difference became highly significant. This difference seemed to be developmentally determined, favoring the girls.

The most primitive form of hair, hair drawn as a scribble, was used more often by boys than by girls. This form is connected with development and diminishes with age. There was an abrupt fall in the use of it in girls after 10 years of age and in boys after 11. The drawing of structure in the hair was used more often by girls than by boys. This trait was introduced in the drawings of girls at the age of 8, but almost only used by boys at age 12.

A curved neck, as an attempt at shaping it, was drawn more often by girls than by boys. This is a developmental trait, not much used by girls before the age of 9 or by boys before 11.

One-dimensional "stick-fingers" were seen more often in the drawings of boys than in those of girls, while girls more often use the two-dimensional form. These forms are clearly connected with development. The only other difference in the use of dimensions was, as mentioned above, the difference in the drawing of the nose.

In summary, very many sex differences manifest themselves in the choice of different forms of the various body parts. In some cases, the differences seem mainly quantitative as, for example, in the drawing of fingers in one or two dimensions, in other cases age or development

FIGURE 31 Elaboration of the hair in the drawing of a girl (Girl, 13 years old).

seems to play only a minor or no role, and the differences appear to be more or less purely qualitative, as, for example, in the drawing of the nose. In most of the cases where the differences are significant, the tendency is for the boys to use a less mature form in their drawings a couple of years longer than the girls. This is true in the drawing of eyes, arms, trunk, neck, and hair, where the girls earlier begin their attempts at naturalistic shaping, while the boys stick to more schematic forms. The same is true in the drawing of one-dimensional fingers, in the drawing of the head as a closed circle, and in the drawing of the forehead, where the boys are behind the girls. These traits all seem to be mainly determined by development and fall into the general pattern of different rates of maturity for the two sexes. In most cases the boy catch up with the girls, so that no difference can be seen in the older age-groups.

As always, the deviations from the basic pattern seem most interesting. Such a deviation is found in the drawing of the head, where the girls continue to use the simple, round form longer than the boys, who earlier attempt a naturalistic shaping. This does not look like a purely developmental difference—first, because it is in the opposite direction of what might be expected, and second, because the girls never catch up with the boys in the drawing of shaped heads. Girls seem to prefer a different way of drawing heads, not only represented by the round or oval form, but also by the more square form with rounded corners. The projection of the chin, which was more frequent with boys, is one of the features contributing to the shaping of the head.

The drawing of the nose also differs from the usual pattern, with the girls drawing one-dimensional noses more often than the boys. This is mostly due to the fact that girls stress the drawing of nostrils, often letting them represent the nose as a whole, while the boys place a much greater weight on the depiction of the shape and body of the nose.

The drawing of simple, round ears was also found more often in the drawings of girls than in those of boys. One explanation for this may be the fact that girls draw fewer figures with ears and therefore lack experience in the drawing of this body part. Although girls were found to draw as many ears on male figures as did boys, there is no doubt that the clear majority of figures that girls draw on their own initiative are female figures, where the ears will often be omitted.

Placement and Position of Body Parts

Sex differences in the placement of body parts were found in the drawing of eyes and mouth, legs and waist. Sex differences in the position of body parts were seen in regard to arms, fingers, and feet.

Eyes placed closer to the outline of the face than to its vertical middle axis were more frequent in the drawings of girls than of boys. There was a tendency for use of this trait to decrease with age, but more so for boys than for girls.

More boys than girls placed the mouth asymmetrically in the face.

While this trait disappeared completely in the drawings of girls after the age of 8, it was still occasionally seen in the drawings of even the oldest boys.

Legs connected to the trunk very asymmetrically, or far away from the correct place, were seen more often in the drawings of the boys, while girls more often drew a more correct connection. These are at least partly developmental traits.

Legs attached to the trunk with correct indication of crotch were found most often in drawings by the girls. This trait shows a connection with age development. Legs attached differently were found most often in drawings by the boys, which may be connected with their more frequent drawing of movement.

Correct location of the waist was found significantly more often in drawings by girls than by boys. This is a developmental trait for both sexes.

Arms stretching horizontally out from the body were found most often in the drawings by girls and also the position where arms are held

FIGURE 32 Arms in a different position in the drawing by a boy, down at the sides in the drawing by a girl (Boy, 11 years, girl, 10 years old).

down at the sides with the angle between body and arms less than 10°, but with space between them. Arms in a different position (neither straight out or down at sides) were found most often in drawings by the boys. This corresponds with the fact that boys more often drew figures in movement.

The drawing of hands where the fingers are completely spread out with the angle between thumb and little finger at least 180° was seen most often in the drawings by girls. Fingers in a different position (not spread out or close together) were found more often in drawings by the boys.

One or both feet seen from the front without any attempt at foreshortening were seen most frequently in drawings by the girls, and when combined with feet seen from the front with attempts at foreshortening, the difference becomes still greater.

In summary, a correct placement of body parts is found more often in the drawings of girls than in those of boys. It is seen in the connection of legs with body, in the drawing of crotch, in the location of waist and of mouth. All these differences seem mainly developmentally determined, perhaps with the exception of the asymmetric placement of the mouth. The treatment of the face and facial features differs much between the sexes, with boys tending toward more expressive and less carefully drawn faces.The spaced placement of the eyes by the girls has a connection with their tendency to draw broad, square faces. The eyes are often placed very far apart in a quite unnaturalistic manner.

The differences in position of body parts show that girls tend toward the drawing of relatively static figures, with arms down at sides or—in young children—straight out from the body—while boys tend to draw their figures in more varied positions. The greater variation is found in the positions of arms, fingers, and legs. Girls, more often than boys, draw feet seen from the front which is connected with a greater preference for the front view for the whole figure, while boys more often draw the figure in profile (see p. 173).

Presence of Details

Differences in regard to the number and kind of details drawn were found in the following areas: eyes, nose, mouth, hair, neck, face, clothing, and jewelry.

The drawing of pupils, eyelashes, eyebrows, and eyecorners was found significantly more often in the figures of girls than in those of boys. Girls start earlier to draw these details and seem to maintain their superiority although it diminishes somewhat with age. The only detail that was found more often in the drawings by boys was the iris, but this difference did not reach significance.

Nostrils were seen most often in the drawings by girls. Bridge of nose was more frequently drawn by boys, and also more boys than girls drew the nose in a continuous line with one or both eyebrows. These traits show no clear connection with age development, except perhaps the last-mentioned.

The lips were drawn more often by girls than by boys. This is a developmental trait, where girls are several years ahead of the boys. Also a cupid bow was drawn mostly by girls. An open mouth was found most often in the drawings by boys, however. Also significantly more boys than girls drew teeth. No age development was seen for the last two traits.

When the drawings were collected, long hair was fashionable for boys and men, and it was, therefore, examined whether any effect of this could be found in the drawings, i.e., how many male figures were drawn with long hair by both sexes. Fourteen male figures, drawn by boys, and two male figures drawn by girls were long-haired. This difference is significant. As mentioned earlier, the boys seemed more influenced by the current fashion than the girls who seemed to prefer the drawing of the traditionally short-haired male figures.

Bows in the hair were drawn more often by girls than by boys, even when the greater number of female figures drawn by girls was taken into consideration. The preferred form was a bow placed in front of the hair, and this form too was found significantly more often by the girls. None of these traits showed connection with age.

No separation between head and neck, i.e., the line of the jaw not drawn all the way across the neck, was seen more often in drawings by boys than by girls. It shows no development with age.

With regard to the details of clothing, more girls than boys drew sleeves, either as a line across the arm or with details added. Also more girls than boys drew a neckline, either as just a line across the neck or marked with further details.

More boys than girls omitted the marking of the waist in the clothing of their whole figures.

Decoration of clothing with various patterns was most frequent in drawings by the girls, and so were different forms of patterns, e.g., the use of a geometrical pattern and the use of patterns other than a geometrical pattern or flowers.

Shoes were seen most often in the whole figures drawn by girls and so were stockings.

In the drawings of male figures, girls drew not only a relatively greater, but a numerically greater, number of details than the boys although they drew only half as many male figures. They more often indicated trousers, both by a line across the ankle and with the addition of further details. Girls also more often drew a jacket on male figures and added details on jacket or sweater.

Under the heading of "special facial details" a number of details were gathered which did not belong to the facial features proper, and which were not seen regularly. They were freckles, wrinkles, round spots for cheeks, beards, or completely irrelevant details such as notes, letters, etc. They are not beautifying details, but rather ones that give the face either a realistic look (freckles or wrinkles) or a humorous, clownish, or degrading one. Both the total number of such details and the number of figures containing them was greater for the boys than for the girls. Completely irrelevant details were only found in drawings by boys (eight drawings) and not at all in drawings by girls. The number of such special facial details rose in the drawings by boys after age 8 and again after 11, reaching their maximum at age 12. For the girls, the development was slower and more regular, culminating at age 11.

The category of "jewelry" encompasses both decidedly feminine objects such as necklaces and bracelets, and objects that are common to both sexes such as watches. Also purely masculine objects were found here, such as police signs, sheriff stars, etc. When the "purely feminine" jewelry was considered alone, girls were found to use it much more often than boys, even when the difference in number of female figures was taken into account. Watches were also drawn more often by girls. The total number of objects under the heading of jewelry was also greater for the girls. The specific "masculine" objects were not seen to be used very often by either sex (in three drawings by both sexes). The girls' interest in jewelry culminates at age 8, but their interest continues to some degree through all ages.

In summary, the use of details shows very clear sex differences. The girls generally emphasize details of eyes and mouth, of hair, clothing,

FIGURE 33 Special facial features in the drawings by boys (Two boys, 12 years old).

and jewelry. They even draw more details in the clothes of the male figure than the boys themselves do. They start earlier to use these details, and they continue to use them more often than the boys. However, it would be wrong from this to draw the conclusion that girls in general use more details than boys; the two sexes seem rather to use different details to emphasize different aspects of their figures.

In the drawing of the facial features, the boys more often show the bridge of the nose and connect the nose with the eyebrows. The possible meaning of the different treatment of the nose by the two sexes will be discussed later. Moreover, the boys more often draw faces with an open mouth, with teeth, and with various details that tend to emphasize the realism of the face or even to show degradation or ridicule. It is obvious that girls tend to emphasize beauty and "niceness" of face, hair, and clothes, while boys pursue other goals through their choice of details. The boys' greater preference for the drawings of long-haired male figures compared to the girls was discussed earlier (see p. 128).

Profile Drawings

When all the drawings of a whole figure showing the whole or part of the figure in profile were combined, the results showed that these forms appeared most often in drawings by the boys. (Excepted were drawings where nothing but the feet were seen in profile). This is the more remarkable as the boys drew fewer whole figures than the girls. In contrast, the drawing of figures seen from the front was more common for the girls, and so was the correct drawing of figures seen from the front where the feet also were seen from the front. There was some connection between age and the drawing of profiles, as no attempts at profile drawings at all were seen at ages 5 and 6; after these ages, however, the use of it was rather constant for both sexes. Both boys and girls preferred to turn the profile to the left. Only one drawing by a girl and 13 by boys were turned to the right, a nonsignificant difference.

Age of Figure

Many more boys than girls drew figures whose age could not be estimated. When only those drawings were compared whose age could be estimated, it was found that girls in half of the cases drew a figure of approximately their own age, while fewer of the boys tended to do so. Also more girls than boys drew figures whose age was slightly older than their own, but who were not shown as adults. In contrast, almost half of the boys drew adult figures, while far fewer girls did so.

That the drawings by boys are less well-defined with regard to age than those of girls corresponds well with the fact that the drawings by boys are also less well-defined in regard to sexual differentiation. Both are probably due to the boys' lesser interest in clothing and hair, which are some of the traits that help define age and sex most clearly.

The tendency to draw figures of undefinable age diminished with age in both sexes, but for girls there was again a rising tendency in this variable during the ages 11–13. This may be due to a growing number of heads only. That the same rise was not discernible in the boys may be due to the fact that at all ages they drew many more figures with indeterminable ages, and that the rise in the number of heads only may be counterbalanced by a better age depiction in their whole figure drawings. In both sexes, a rise in the tendency to draw the figure as older

FIGURE 34 Profile drawing by boy (Boy, 10 years old).

than the drawer, but not as an adult, was significant with increasing age.

The actual number of drawings showing the figure as an adult rose slightly in boys with age, but compared to the total number of drawings with definable age, the percentage of adult figures dropped with age. In girls, the number of adult figures culminated at age 8, but the total number of adult figures drawn by girls was so small that no age development could be seen.

Height and Width of Figure

Boys tended to draw figures that were somewhat higher and wider than girls, which was rather remarkable when at the same time they drew a greater number of heads only; but apparently this did not lead to a reduction in size. The greater width may be connected with their greater tendency to draw movement, e.g., arms stretching out.

Use of Baseline

The total number of figures with baselines was almost identical among the sexes, but the form of the baseline differed somewhat, with boys most often using one or two definite lines, while girls sometimes drew a more diffuse shading around or below the figure.

Positioning of Figure

A central positioning on the paper with center of drawing in center area of paper was most frequently seen in the girls. Positioning in the middle third of the paper, when it is horizontally divided into three equal parts, was also found most often in the girls, while positioning in the lower third of the paper was used relatively more often by the boys.

More boys than girls placed their figure on the edge of the paper which was then used as a baseline. This variable is not identical with positioning in the lower third of the page. A tiny figure placed in the lower third need not stand on the edge of the paper, and a big figure, standing on the edge of the paper may well have its "point of gravity" in the central third of the page and be scored accordingly. The use of positioning on the edge of the paper rose somewhat with increasing age.

Only in the boys' drawings were such traits found as framing of the figure or placement on a pedestal (ten drawings). Boys thus showed a greater tendency to support their figures either by a definite baseline, by placement on the edge of the paper, or by an actual framing of the figure.

FIGURE 35 Special positioning of the figure on a pedestal (Boy, 13 years old).

Transparencies

More drawings by girls than by boys were completely without transparencies, and the total number of transparencies in the drawings by the boys was twice as large as the number in the drawings by the girls. The most common transparency for both sexes was the head showing through hair or hat, which also appeared almost twice as often in the boys' drawings. They also more often showed one or both arms crossed by the body. This may be due to their more frequent drawings of profiles and figures in movement, which easily leads to a transparency of the arm.

Another trait which was also seen more often in the drawings by boys, however, and which may not be so easily explained, was the tendency to cut off arms or legs from the body with a line without this being caused by clothing or for any other apparent reason. The use of transparencies culminated at age 6 in both sexes and declined from then on, until girls completely stopped drawing transparencies at age 13. For all age-groups, the number of transparencies was greater for boys than for girls.

Corrections and Erasures

The number of drawings without erasures or corrections did not differ significantly between the sexes, neither did the total number of corrections. But boys, more often than girls, corrected or erased in their drawings of the nose. The drawing of the nose may be more difficult for boys who tended to draw bigger and more shaped noses than girls.

The number of corrections increased with age in both sexes until the age of 8, when a relatively stable level was reached. For the boys only, a new rise was seen at the ages of 12 and 13.

Symmetry

A drawing characterized by rigid symmetry was found more often in drawings by the girls than by the boys. The total number of symmetrical drawings, rigid and nonrigid, was also greater for the girls. This variable is partly dependent on other variables, most notably on the drawing of profiles and of movement, which boys were found to use more often. This may explain part of the difference, but the general impression is also of a greater symmetry and order in the girls' figures when both sexes draw figures seen from the front and without movement.

Movement

The drawing of an upright, standing figure with no movement, seen either from the front or in profile, with arms at the sides or straight out from the body, was seen much more often in drawings by the girls. In contrast, a figure with arms or legs (or one of either) placed in a position other than down at the sides was seen exclusively in drawings by the boys.

FIGURE 36 Typical example of a symmetrical drawing by a girl (Girl, 8 years old).

It is not quite clear whether there is a development toward the drawing of more movement with greater age. The girls drew so few figures in activity that no conclusion regarding age development may be made. In the drawings by boys, movement seemed to culminate during the years 8–10, which seems to indicate a rise with age. After the age of 10, the greater number of portraits naturally leads to a decline in the depiction of movement.

It was observed that profile drawings and movement tended to occur together, and I therefore examined if the two traits were interdependent. I examined this only for the 425 drawings showing a whole figure. The results showed that the hypothesis of a closer connection between them than what might be expected by chance is very strongly supported in the drawings of both sexes.

The question remains, however, as to how the relationship is best understood. It is obviously easier to show movement in a figure seen in profile than in one seen from the front. The depiction of, for example, walking in a figure seen from the front requires the use of foreshortening and will, even then, easily lead to a clumsy result. Profile drawing might therefore be regarded mainly as a tool to help in the depiction of movement. On the other hand, a profile drawing easily looks artificial if no movement is shown; if, for example, both legs should be visible, one of

	no movement	*movement*	
fig. not in profile	133	21	
profile drawing	12	30	*boys*
fig. not in profile	195	16	
profile drawing	5	13	*girls*

Boys: chi² 54.294 *Girls:* chi² 56.947
p<.001 p<.001

FIGURE 37 Table showing the connection between the drawing of profiles and movement.

them must be moved. As seen in figure 37, the use of movement is more frequent than the drawing of a profile, and this might support the idea of the drawing of movement as the primary goal. Still, some profile drawings are made without any indication of movement, and this is even more frequent when the drawings of heads only are included. It is thus not easy to distinguish between cause and effect, but, at least the relationship between the two variables must be recognized, and the interpretation of either of them must consequently be more cautious.

Line Qualities

All the line qualities (thickness, pressure, length of stroke, and firmness) showed significant sex differences.

The use of lines of medium thickness was found most often in the girls, while the drawing of rather thick lines was seen most often in the boys. This trait decreased with age in the girls, but not in the boys. Varying thickness of line was also seen most commonly in the drawings by the boys.

Medium pressure was seen almost twice as often in girls' drawings than in those of boys. Boys tended to use stronger pressure, particularly in the younger age groups, but the difference did not quite reach statistical significance.

The use of long, unbroken lines was seen most frequently in girls, short, sketchy strokes most frequently in boys, and very short, crabbed lines only in boys. The use of short, sketchy strokes increased clearly with age in boys, but not in girls. The girls seemed to prefer the use of long strokes during all ages, while boys used this form considerably more rarely with greater age.

Slightly insecure lines were seen most often in girls' drawings, while very insecure lines were more common for boys. The latter trait diminished with age, but more completely so for girls than for boys.

Shading

The number of drawings without shading was almost identical for the two sexes, encompassing about one-third of all drawings. The total number of scores for shading was also very similar, but some differences could be seen in regard to the parts of the body shaded.

Shading of the eyes was mostly used by the girls, and so was shading of beard or eyebrows. The shading of eyes occurs in two different forms, one used by young children who fill out their big, round eyes, perhaps in order to avoid empty, staring eyes at an age when they cannot yet all draw pupils. This form, which was mostly found in the drawings by boys, disappeared with increasing age as the eyes acquired better shape and details such as pupils. The other form, which was mostly used by the older girls, is a lighter form of shading, apparently used to emphasize the eyes. This use of shading increased with age in girls, but not in boys. The shading of eyebrows seems to have a similar purpose. It was also predominantly found in the older girls' drawings.

Shading of the body below the waist was seen most often in drawings by the boys, and when the number of drawings which were shaded above and below the waist were combined, the difference was still pronounced. It is noteworthy that a greater number of boys than girls shaded the body below the waist as the boys on the whole drew fewer whole figures than the girls (229 drawings by girls, 197 by boys were whole figures).

Shading of details on clothes was used more often by girls. This may be regarded as a way of underlining such details in much the same way as shading of eyes and eyebrows.

Shading of arms/hands was on the other hand more common for the boys. The shading of body and arms/hands culminated in the drawings of the 9-year-old boys where—as mentioned earlier—the number of shadings seem out of proportion. This is most probably incidental, due to the small sample of children in the study. It should not be concluded from this that 9-year-old boys generally tend to use shading more than other age groups.

No sex differences were found in the different qualities of shading (pressure, boundaries, and density).

Integration

Good integration in the drawings was seen most often in the boys, while rather well-integrated drawings were more frequent with the girls. Poorly integrated drawings were, however, also seen mostly in the boys. The number of well-integrated figures rose with age in both sexes, while the number of poorly integrated ones diminished. The latter disappeared almost completely in the girls, but continued to be found among the drawings of even the oldest boys.

Motoric Control

The number of well-controlled drawings showed no differences between the sexes, but drawings with a medium degree of control were seen most often in girls. Drawings with a poor degree of control were most frequent in the boys. The number of well-controlled drawings rose with age, while the poorly controlled ones disappeared almost completely, but earlier for girls than for boys. These traits seem to be developmentally determined.

OVERVIEW OF SEX DIFFERENCES

The sex differences found represent tendencies, but not absolutes. In few cases, a trait is represented in the drawings of children of one sex only, and this may even be due to the limited sample of children and cannot necessarily be generalized. In most of the traits described, even though the sex differences found may be clearly significant, smaller or greater overlapping between the sexes is found. Although in some drawings the sex of the drawer can easily be guessed from the characteristics of the figure, many drawings cannot immediately be recognized as being made by either a boy or a girl. With these limitations in mind, however, it is true that many and convincing differences are found between the drawings of the two sexes, considered as groups, differences that together form a meaningful pattern which can be dynamically understood.

Because of the limited sample of children in each age-group, traits that stand out as particularly characteristic of specific age-groups in this sample should not be considered necessarily characteristic of that age-group in general. Such variations may be due to individual peculiarities in a few children. This does not limit the value of the overall picture which is made up of many details, but it would add no meaning to compare the sexes year by year as, for example, Machover (1953, 1960) does (also with dubious validity).

Another important point is the fact that a sharp distinction between quantitative and qualitative sex differences is difficult, if not impossible, to maintain. Some differences are very clearly quantitative, e.g., the presence of arms, which shows a clear increase with rising age, with the girls having an advantage of a couple of years. The boys catch up completely with the girls, however, and the actual difference between the sexes is only manifest during a few years.

Other differences are equally clearly qualitative. This is true, for example, of the different forms of noses drawn, where each sex prefers different forms, and where no clear age developments can be seen. One sex does not simply catch up with the other, but they seem to develop in different directions.

Other traits again show an intermediate pattern with some age development, but with the sex difference persisting through all ages. An example is the drawing of heads only which shows a rise with increasing age in both sexes, but where, through all ages, more boys than girls prefer this form. Another example is in the drawing of details of clothes, where boys at all ages draw fewer details than girls, although the number of details also rises in their drawings. In such cases, it does not seem reasonable to explain the differences only as the effect of a lag of maturation in one sex.

A clear distinction between quantitative and qualitative sex differences will therefore generally not be attempted. The sex differences can better be described as placed on a continuum from predominantly quantitative ones at one end to predominantly qualitative ones at the other, with many transitory steps in between.

When the most clearly quantitative differences are regarded, the girls are obviously ahead of the boys in many aspects of drawing. The tendency is even clearer than the results here show, because for many variables the difference that favors the girls does not reach statistical significance. This is most probably due to the limited sample of children, both in regard to ages included and number of children at each age level. In order to see the maximum of quantitative sex differences, a greater number of particularly younger children should have been included, as many of the quantitative sex differences seem at the point of disappearing at the ages of 6 and 7. This is particularly true for the presence of major body parts. The girls seem to be ahead of the boys in the drawing of more body parts than can be seen from the results here, but the actual numerical differences are small and disappear in the higher age-groups. In this material, only the presence of arms and clothing were found more often in drawings by the girls. They also showed a general advantage in regard to form-level, tending to attempt a naturalistic shaping of many body parts earlier than boys. This was true for the drawing of eyes, arms, body, mouth, neck, and hair. They drew figures in two dimensions earlier than the boys, and they stopped drawing earlier the head as a closed circle with hair stuck to the outline or with the outline seen through the hair. They placed the legs correctly on the body, drew the crotch, and placed the waist correctly on the body before the boys. Many of these traits are, of course, among those described as developmental traits in chapter 5. In accordance with the results described there, it can be concluded that girls show a somewhat faster development in drawing a human figure in a number of aspects. After this is said, however, it seems most fruitful to describe the remaining sex differences without any emphasis on what is quantitative or qualitative.

With the overlapping between the sexes kept in mind, clear and consistent differences can be seen between them in their overall treatment of the human figure. Girls tend to draw a whole, relatively static figure, seen from the front and with arms down at sides or straight out from the body. The front view gives the possibility of maximal display of body and face. These figure parts are further emphasized both by means of a relative exaggeration of size and through emphasis on hair, clothing, and elaboration of details. A relatively short, often curved neck, adds to the compactness of the figure. Girls are found to draw clothes on their figures earlier than boys, to add more pieces, and more often to draw a complete dress and to show awareness of what is fashionable. They more often draw various details such as sleeves, neckline, indication of waist, shoes, and stockings, and even on the male figures the actual number of clothing details is greater in the drawings of the girls in spite of the smaller number of them. Also the girls' interest in decoration of the clothes both with geometrical and other patterns is greater than the boys', as is their depiction of jewelry. Their use of shading of details of clothes also seems to have the purpose of giving emphasis to them.

The head and face are treated very differently in the drawings by boys and girls. Not only do girls draw the head relatively bigger than boys, but they also give it a round or somewhat square form instead of attempting a naturalistic shaping with a narrowing toward the chin. The big, round face may form a better background for the elaboration of the facial details. Girls do not emphasize all facial details, as it is often stated, but they do emphasize mouth and eyes. They draw two lips more often and add a cupid bow. The eyes are better shaped and proportioned and of better size, but they are often spaced quite widely apart in the face. The girls draw pupils, eyelashes, eyebrows, and eye-corners considerably more often than boys, and they shade eyes or eyebrows, apparently also with the purpose of emphasizing them. Contrary to this, nose and ears tend to be minimized, and ears are often omitted on the drawing of female figures although girls seem to draw them as often on male figures as boys do. But they also draw smaller ears and stick to a more primitive form. The nose is often drawn very small, only as a single line or as one or two dots. Nostrils are emphasized, but not the shape of the nose.

The differential treatment of the hair by the two sexes points in the same direction of the girls stressing the importance of the head. They more often draw hair with structure and hair that is arranged in a specific way, and they do not stick to a crude scribble as much as the boys. They draw long hair on the female figure, they place bows in the hair, particularly in the front, but also at other places.

Girls, more frequently than boys, draw figures whose age and sex can be estimated. As mentioned in chapter 4, this may be a consequence of their greater interest in clothing and hair which are some of the details that help in the identification of sex and age. The age given to the figure varies also, with girls tending to draw figures of their own age or slightly older in contrast to the boys who more often draw adults.

Although both sexes mostly place their figure centrally on the page,

FIGURE 38 Typical drawings by girls (Girls, 10 and 8 years old).

girls do so more than boys. They also tend to draw figures that are symmetrical, even sometimes rigidly so, more than the boys.

The girls' drawings generally have a more orderly and neat appearance. This is partly a consequence of the greater uniformity and symmetry and less varied positions, but has also something to do with differences in the graphic traits. Girls draw fewer transparencies, they draw more even lines, and tend to use weaker pressure. They use longer, more unbroken strokes and draw with greater security. They draw fewer figures with poor integration and poor motoric control.

One of the most striking characteristics of the boys' drawings, compared to the girls', is their greater variation. It is obvious just from a quick glance through the collection of drawings, but can also be documented through the description of the variables. It has already been seen in regard to the part of the figure drawn where more boys than girls draw heads only or other parts, such as figures to the waist or cut across the legs. More boys turn part of or the whole figure away in profile, and they introduce greater variation in the positioning of arms and legs. They place their figures less uniformly centered on the page, but more often in the lower third or placed on the edge of the paper. Only the boys in this sample were found to frame their figures.

Boys tend to emphasize different parts of the figure from girls, not head and body, but limbs and neck. They draw a long, thin neck, long legs and big feet and hands. Instead of the rather compact, short-legged figure of the girls, boys tend to draw a long, outstretched figure. More often than the girls, they omit a line of separation between head and neck and between neck and body (neckline). The emphasis on the limbs is further stressed through the use of movement. Boys draw slightly bigger and broader figures than girls.

Boys also emphasize different details of the face and head from girls. First, they try to shape the face realistically and show, for example, projection of the chin more often. Their tendency to draw smaller heads, on the other hand, leads to a more infrequent inclusion of the forehead. The treatment of the mouth differs greatly from that of the girls. Instead of a small mouth with a cupid bow, they draw a big one, sometimes asymmetrically placed in the face, often open and provided with teeth. The eyes are relatively neglected and are more often drawn as primitive round circles. The nose and ears, on the other hand, are drawn with greater care. The nose is often big, and attempts are made at a two-dimensional shaping; it is often drawn in connection with the eyebrows, but the nostrils are less emphasized. Also the ears are drawn with attempts at shaping, and they are bigger than in the girls' drawings. Corrections are more frequent in the nose, also pointing in the direction of concern with the execution of drawing it. The boys, thus, not only in the total figure, but also in the head, place greater weight on the protruding parts, while the girls tend more to emphasize the compact mass.

Boys also introduce more details in the face that may add to its realism, such as freckles and wrinkles, or they add completely irrelevant details such as notes and letters. Such details were not found at all in the drawings by the girls. The hair is relatively neglected by the boys with the exception of some boys drawing long hair on their male figure in accordance with the then prevailing fashion.

In general, the boys show less order and control in the execution of their drawings. Their figures contain more transparencies, and the body and the arms/hands are more often shaded. They tend to use wider and more uneven lines, they use more often short sketchy strokes, in some drawings even very short, crabbed lines, a form which was not found in the girls at all. They also more often use very insecure lines and poor motoric control. Also here, more variation is found, with the boys showing more examples of both good and poor integration, while girls show a more uniform medium level.

In attempting to describe the essence of the differential treatment of the figure by the two sexes, it can be said that the "point of gravity" in the girls' figures rests in the figure itself, and mostly in the massive head and body, which are presented to the observer with emphasis on beautifying details. The figure radiates immobility, calmness, order, regularity, and "niceness."

The "point of gravity" in the boys' figures, on the other hand, seems to be placed outside the figure itself. The figure is not adorned in itself, but the means of locomotion are emphasized, there is movement, and the figure is turned away in profile—the attention is directed toward the surroundings rather than toward the figure itself. The impression is of less order, but rather of a certain unrest and irregularity.

Before attempting an interpretation of these differences, a word might be said about the importance of sex differences as they manifest themselves in drawings. In recent years, sex differences have been widely discussed. Sometimes the tendency has been to minimize them or to quickly and superficially explain their existence as a consequence of upbringing and as the effect of social and cultural factors. Sometimes they have been regarded as quite interesting, but nonetheless rather peripheral phenomena, the existence of which more or less disturbs the coherent picture of children as first and foremost children (as opposed to adults). In psychological testing, sex differences tend to be seen as rather disturbing factors, which either are completely ignored or—

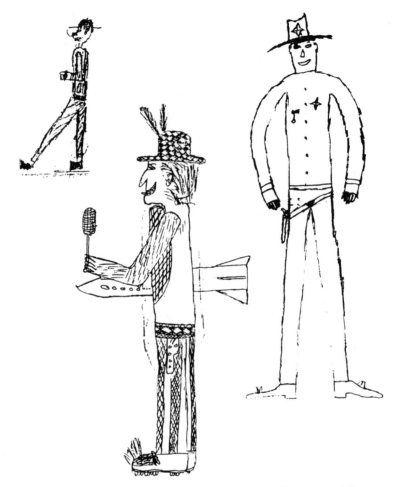

FIGURE 39 Typical drawings by boys (Boys, 8, 12, and 10 years old).

if that is impossible—are regarded as inconvenient and complicating factors.

The manifestation of sex differences in children's drawings does certainly not confirm the impression of them as neither peripheral nor unimportant. They pervade all aspects of the drawing of the human figure. Few variables are found which are not more or less differently treated by the two sexes. It seems more appropriate to regard the differences as fundamental factors which manifest themselves in very many aspects of the child's functioning and which are an integrated part of his personality. They manifest themselves early and continue to be seen.

INTERPRETATION OF SEX DIFFERENCES IN DRAWINGS

The many sex differences in figure drawings cannot possibly be explained satisfactorily only by referral to the child's observation of the persons around him. Their interpretation must necessarily be connected with the drawers' differential experiences of their own bodies, otherwise the sex differences become simply meaningless.

For girls, body (and head) seem highly cathected, worthy of decoration and placed right in the center of the page, facing the observer, thus expressing a high degree of narcissism. The value of the body for the girls can be regarded as a natural consequence of its future role as the container of children. But, at the same time, both the body and face seem to be used as means of sexual attractiveness. There is much emphasis on hair, which—since the time of Samson and Delilah—has been recognized as a symbol of sexuality. The beautifying details of the face, mouth, and eyes are particularly stressed. These features are, at the same time, the main features of contact, and the emphasis on them may thus also be interpreted as a sign of interest in human contact. The general appearance of order and neatness—and the absence of signs of aggression—may also be seen as ways of emphasizing the positive qualities of the figure.

Although aggression seems minimal, there are some elements that point in the direction of sexuality. The hair has already been mentioned, but also some of the decorations used, notably the many bows, seem to have such a function. The bows are often placed conspicuously in front of the skirt, just at the location of the genitals, and may in all probability be a symbol of these. Not rarely, the bow is displaced upward and placed in the middle of the excessive mass of hair. That the use of bows as decoration either in hair or on skirt should be a reflection of the current fashion is out of the question. Sometimes the bow is replaced by other objects, e.g., a big safety pin or the end of a belt hanging down.

In contrast to the drawings by the girls, those of the boys show many signs of aggression. Variables that point in this direction are, e.g., big hands, long arms, and teeth, all of which are included among Koppitz's (1968) emotional indicators as signs of excessive aggression.

The boys were also found more often than the girls to omit the lines between head and neck and between neck and body. The drawing of these lines is usually regarded as a sign of concern with control of bodily impulses. Their omission thus supports the impression of less control of aggression (and probably of sexual impulses also). The more frequent depiction of movement also supports the impression of a higher motoric activity level.

The tendency of the boys to draw irrelevant or ridiculing details of the face, or to draw caricatures, also accentuates their greater aggressiveness, the line between humor and aggression being difficult to draw. The somewhat greater size may also be seen as a sign of greater self-assertion. In the graphic variables, the lesser control or greater aggressiveness is manifested through less motoric control, poorer integration, greater pressure and line width, as well as greater variability in line quality. Where the girls seemed to want to emphasize the beauty and "niceness" of the figure, the boys rather seem, as far as possible, to avoid giving that impression.

But not only do the drawings by the boys show a greater activity level and aggression, they also contain more signs of conflict. Among the signs of conflict are the shading of body and of arms/hands, which were found in all probability to be related to emotional disturbance. Also, the greater use of support to the figure in the form of framing, a definite baseline, or positioning on the edge of the paper, can be seen as signs of insecurity. The use of very short, crabbed lines, which was only seen in the boys' drawings, also points in the direction of insecurity or anxiety.

The more frequent omission of the body may be due to its being less cathected, but it may also be due to a greater anxiety connected with the drawing of the body, as reflected also by the more common shading of it. This can only be a hypothesis. What is obvious, however, is the tendency of the boys to direct attention away from the figure itself and toward objects (or persons) in the environment.

Also the drawings by the boys contain symbols of sexuality. Boys were found to emphasize the protruding parts of the face, chin, ears, and nose, and notably the nose has often been interpreted as a phallic symbol. As boys were found to underline the size and shape of the nose, while girls were found to neglect exactly these aspects of it, it is natural to see it as such. Girls instead tend to emphasize the nostrils, even to such a degree that they represent the nose as a whole. It thus seems as if the sexual symbolism of the nose is valid not only for boys but also for girls, both sexes choosing the aspect of the nose which corresponds most to their own genitals. The symbolism in the drawings by the girls is far less obvious, which may have contributed to the fact that the sexual symbolism of the nose for the girls is rarely or never mentioned. The form of the nose is often seen as the reason for its symbolic value, as is its position between the eyes, a fact which is often recognized on obscene drawings on streets and walls. A contributing factor—for both sexes—may be the experience of the sneeze which is probably the body sensation which comes closest to orgasm.

Only some of the boys' drawings contain other objects, e.g., guns and knives, which are commonly (and probably rightly) interpreted as sexual symbols; they are not mentioned here, because they occur so rarely in the material that no significant sex differences stand out.

DIFFERENTIAL TREATMENT OF MALE AND FEMALE FIGURES

The differential treatment of figures of the two sexes is an interesting and essential aspect of the examination of the relative roles played by the drawer's body image and his perception of the outer world (and the persons in it). As boys cannot experience "from the inside" what it feels like to be a girl, and vice versa, traits that are ascribed mainly to the other sex should be expected to rest mostly on observation of the persons of the opposite sex. On the other hand, traits that are repeated in all human figure drawings, regardless of their sex, may to a greater degree be expected to reflect the drawer's inner experience of what it feels like to be a person. This is not to deny the role played by identification, also with persons of the other sex, but even this must rest on observation and cannot be experienced really "from within."

A study of the differential use of all the items in the Danish study was found impossible, due to their large number. But in order to get to know whether the figures were treated differently at all, and—if so—then to get some possible hints as to those aspects where the differences could be found, an examination was made of the distribution in male and female figures of a limited number of variables. The same 52 developmental variables were used here as in the study of the reliability of developmental traits. In this study also only the whole figures were used, and drawing no. 3 was omitted to avoid possible complications connected with the drawing of the self. This left 70 male and 68 female figures from the boys, 83 male and 82 female ones from the girls. The chi²-test was applied, and the 5% level of discrimination used.

Among these variables, the differentiation between male and female figures was found greater for the girls than for the boys. Among the boys, only the following three items were found to differentiate significantly:

1. ears more long than wide,
2. pleats or folds in clothes, and
3. movement.

Among the girls, eight traits were used differentially:

1. presence of ears,
2. ears more long than wide,
3. two lips drawn,
4. drawing of a cupid bow,
5. eyelashes drawn,
6. special facial features,
7. patterns in clothes of any kind, and
8. pleats or folds in clothes.

Of the traits used differentially by the boys, two occurred most frequently in their male figures, one in their female figures. Of the traits used differentially by the girls, three were found more often in their male figures, five in their female ones.

Actually, the correspondence between the sexes is greater than it appears from the significant numbers because for all the variables mentioned a similar tendency exists in the drawings by the other sex, even though it does not reach significance. For example, the girls also more often draw their male figures in movement than their female ones, but their total number of figures in movement is too small to reach a significant level. This means that if the number of drawings had been greater, in all probability a greater number of differentiating traits might have been found, and the correspondence between the sexes would have been greater.

The more frequent drawing of ears in male than in female figures (and the correspondingly greater number of well-proportioned ears) was described earlier and attributed to the shorter hair on male drawings (see chapter 5). Although the presence of ears in male figures drawn by the boys is not significantly more frequent here, it is almost so, and it does reach a significant level when those drawings are also included which show only part of the whole figure.

The results show that the first question—whether figures of either sex are treated differentially—must be answered affirmatively. The other question—in what aspects the differentiation takes place—cannot be fully answered on the basis of this limited study. It looks, however, as if the differentiation is most pronounced in the use of details, e.g., in face and clothing, while the more fundamental characteristics of body proportions and shapes are more alike in figures of both sexes. Girls also draw their male figures with relatively big and roundish heads, with a short neck and relatively short arms and legs, while boys draw their female figures as long-legged as their male figures, with as small heads, etc. These aspects of the drawings may be less immediately conspicuous and perhaps to a greater degree reflect the drawer's body image than the details that rest on the child's more or less conscious observation.

The one aspect which does not quite fit into this pattern is movement, which must be regarded as one of the more fundamental aspects of the figure, but which by both sexes seems to be mostly associated with masculinity (although the differentiation by the girls did not quite reach significance). An analysis of the use of this trait illustrates well the complications in the interpretation of the sex differences. Movement is in general found more often in the drawings by boys than in those by girls. This may suggest that movement (or physical activity) is a more essential aspects of boys' body experience than of girls'. But when movement by both sexes is used more often in their male figures than in their female ones, it suggests that observation of the actual activity patterns of the two sexes also plays a part. The area of differential treatment of the figures of either sex should give rise to further research.

COMPARISON WITH THE LITERATURE

The quantitative sex differences found in the Danish study correspond to the results described by Goodenough (1926), Harris (1963), and Koppitz (1968), but are in contrast to the results from the earlier studies. The girls were found to be ahead of the boys in regard to inclusion of major body parts, in form-level of most parts, and in proportioning. These quantitative differences are found so consistently in all later studies that they must undoubtedly be regarded as valid. The above-mentioned authors do not agree completely as to when the boys catch up with the girls; but, as discussed in chapter 5, the reason for this disagreement lies mainly in the different selection of traits. Some possible reasons for the differences in results between the earlier and later studies were discussed earlier.

The study of sex differences gives added weight to the hypothesis, however, that the superiority of the girls may be partly due to the subject chosen, which may be more in the center of interest for the girls than for the boys. It was found that the girls' attention seemed to be centered on the person, while the boys' seemed more directed away from the person, toward the surroundings; this may indicate that they may be more interested in and perhaps better at drawing things other than human beings. Kerschensteiner (1905) found the sex differences even greater in favor of the boys when it came to the drawing of objects such as houses and greatest in the drawing of a technical object, a streetcar. Although this study cannot answer it, the question may reasonably be raised as to whether boys still do not surpass girls in the drawings of technical objects such as cars, airplanes, etc. Boys much more often draw such things and seem much more interested in the correct depiction of details on objects than girls who more often draw persons, flowers, houses, etc. So the superiority of girls in drawing development is not necessarily general, but in all probability also dependent on the object chosen.

Kerschensteiner's finding that girls were better at using decoration corresponds well to the fact that girls also decorate the human figure more than boys. This may be looked upon as a general tendency to use decoration which manifests itself in various fields, also in the drawing of the human being, or, in contrast, the decoration of one's own body may be regarded as the primary starting point, which then generalizes to other objects and the surroundings in general (see chapter 8 for further discussion).

Burt's (1921) observation that boys showed more imagination and originality in their work was also supported here.

It was mentioned by several authors that girls were better at depicting details. This does not seem to be true, however. Also in the Danish material, the girls were more interested in the drawing of some details of the face, and in details of the hair and clothes, but, as was demonstrated, boys emphasized other details on the figure; and if drawings of technical objects had been compared for the presence of details, boys would, in all probability, be better in the depiction of details there. That the drawings of girls are more orderly and therefore perhaps better allow the details to stand out clearly is another factor that can play a part.

When it comes to the qualitative—or semiqualitative—differences, it is striking to see the very great correspondence between the Danish results and those from other studies.

Goodenough (1926) found boys more apt to draw profiles, to draw the figure in movement, to draw long arms, and to draw transparencies. For girls, she found typical the drawing of the nose as two dots, relatively small feet, many eye details, hair arranged or curly, cupid bow mouth, relatively large head, and relatively short arms and legs. These traits all show complete correspondence. Goodenough did not study very many drawings for sex differences and also limited herself to a narrower age range, which may account for the more limited number of sex differences described by her. A few traits that did not show significant differences in the Danish material, but are described as showing differences by Goodenough, are the drawing of accessories or of scenery and background, which she found more typical of boys. That the drawing of a necktie does not appear in the Danish material as typical of boys is, of course, due to the general disappearance of this piece of clothing at the time that the drawings were sampled. An exaggeration of the size of the eyes by the girls was not found in the Danish material, where rather the boys tended to draw big eyes. This may have to do with the age differences of the samples, as most big eyes drawn by the boys in the Danish sample occurred among the younger boys, who were not included in Goodenough's study.

Both similarities and differences are found in comparison with Harris's (1963) results. Harris distinguished between the drawings of male and female figures, however, which makes the results not always directly comparable. In the drawing of both male and female figures, Harris found the girls to do better in the depiction of facial features and in hair and hair-styling. They also excelled in motor coordination on both sex figures. The boys were found more likely to draw the nose in two dimensions. In the male figure, Harris found the girls drew the arms better in proportion, and they showed fewer transparencies. The boys were more likely to portray action in the arms. All these traits also correspond with the Danish results.

In the drawing of a male figure, Harris found the girls better in the drawing of the jaw and in the proportioning of the ears, which the Danish boys were found to draw better than the girls. Also in contrast to Harris's results, Danish girls were found to do better in the proportioning of the feet, boys showing a tendency to exaggerate their size. The girls in the Danish material also more often included the heel, although the sex difference was not significant.

The drawing of the female figure shows great correspondence. Harris found that girls more often depicted jewelry and neckline, and on the whole scored more points on clothes and costume, especially after the ages 8 or 9. They also more often included secondary sex characteristics.

In her study, Koppitz (1968) found the following traits to be typical of boys: profile drawings and drawing of the knee and the ear, while the traits that were typical for girls were: drawing of hair, pupils, eyebrows, two lips, and clothing. Except for the drawing of the knee, which is not found very often in the Danish material at all and shows no sex difference, there is complete agreement with some of the Danish results, but her study of sex differences is not so comprehensive either. That she finds ears most often in the drawings of boys may be due to the fact that she probably most often got male figures from the boys. She herself offers the hypothesis that it may be due to the drawing of shorter hair on the boys' figures.

It was found in the literature that girls generally differentiated better between the sexes than boys. This result was also very clearly confirmed in the Danish study, which shows that, after the age of 7, all the girls' figures could be differentiated as to sex, while the boys' drawings at no age could be totally differentiated. Doubt was already raised as to the interpretation of this as a sign of greater awareness of sexual identity in girls.

In regard to the first drawn sex, earlier studies showed no very consistent sex differences among younger children, but when adolescence was approached, boys more often drew their own sex first, girls less often. In the Danish study, the sex difference did not reach statistical significance, so no general conclusions can be drawn. But a tendency was seen for boys, with increasing age, more often to draw own sex first, and for girls to do the opposite.

Weider and Noller's (1950, 1953) studies of profile drawings confirmed the greater frequency of profile drawings by boys which was already described by Goodenough (1926). The Danish results are in accordance with them, except for the fact that in this sample not so large a proportion of the boys drew profiles as in the studies by Weider and Noller, nor when similar age-groups are compared.

The descriptions of sex differences by Machover (1953, 1960) and Koppitz (1968) are in many ways comparable to the Danish results; but the meaning attached to them and the explanations offered differ from the present author's. As mentioned before, both of the authors relied on psychoanalytic theories, but on different schools, stressing different aspects of personality. Machover, applying Freudian theory, stressed the importance of body image, unconscious motivation, and the role of instinct, while Koppitz, drawing on ego-psychology, gave greater weight to the role of ego-functions, conscious motivation, and interpersonal relations. Common to both authors is their lack of use of information from other sources, such as general developmental psychology and sexology.

Common to both of them is also their obvious dissatisfaction with the drawings of the girls in particular. Both of them seem disturbed by the girls' preoccupation with clothes and hair, which they seem to regard as somewhat inferior. Koppitz's studies of sex differences are the least comprehensive and will be treated first.

She states explicitly that the qualitative sex differences are not biologically determined, and she attributes them mainly to social learning, reflecting Western middle-class values. She sees them as reflecting attitudes that have been learned unconsciously in early life from the social and cultural environment in which children live. She states that girls formerly drew figures with many more clothing details than today and warns against the attribution of too much psychological significance to the presence or absence of hair and clothing items. That girls formerly drew more details on clothes than now lacks documentation and seems rather improbable in light of their great occupation with it in all studies, including the present. What is more important, however, is that it is not the presence or absence of specific details which is interesting, but the incontestably greater attention to this area of drawings, which seems so strikingly constant. Koppitz much too superficially attributes significance mainly to the environment, and her attitude seems to imply that if only girls were brought up differently and with other expectations than exist today, their (too great) interest in clothes and hair would diminish. She does not at all take into consideration the child's experience of inner reality and of his or her body and its effect on figure drawing. Koppitz uses no argumentation in support of her rejection of the biological basis for the sex differences. The fact that she only describes a few of them makes it, however, easier for her to see them as the result of learning.

Machover's (1953, 1960) results were described in detail in chapter 4. There is correspondence between the Danish material and her findings of greater aggressiveness and more signs of conflict in the drawings by boys and greater interest in display of the body and face by girls. But many of her more specific interpretations seem to be postulates with no substantiation behind them and—as mentioned earlier—her view of the development of children of both sexes is quite negative, emphasizing many traits as defensive and as indicating conflict, and it does not allow room for the interpretation of healthy or positive aspects of normal development.

To a great extent, her interpretations have been related to specific aspects of American culture. She stresses in particular the fact that American children grow up in a world dominated by women both at home and at school. She also stresses the contrast between the expectations of society toward boys and men, who are expected to be obedient as children, but dominant and aggressive as adults. The girls get into trouble as adults because they have never learned to trust themselves and their own impulses and initiatives.

These cultural patterns are not similar in Denmark, and the conclusions that Machover draws regarding the causes of the sex differences seem therefore not generally valid. She ascribes, for instance, great importance to the boys' resentment toward the childhood world dominated by women; but the greater aggressiveness by the Danish boys cannot be explained in the same way, due to the fact that the same female dominance is not found in the case of Danish children.

Danish fathers take a greater part in the education of their children than American fathers, as has for example been shown in a comparative study (Kandel and Lesser 1972), and in the schools approximately equally many male and female teachers take care of the children. The adult society is, on the other hand, less violent, and less dominance and aggression is expected from men who are not necessarily expected to be the only providers of the family. In general, the working life is less merciless, and greater economic security is offered by society if unemployment, sickness, or other accidents should occur. This means both that the contrast between the children's world and the adult world is less sharp than in the United States, and that the boys do not, to the same degree, feel the lack of masculine models, nor do they have to protest as violently against female authority. For the girls, there are also differences between the two societies. Danish girls are, to a much greater degree than was the case in the United States in the fifties, expected to be able to care for themselves when they grow up, to get an education, and to take part in the working life outside the home.

This means—not that Denmark is an ideal society in these respects—but that when the drawings from the two countries, in spite of the cultural differences, still show very many exactly identical sex differences, great caution must be taken in the interpretation of them as consequences of these cultural factors.

Therefore, two changes in outlook on the sex differences are suggested: they may be regarded as less culturally and more biologically determined, and they may be regarded not as much as expressions of defense or conflict, but rather as positive expressions of natural and biologically relevant sex differences.

If this is applied to the drawings of the girls, it means for example that the cupid bow mouth must not necessarily be seen as a transformation of a concave, dependent mouth, but may as well be a way of underlining the mouth which is normal and not defensive. Neither must the buckle be seen as a navel, a sign of immaturity, but may be a (positive) symbol of the genitals. That girls should have fantasies about pregnancy, which may be expressed through decorations on the skirt, need not be regarded as something negative, but seems natural without necessarily leading to a life where motherhood is the only purpose. The girls' interest in the body and its clothes may be regarded as something positive, an expression of their estimation of their own body as something valuable and precious, worthy of care and decoration, as the future container of new life. This interest, not only in one's own body, but in oneself as a person, may generalize to an interest in other persons as well and to an interest in emotional and personal matters that is valuable.

On the other hand, the boys' turning away from the body and focusing on outer objects, on action and movement, need not be regarded as a defensive maneuver either, but may as well be seen as a natural interest in the outer world and its objects, which is just as necessary as the interest in persons and emotions.

Of course, if carried to the extreme, both attitudes can become caricatures; the girls' ending in extreme narcissism and overconcern with the body or in hysterical symptoms, the boys' in lack of contact with feeling, in abstraction and lack of interest in other human beings. But these possible dangers should not from the outset prevent us from seeing the different possibilities and starting points for the two sexes; the exaggerations may just as well be a consequence of neglect or lack of acknowledgment as of too much cultivation of them.

PART THREE

Children's Human Figure Drawings Related to General Psychological Theory

SEVEN

Drawing Development Related to General Developmental Psychology

Drawing development should not—as has usually been the case—be considered in isolation, but can profitably be related to general theories on child development. It can then be seen to follow the same principles as other aspects of development.

A choice must be made between different theories. Piaget's theory might be considered relevant because of its great emphasis on concept development, but it is too narrowly cognitive in its approach to do justice to all aspects of drawing development. Psychoanalytic theories, on the other hand, which emphasize dynamic aspects and motivational factors, are not specific enough in their treatment of, for example, concept formation and the development of other ego-functions. In accordance with the view of drawing as an activity that requires motoric, sensoric, cognitive, and emotional functioning of the child, the theory applied must be wide enough in its scope to encompass all these different developmental aspects.

The theoretical principles set forth by Werner (1964) are found to be best suited to this purpose. Werner not only describes ontogenetic development, but is concerned with different levels of functioning as reflected also in various cultures ("primitive" cultures versus more technically developed ones) and in various levels of mental functioning, such as normal function compared to schizophrenic reactions, but these latter aspects need not concern us here.

Another advantage of his theory is its emphasis on such aspects as concept development and symbol formation which are particularly relevant for the study of drawings.

SOME ASPECTS OF WERNER'S DEVELOPMENTAL THEORY

Werner's (1964) theory concerns mainly the structural aspects of mental organization and the principles of development and not the mental content. Development is characterized not only by quantitative changes, but also by qualitative shifts. It may be described as consisting of successive "patterns," each resting on the previous one, but, nonetheless, also containing completely new aspects. Child development is seen as consisting of phases, which may have the character of crises when the old structure is broken down to be rebuilt.

Werner describes development as governed by the following main principles: (1) a gradual increase in differentiation and (2) a gradually increased hierarchic organization. This is true of the development of part functions as well as of development as a whole.

The different developmental levels are characterized by the following pairs of qualities, the first of which in each case describes the more primitive level, the second the more advanced:

1. syncretic—discrete
2. diffuse—articulated
3. indefinite—definite
4. rigid—flexible
5. labile—stable.

Syncretism means that two or more phenomena, which later are to be separated, still make up an undifferentiated totality. Discreteness, on the other hand, means that a differentiation has taken place. Diffuseness and articulation define the formal aspects of a structure. A diffuse structure is relatively uniform and homogenous; the parts are indistinct and have no clear self-subsistence. Every part has more or less the quality of the whole—or, differently expressed—the pars-pro-toto principle is governing. In contrast, articulation means that distinguishable parts constitute the whole.

These principles are also valid regarding the most essential aspects of functioning in the small child. Perception, imagination, motoric function, and emotionality are not clearly differentiated. Subject and object are more or less syncretic, meaning that the child only gradually learns to differentiate between himself and the most important persons in his surroundings and between living persons and nonliving objects. This is also in agreement with the psychoanalytic theories about symbiosis and the gradual process of separation-individuation. The process of differentiation which takes place is slow and gradual and runs through the whole of childhood.

Perception and motoric action are connected in a way which means that for the small child objects are not abstracted and isolated parts of the environment, but "signal-objects," i.e., objects that elicit manipulation and action. Their qualities cannot be adequately sensed only through visual perception, but must be touched and manipulated. This means that the child reacts first to the dynamic properties of objects and only later to their more abstract qualities such as shape, size, color, etc. Many of the young child's activities can be understood only through the assumption that the motor, emotional, and sensory factors are blended into one another. The younger the child, the less purely objective and self-subsistent things become, and the more highly conditioned in their significance by emotional and motor reactions.

Not only motorics, but also emotionality influence perception, leading to the special way of experiencing which is characterized by the word "physiognomic." This means that objects are perceived as possessing emotional qualities which usually are regarded as only belonging to persons or animals. This is another example of the lack of differentiation between animate and inanimate. Physiognomic perception is regarded as an essential factor in the process of symbol formation. This way of experiencing is not reserved for children, but they seem, more easily than many adults, to perceive in this way. With increasing age, the tendency to see objects as mainly determined by their more abstract qualities increases, but even completely abstract figures such as triangles, squares, or circles tend to be perceived as possessing emotions and as acting purposefully by adults, too, if they are set in motion, as shown by, e.g., Heider and Simmel (1944). They may even be directly personified.

Werner characterizes at least three different levels of functioning: on the motor-sensori-affective level, on the perceptual level, and on the conceptual level. Concept formation takes place at all ages, but is based on different functional patterns at different ages.

At the first level, thought processes are always more or less fused with functions of a sensorimotor and affective type. The organization is characterized by diffuseness, which may for example be shown by a single part or quality representing the whole—the pars-pro-toto principle. If children, for example, are asked to distinguish between various geometrical shapes, they react to a diffuse impression of the totality, such as "pointedness" or "roundness" rather than to other qualities, as late as age 5–7. They cannot make an actual perceptual analysis and cannot very well analyze a pattern into its parts. If they should copy geometrical forms, their drawings are similarly characterized by, for example, the qualities of "pointedness" or "roundness" which are generalized in the totality of the drawing. Such qualities are intersensory, which means that, although they may have been sensed visually, they may also find expression motorically and influence the way in which the child draws. "Pointedness" may, for example, find expression through the child's pricking holes in the paper, "roundness" through a light use of the pencil.

The pars-pro-toto principle never seems to disappear completely in the use of pictures. The adult person does not believe himself to be totally hidden if his head is hidden as the small child does; but it is found completely satisfactory if a picture of a person only shows his head in the form of a portrait. The head seems to be endowed with so much importance that it may well represent the whole person.

Studies of copying by kindergarten children have shown (Muchow 1926) that a tendency toward homogeneity and greater diffuseness may be revealed:

1. In the the strong emphasis on qualities-of-the-whole:
   (a) making figures more uniform, indivisible,
   (b) closing of open figures.
2. In the homogenization of directions and parts by:
   (a) making parts alike,
   (b) simplifying directions,
   (c) using symmetry.

Perception and imagination are also more closely bound up with each other than later. Werner states that a primordial functional unity exists in the sensory and imaginative fields and that out of this undifferentiated function arise the true memory and the fantasy image (the knowing of an inner world) in contradiction to objective perception (the knowledge of the outer world). As affectivity is again closely connected with both perception and imagination, affectively caused changes may well be found in the images, so that, for example, things or persons that are valuable to the child are experienced as bigger than less important ones. Werner talks about this phenomenon as the "emotional perspective." As the experience of the bodily sensations of course is part of the total sensoric pattern, it means that the body image also may be subjected to such distortions.

At the second level of concept formation, the perceptual level, a relationship is formed through perception, i.e., the relation between two or more parts is grasped in a certain configuration. These configurations are organized according to certain perceived characteristics of the objects and on the basis of certain innate tendencies, based on qualities such as similarity, proximity, and "Prägnanz." At this stage, perception may still be influenced by affection, and the relationships perceived may not only be based on perception of abstract properties such as shape, size, and color.

Only at the last stage of concept formation are the relationships based on abstract qualities and not bound to the concrete situation or to the person's affects—or are so to a lesser degree. Or, stated in Werner's own terminology: "The difference between grouping based upon "concrete abstraction" and a generalization at the purely conceptual level is this: concrete grouping reveals a certain quality through the configuration of the elements possessing that quality, whereas in a true generalization the quality (e.g., a color) common to all the elements is deliberately detached—mentally isolated, as it were—and the elements themselves appear only as visible exemplifications of the common quality" (1964, 243). In general, children's concepts are thus more picture-like and less abstract than those of adults.

DRAWING DEVELOPMENT RELATED TO DEVELOPMENTAL THEORY

This general view of development corresponds very well with what is known about drawing development. It has generally been described as progressing through phases that not only quantitatively, but also qualitatively differ from each other (scribbling stage, schematic stage, and naturalistic stage), although these patterns do not emerge clearly in the kind of studies that describe the development of single aspects at a time (such as the present one and those of Goodenough 1926; Harris 1963; and Koppitz 1968).

In a way, a study of drawing development, which is based on a description of the development of the single elements, runs counter to the very principle of development as here stated, characterized by the totality as the point of origin, the basic entity, which is the precursor of its component parts.

Drawing development may also show crises, such as when well-developed and elaborate scribbles are replaced by hesitating and primitive attempts at representation—or when automatic and fluent schemata are succeeded by strangely distorted shapes in the early attempts at naturalism.

Early drawings are characterized exactly by qualities such as syncretism, diffuseness, rigidity, and lability when compared to later and more developed ones.

Syncretism is found in the drawing of both the total human being and of its parts. At the earliest stage of figure drawing when the person is only drawn as a circle, possibly supplied with facial features and legs, it has been much discussed why the body is "left out" or is included so late in the drawing compared to head and limbs, and it has been argued that children experience their body less than their head and limbs. But, according to this theory, the question is asked wrongly. The body is not left out, but head and body make up an as yet undifferentiated totality, which is simply drawn as a circle (as the simplest available form). In exactly the same way, arms and hands (or legs and feet) are, at first, only drawn as single lines and not until later differentiated into their various parts.

We may ask, however, to what extent the early undifferentiated forms are determined by the child's way of perception or by his limited motoric ability. The child's concrete, emotionally toned perception of persons and his tendency to be also influenced by tactile sensations may well lead him to experience persons as characterized first and foremost by qualities such as roundness, softness, and warmth, qualities that physiognomically are most appropriately expressed by round forms. This would be a confirmation of Grözinger's (1971) theories of the early drawing stages. But if the undifferentiated form is due mainly to limitations in motoric development, the circle is chosen because it is the simplest shape to draw —a viewpoint which would correspond to Arnheim's (1954). There is some evidence that perceptual differentiation precedes motoric abilities in the same way as a language is understood passively before it is mastered actively, because children may occasionally express dissatisfaction with their own drawings, which are seen to deviate from the objects they are meant to represent. Or—to state it differently—at all stages, differentiation in perception is a necessary, but not sufficient condition for subsequent differentiation on the visuo-motor level.

In small children's drawings, at the preschematic stage, the relations between the various parts of the drawing are very labile; arms and legs may be connected to the figure almost anywhere, and facial features may even be placed outside the face. Size relationships are often grossly disproportionate, but may vary from one drawing to the next. This lability seems to be gradually replaced by a rigidity which is most pronounced at the schematic stage, when both position and shape of the body parts can only with difficulty be changed by the child, and often are not even changed when the figure is meant to be seen in activity.

The lability is also found in the content of the early drawings which may change from minute to minute. The lack of deliberate planning and the dependency on the present, concrete situation is striking.

The lack of differentiation is not only seen in the frequent use of simple shapes and long lines for more complicated body parts, but also in the preference for symmetrical positioning of arms and legs. Moreover, directions are simplified; arms are for example shown as straight lines without bends or angles.

In addition, the other traits that emphasize homogeneity, as described by Muchow (1926), are seen in the early drawings, e.g., closing of open figures (the head is seen as a closed circle through the hair or hat) and the use of similar symbols for different parts (both hands and feet are drawn as circles).

These phenomena correspond to Lowenfeld's (1947) description of the preschematic stage as characterized by such a lack of differentiation between the single parts that they cannot be recognized if isolated from the total drawing.

From the schematic stage and during the first part of the naturalistic stages, the differentiation process seems most striking, resulting in an abundance of concrete detailing. When approaching puberty, the organization into more superior totalities seems to dominate, often to such an extent that some of the earlier details become totally subordinated and disappear again.

The "emotional perspective" can be seen directly in drawings. Lowenfeld (1947) emphasized how the child uses change of size, omissions, or distortion of form in his drawings, and it is, of course, in complete correspondence with the basic theories behind the projective use of drawings. This emotional perspective may also explain one of the more common size distortions in children's drawings, the overestimation of the size of the head. This may be a consequence of the emotional and sensory importance of the head, as the receiver of the majority of sensual impressions as well as the site of thought and imagination. For the small child, there is no clear distinction between "outer" and "inner" in the personality, i.e., between physical and psychic qualities. Thoughts are, for example, believed to take up space and to be material. There is therefore no distinction either between psychic and physiological space. The head takes up much space, psychologically speaking, and this is reflected in the physical size that it is given on the paper.

The uncertainty about who the drawing actually represents in the case of children may also be a consequence of the lack of differentiation between the child and his closest relatives. It was suggested earlier that this was due to a certain future-orientation on the part of children who may draw ideal figures and ascribe adult ages to their drawn figures. This may still be the case, and is perhaps particularly so for older children in adolescence and preadolescence. Their drawings of popular singers or sports heroes probably represent ego-ideals most of all. But the small child's ascription of adult age to his figures and the whole lack of clarity as to who the figure represents, may be due to a similar diffuseness in the child's own experience. The confusion that the observer feels may not only be his own, but a reflection of the still partly existing fusion between child and parent, which is expressed in the drawing. If this is true, the question of who the drawing represents will never find a unanimous, unequivocal answer.

DRAWING AS LANGUAGE

Drawing development was early compared to language development (e.g., by Rouma 1913). Drawing is commonly experienced as a form of communication, and there is the very obvious similarity between spoken language and drawing in that both systems use symbols, i.e., objects that represent or refer to other objects, the referents. There is the further similarity between them that they both start as purely expressive functions without any representational purpose, such as babbling and scribbling, respectively.

On the other hand, there is the important difference between verbal language and drawing that language has already been structured into a more or less fixed system of symbols, while in drawing the individual must personally create the symbols he is going to use. (That drawing does not, in general, rest on a system of fixed symbols does not, of course, exclude the fact that children imitate each other and in that way include more or less common or stereotyped forms in their drawings.) This makes drawing particularly interesting from the viewpoint of symbol formation.

Symbol formation was also studied by Werner, together with Kaplan (1964). In analogy with concept formation they also found symbol formation, in its earliest stages, characterized by syncretism and physiognomics. They applied their theories also to the spoken language and describe early names as physiognomic in character, i.e., of a concrete-affective dynamic nature and contextualized, in other words lacking communicative value outside of their concrete context of application.

The validity of this theory on the development of verbal language has been disputed, a discussion which need not concern us here; but it has been found that adults, when asked to make simple linear symbols for certain concepts, create symbols according to their physiognomic qualities. This means that the lines of figures chosen as symbols share dynamic-physiognomic qualities with their referents. Most well-known in this connection are probably the studies by Krauss (1930) and Lundholm (1921).

The created symbols were not chosen for their geometrical, abstract qualities, but for their dynamic-affective ones. This means, on the other hand, that no unequivocal relationship exists between symbol and referent. Geometrically similar forms may be used to symbolize different objects, and the same object may be symbolized by different linear patterns. Different qualities may be emphasized by the same concept, leading to symbolization by different linear patterns. In spite of this "fluidity" of representation, however, the choice of symbols is not com-

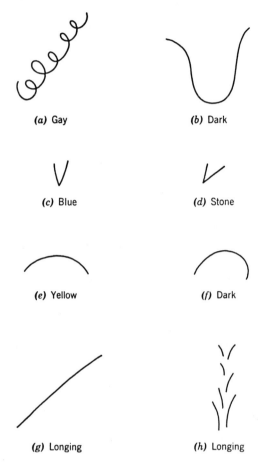

FIGURE 40 *(a)* and *(b)* Typical expressive forms. *(c)* and *(d)* Geometrically similar, physiognomically dissimilar patterns. *(e)* and *(f)* Geometrically similar, physiognomically dissimilar patterns. *(g)* and *(h)* Geometrically dissimilar, physiognomically equivalent patterns. (From H. Werner and B. Kaplan. [1983]. *Symbol formation.* Hillsdale, N.J.: Lawrence Erlbaum Ass.)

pletely arbitrary, but shows a certain consensus. For example, many persons will choose symbols that have certain characteristics in common to represent the same concept, i.e., through the choice of angular, jagged lines to represent a concept such as "raging."

These considerations on the qualities of nonverbal symbol-formation are, of course, essential in the understanding of drawing, particularly of

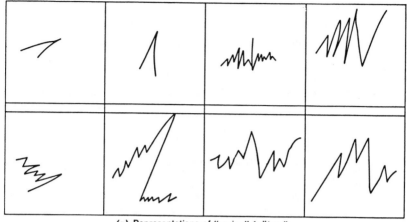

(a) Representations of "raging" (wütend)

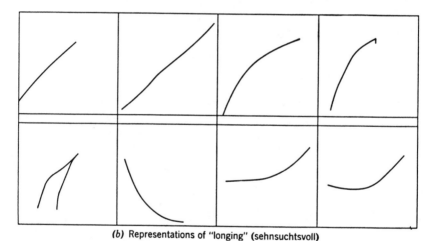

(b) Representations of "longing" (sehnsuchtsvoll)

FIGURE 41 Representation of two concepts by various subjects showing generic, externally visible consensus on production. (From H. Werner and B. Kaplan. [1983]. *Symbol formation.* Hillsdale, N.J.: Lawrence Erlbaum Ass.)

drawing as a projective technique. They explain, on the one hand, how the drawing of a concept such as the human figure may include physiognomic features and thus contain elements that are not similar to a person in a more abstract manner. The way in which different qualities of the concept may lead to the choice of different symbols is immediately understandable with so complex a concept as the human figure, which is both highly charged emotionally and very different for different children. One child may emphasize aggressiveness, resulting in a drawing with sharp, pointed lines and angular forms, while another, emphasizing warmth and softness, may draw with soft, rounded lines and rounded shapes. The "multiformity", i.e., the possibility of using different patterns to refer to the same context, explains the difficulty or impossibility of a general "sign-interpretation" of figure drawings.

On the other hand, the consensus which is also found between many persons in their symbolization of concepts may explain why it is sometimes, nonetheless, possible to generalize. It seems as if one of the conditions for consensus is the existence of a rather strong emotionality of the concepts depicted. An example might be the concept of aggression. Another emotionally highly laden concept might be "anxiety" which physiognomically may to many people be connected with darkness. This might explain the general use of heavy, black shading in figure drawing as a sign of anxiety.

Analogic and Digital Language

In the comparison between drawing and language, it seems useful, as Watzlawick, Beavin, and Jackson (1967) do, to distinguish between digital and analogic communication.

In digital language, arbitrary signs are used as symbols, and they are manipulated according to a logical syntax; no likeness whatsoever need be found between the sign and the object it represents. This corresponds to ordinary spoken and written language. This view of the verbal language as a digital language is in contrast to Werner and Kaplan's (1964) theory of language development; but this difference of viewpoint is irrelevant in connection with drawings.

In analogic communication, however, there is some kind of similarity between the signs and what they represent. An analogic language will be more or less understandable according to its greater or lesser similarity to its representations. A drawing can—within limits—be universally understood. Watzlawick, Beavin, and Jackson do not describe in greater detail what kind of likeness exists between an analogic language and what it represents; they do not distinguish between similarity in regard to physical, objective qualities and other forms of similarity. Werner's

(1964) distinction between likeness of abstract properties and of physiognomic, dynamic-affective properties is here a valuable supplement.

In the same way as physiognomic perception is regarded as dominant at the early stages of development, analogic communication is considered to have its roots in far more archaic periods of development than digital communication. Watzlawick, Beavin, and Jackson (1967) consider it therefore to be of much more general validity than the relatively recent and far more abstract digital mode of verbal communication.

Digital language is characterized as particularly well suited to the sharing of information about objects. On the contrary, when it comes to relationships, we have to rely almost exclusively on analogic language. "Whenever relationship is the central issue of communication, we find that digital language is almost meaningless" (Watzlawick, Beavin, and Jackson 1967, 63).

Digital language has the advantage of being both perfectly precise and logical. This may not always be the case in oral language, which is rarely only digital, but the principles are carried to completion in computers that work according to the digital system. This means, among other things, that all the 16 possible logical truth functions can be expressed in a digital language. In contrast, the analogic languages have nothing comparable to the logical syntax of digital languages. They have no equivalents for such vitally important elements of discourse as "if-then," "either-or," and—most important—no negation is possible. In facial expressions, for example, tears may express sorrow or joy, a smile may convey sympathy or contempt (or aggression), etc. Analogic communication has no qualifiers to indicate which of two discrepant meanings is implied, nor are there any indicators of time, of past, present, or future.

Watzlawick, Beavin, and Jackson also discuss the difficulties of translation from analogic to digital communication:

Analogic message material, as already mentioned, lacks many of the elements that comprise the morphology and syntax of digital language. Thus, in translating analogic into digital messages, these elements have to be supplied and inserted by the translator, just as in dream interpretation digital structure has to be introduced more or less intuitively into the kaleidoscopic imagery of the dream.

Analogic message material is highly antithetical; it lends itself to very different and often quite incompatible digital interpretations. Thus not only is it difficult for the sender to verbalize his own analogic communications, but if interpersonal controversy arises over the meaning of a particular piece of analogic communication, either partner is likely to introduce, in the process of translation, into the digital mode, the kind of digitalization in keeping with *his* view of the nature of the relationship. (1967, 99–100)

Another of the basic mistakes made when translating between the two modes of communication is the assumption that an analogic message is by nature assertive or denotative just as digital messages are. Examples are given of analogic messages that may well be regarded as analogous to a proposal or a question in the digital world.

In translating analogic into digital material, logical truth functions must be introduced which are absent in the analogic mode. This absence becomes most conspicuous in the case of negations. In nonverbal language, the clearest way of expressing a negation is through a demonstration or proposal of the action to be denied, which is then not carried through to its end. This is exemplified by the behavior of animals where the ritual is described as the intermediary process between analogic and digital communication, simulating the message material, but in a repetitive and stylized manner that hangs between analogue and symbol.

It is also emphasized that, in general, the first consequence of a breakdown in communication is a partial loss of the ability to metacommunicate digitally about the contingencies of the relationship and a return to an analogic mode of communication. This is what takes place for example in hysterical symptom formation. C. G. Jung, throughout his work, stresses that the symbol appears when "digitalization" is not yet possible. But symbolization may also take place when digitalization is no longer possible.

The distinction between the two kinds of language seems very useful with regard to drawings. In the past, they have sometimes been treated as a digital, sometimes as an analogic language. In Goodenough's (1926) intelligence test, drawings are used as a—very simple—digital language, where each trait has an all-or-none function. Each item of the test is regarded as a message, giving the information whether the mental concept of this body part exists in the drawer or not. It is characteristic that when used in this way only cognitive aspects are communicable, while nothing is conveyed that has emotional significance. The system obtains the high degree of precision that characterizes digital languages, but as it is a very primitive digital system, the amount of meaning that can be communicated through it is correspondingly limited. As drawings, by their very nature, represent an analogic communication, it seems only to lead to a loss of information to press them into the form of a digital language.

When used as a projective technique, however, drawings are regarded as an analogic language, characterized by the qualities that belong here. It follows from this that attempts to find a "system" of signs that can be interpreted unequivocally are deemed to be futile.

The lack of negation is one of the qualities that creates the most serious difficulties in the understanding of a drawing's message. It cannot immediately be seen whether a drawing of a cruel monster should be regarded as something that is wished or feared—if it represents the drawer's wish to be such a threatening figure or his fear of being attacked by one—or both. Perhaps the totality of several traits pointing in the same direction can give one of the possibilities greater probability than another, in exactly the same way as gestures and tone of voice can support each other. This is, of course, another way of stating the fact already emphasized by Machover (1949) that a drawing may show both impulses and defenses against them.

The lack of possibilities of expressing time relationships makes it also difficult to give a precise interpretation of a drawing's message. A drawing may represent a present state of the drawer, a former state, or perhaps some future possibilities that are tried out symbolically on paper instead of being acted out.

The difficulties in interpreting drawings are very precisely described by the authors in their description of the difficulties inherent in the translation from one mode of communication to the other—here from the analogic to the digital. The interpreter must add such an essential aspect of the communication as negations, and it is he or she who must distinguish between what is meant as a forceful statement by the drawer regarding his present situation and what is meant as a cautious proposal regarding the future. There is the ever-present danger of too great subjectivity—of interpretations that fit the interpreter's wishes and needs and not the drawer's. As emphasized by the authors, however, it is continually necessary to continue the translation from one mode into the other, and we neither can nor should stop the attempts at going from drawings to verbal messages and vice versa.

CONCLUDING REMARKS

When drawing development is related to these more general theories of child development and conceptual development, it can be seen, first, that this limited aspect of development fits easily into a broader and more comprehensive frame of reference. Second, it is not necessary to relate drawings to different or opposed theories, if only the applied theory is wide enough. Drawings seen as manifestations of concept formation and also as manifestations of emotional and motivational aspects of the personality may well be contained in one theory, if the theory of concept formation is wide enough to include earlier stages of concept formation than the latest and most narrowly cognitive stage.

When this is done, many of the aspects of drawings that have often been regarded as inexplicable or contradictory become understandable and meaningful, such as the form of early drawings and the different possible uses of drawings.

The description of concept formation as passing through several stages with different characteristics contrasts sharply with the description offered by Harris (1963) where concept formation is seen as basically similar for all ages, and no distinction is made between different developmental levels. His model seems mainly to correspond to Werner's (1964) last stage of concept development, which is based on the truly abstract qualities of objects and which requires the ability for real conceptual analysis. In this way, only the purely cognitive aspects of concept formation are taken into consideration, with the consequent neglect of contributions from other personality factors. Drawing development is then only partly understood, and deviations from the purely conceptual schemata must be considered as defective and cannot be regarded as valid representations of other levels of experience. It is a way of description that sees concept formation as a process isolated from emotional and motivational aspects of personality.

The fact that children's concepts are more influenced by perception and more pictorial in their form than those of adults explains partly the greater role that drawing plays in the lives of children than in those of most adults. It is easier to express a perceptually experienced relationship in pictures than to translate it into a more digital, logical, and abstract verbal language.

At the time of development when children become able to form truly abstract concepts, during adolescence and preadolescence, the use of drawings as a means of expression is often drastically reduced and replaced by the spoken and written language.

Drawings can, because of their concrete nature, never be used to depict truly abstract concepts directly. They must always, to a much higher degree than the verbal language, remain bound to perception and sensation and thereby also to bodily experience, to motion and emotion. Also adults were found to resort to physiognomic perception and expression when forced to use drawings as their medium of concept formation. This, of course, sets limits to the use of drawings as a means of communication.

On the other hand, the description of drawings as an analogic language also points to some of the advantages that drawings possess over verbal language. In the realm of emotions and human relationships, drawings can be much more expressive and can convey emotional states and feelings which can only with difficulty be translated into verbal language. Drawings seem to be connected with more basic and earlier layers of the personality and to be directly connected with fundamental bodily and emotional experiences of which the drawer may not even be conscious. As was pointed out, analogic language is used both before digital communication is possible and when for some reason it has broken down. This points to the value of the use of drawing as a diagnostic and therapeutic tool. Feelings and vague emotional states are more easily translated into the analogic language of drawings than directly into the digital verbal language.

In our culture, the use of logical and abstract thinking and of purely theoretical and intellectual functioning is much cultivated and much more highly valued than the integration of the total personality with the inclusion of mature emotionality and of the ability also to function sensually and perceptually. The one-sided emphasis on intellectual performance leads to highly developed technical skills and needs the development of digital languages which have so far found their perfection in computer languages.

As necessary as this is, it is regrettable that it so often happens at the cost of other forms of development and results in the neglect of other fundamental aspects of personality. The continued use of drawings and other pictorial means of expression might act as a valuable, positive counterbalance to this tendency, and it seems absurd that the use of such fundamental means of expression should be reserved for those who are already in need of therapeutic help.

EIGHT

Comparison with Studies of Sex Differences

In the preceding chapter, drawing development was related to concept development in general, which was found to be a meaningful frame of reference. But this more superordinate frame of reference is not adequate to explain all aspects of children's human figure drawings. The sex differences in the drawings, for example, are not satisfactorily explained only by references to concept development in general. They must be seen in the light of our knowledge about that particular aspect of concept development which has to do with one's concept of oneself as a person of one or the other sex, and also in the light of our knowledge of sex differences in general.

Sex differences have been looked upon through very different theoretical frames of reference. On the one hand, developmental psychology has a long research tradition in this field, based on a broad range of studies, from biological, sexological, and animal research at one end, to observation of children's behavior, use of ratings, self-ratings, and projective techniques at the other. On the other hand, since the days of Freud, the discussion of sex differences has been a major topic in psychoanalytic research, which with quite different tools has built up a substantial amount of knowledge on the subject. Most applied clinical psychology relies at least as much on these theories as on the results from the more positivistically oriented research. Moreover, the sex differences in drawings have been interpreted on the basis of both frames of reference, although rarely by the same persons. An attempt will be made here to combine the results from the different theoretical and methodological approaches.

The subject of sex differences is emotionally provoking and can start heated discussions about, for example, the relative influence of biological and social factors. There have been tendencies to maximize psychological sex differences, to underscore their "nature-given" quality, and—often—to use this outlook as a means of limiting opportunities for women in society. More recently, the tendency has rather been in the direction of minimization or even total denial of psychological sex differences, while the differences that could not possibly be denied rapidly were explained as being caused exclusively by socialization.

It is, no doubt, very difficult to establish neutral and "objective" theories in this area, where the theorists always have the disadvantage of belonging to one of the groups described. One of the clearest examples of this bias is, of course, Freud, who could so much better describe the envy of women toward men than the opposite, and it is probably not incidental that the appearance of female theorists has been necessary (e.g., Melanie Klein) before more balanced descriptions of the development of the two sexes were set forth.

Of course, the present writer is as much subjected to this difficulty as anybody else and can do no more about it than point to its existence. It is rarely mentioned as a factor of importance in connection with specific studies, perhaps because of faith in the objectivity of science and the impartiality of scientists, but its importance should not be overlooked. Hypotheses, methods, and interpretations always contain some degree of subjectivity even in the most well-controlled studies and may favor one sex on behalf of the other. In some of the earlier studies of drawings, for example that of Kerschensteiner (1905), this bias is clearly observable, and probably in the future it will be found equally obvious in some of our contemporary research. The importance of this factor is also mentioned by Dwyer (1979) who writes: "Research on sex-related differences more than most other fields of psychology suffers from researchers' personal and professional prejudices, sex stereotyping, and etnocentricity" (p. 343).

In this chapter, some of the facts that are known about cognitive sex differences will first be set forth, followed by a description of sex differences of personality.

COMPARISON WITH STUDIES OF COGNITIVE SEX DIFFERENCES

Harris (1963) and Goodenough (1926) mainly saw the quantitative sex differences in children's human figure drawings as reflections of cognitive differences. Harris suggested that girls were ahead in verbal and conceptual development, partly due to a faster rate of maturation and partly to an actual verbal superiority. He admitted that the qualitative sex differences were not satisfactorily explained by cognitive differences between the sexes and hinted at the necessity of introducing other and more dynamic theories of personality organization that included such factors as different libidinal investment in different body parts, and differences in body image and in sexual symbolism between the sexes, but he did not go further with these considerations.

In order to clarify to what degree sex differences in drawings reflect sex differences in cognitive functioning or rate of development, a comparison must be made with what is known about sex differences in these areas from general developmental psychology.

Most of the following results from the research on sex differences are from Wittig and Petersen's (1979) comprehensive overview of studies on sex differences in cognitive functioning.

On the physiological level, some developmental differences are well known. Anthony (1970) writes that the developmental rates of the sexes are markedly different judging from bone age, dental age, and the development of the reproductive system. At the age of 6, girls are one developmental year ahead, and at the age of 9, the difference becomes 18 months. He states that during first grade, eleven times as many boys as girls are referred to observation for social and emotional immaturity.

Waber (1979) states that there is a clear difference between the sexes in the maturational rate of neuromotor functions, females being uniformly more advanced. In children, girls stop making involuntary associated movements earlier than boys. The superiority of girls is particularly marked at ages 7 and 11, but has become minimal by age 15. The female curve of neuromotor development shows a steady growth, while the male curve is characterized by rapid spurts, separated by plateaus and dips.

Girls also show a maturational superiority over boys in the ability to execute sequential motor tasks, e.g., repetitive or successive finger movements; such movements require both temporal sequencing and spatial coordination. In some tasks, the difference decreases by age 10, when the boys have caught up, in other tasks by age 12.

Wittig and Petersen (1979) state that the three main areas in cognitive functioning which have been found consistently to show sex differences are verbal, mathematical, and spatial abilities. Of these, the only one showing superiority of girls is the verbal area. In a review by Oetzel (1962) of 26 studies, girls were found to be superior in language development in 23 of them.

Among children, the female superiority appears most clearly in the mechanical aspects of speech and language, e.g., in articulation, reading, and writing. Girls are found to do better in tasks such as rapid automatized naming of colors, objects, letters, numbers, and animals. There are similarities in the development of linguistic and fine motor skills, which show the same maturational pattern: (1) females are consistently more advanced, (2) the sex differences are most pronounced between 5 and 7 years and between 10 and 12 years, and (3) the sex differences diminish at puberty as males catch up with females. Also the smoother developmental pattern that was found for girls in fine motor skills is seen in linguistic skills. Waber (1979) suggests that a common neurological substratum may underlie the development of both linguistic and fine motor skills, and that its maturation proceeds more rapidly in females than in males.

Doubt has been raised regarding the finding that males catch up with females at puberty. Some studies show that by imposing greater difficulty on the task, the female superiority may also persist after puberty (Peretti 1969). The disappearance of the sex difference may therefore be due to a ceiling effect. Girls are also found consistently to be more rapid readers than boys at least up to college-entry age (Moore 1940).

While differences in mathematical abilities do not seem relevant in connection with drawing ability, the differences seen in spatial ability may be connected with drawing performance. Maccoby and Jacklin (1974) write that, beginning with adolescence, consistent mean differences between the sexes are seen in spatial ability: males perform better on tests of nonanalytic spatial ability (the ability to visually rotate an object or figure without the aid of verbal mediation) in eight out of ten tests with subjects 13 years old or more. Studies of analytic spatial ability (where language may be used) show males scoring higher in 22 of 43 studies, females in one. Later studies support their conclusions (Petersen and Wittig 1979). This sex difference persists throughout life; in studies of old people, elderly males have been found to be superior in tests involving spatial abilities (Cohen and Wilkie 1979).

More recent studies have shown, however, that children also show sex differences in regard to spatial ability. In a sample of 7,119 children, 6–12 years old (Roberts 1972), boys over the entire age range were found to be better at the block design subtest of the WISC. Quite similar results were found in another study by Strauch (1976) according to Vanderberg and Kuse (1979) examining 2,200 children, aged 6–16 years.

The male superiority in spatial ability appears in three kinds of tests: those involving (1) spatial visualization, (2) perceptual disembedding, and (3) mazes. Twin studies have shown that a hereditary factor is active and that environmental factors are less influential than in many other abilities (Vandenberg and Kuse 1979). It is hypothesized that there is a general visualization factor which encompasses at least seven primary mental abilities that have been identified through factor analysis. These are: (1) figural relations, (2) visualization, (3) spatial orientation, (4) flexibility of closure, (5) speed of closure, (6) perceptual speed, and (7) figural adaptive ability. Tests designed to measure these abilities consist of tasks requiring the subjects to imagine movement in space, to find configurations embedded in another configuration, to bring about closure among parts of a configuration, or to quickly scan several configurations and locate a particular one.

While a left-hemispheric specialization has been demonstrated clearly for linguistic abilities and motor-sequencing skills, no analogous right-hemispheric specialization has been shown for the spatial tests in which sex-related differences appear. Spatial abilities are dependent on the function of both hemispheres, but each of them is associated with characteristic styles of processing visuo-spatial configurations. This has been observed most clearly in patients who have had the interhemispheric connections surgically severed (Nebes 1974). The left hemisphere is oriented to detail. It breaks a visual configuration into its component parts and attends to its internal features. The right hemisphere is oriented to the whole pattern of the configuration. It attends to the external aspects of a configuration, simplifying internal details.

Sex-related stylistic variation was found in a study of normal right-handed children, 5–13 years of age, in the drawing of Rey-Osterrieth's figure (Waber 1979). At the youngest ages, girls reproduced more parts of the design, thus scoring higher on accuracy than the boys. They had more internal details and drew more discrete parts, while the external configuration of the design seemed to be more important for the boys. By age 8, no sex differences were seen in scoring categories, and most children could draw all the parts. By age 11, a sex-related difference in style was found, boys drawing in long, sweeping, continuous lines, while girls drew theirs part by part. By age 13, these stylistic differences had again disappeared. Males tended to exhibit a style characteristic of right-hemispheric processes, and females a style characteristic of left-hemispheric ones. These sex-related differences were linked to age; they appeared particularly at ages 5 and 11, the ages when there are also marked disparities between the sexes in neuro-motor maturity (Connolly and Stratton 1968; Waber 1979). Performance in the Rey-Osterrieth test depends to a large extent on visuo-motor integration, therefore it is likely that maturational variation in the motor system plays an important role in the etiology of sex-related differences on this test as well.

On the basis of this evidence, it seems reasonable to suggest that some

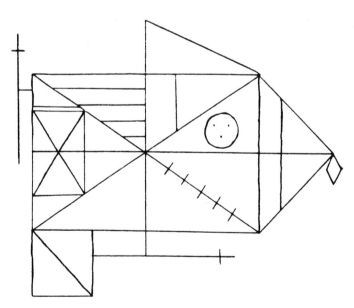

FIGURE 42a   Rey-Osterrieth complex figure. (From Waber 1979.)

A

B

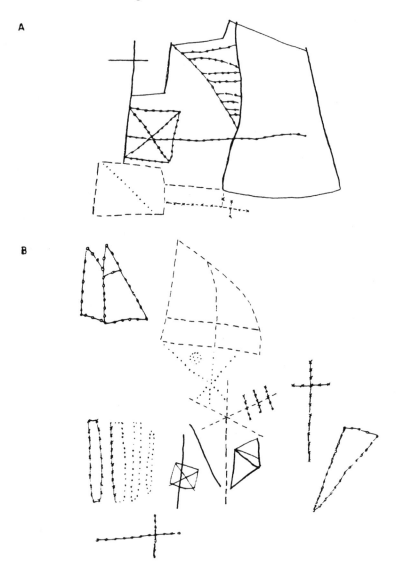

FIGURE 42b *(A)* An example of a copy of Rey-Osterrieth figure drawn by a 5-year-old boy. *(B)* An example of a copy of Rey-Osterrieth figure drawn by a 5-year-old girl. ──────: first color. ─────: second color. —x—x—x—x: third color. . . . . . : fourth color. —O—O—O—: fifth color. (From Waber 1979.)

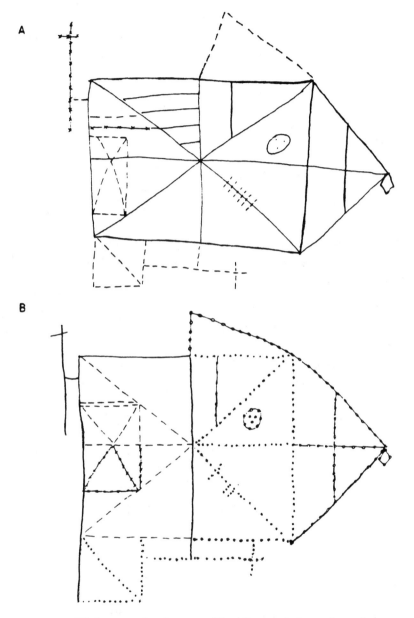

FIGURE 42c *(A)* An example of a copy of Rey-Osterrieth figure drawn by a 10-year-old boy. *(B)* An example of a copy of Rey-Osterrieth figure drawn by a 10-year-old girl. ————: first color. ------: second color. —x—x—x—x: third color. . . . . . . : fourth color. —O—O—O—: fifth color. (From Waber 1979.)

of the sex differences in drawing performance may be due to differences in maturation. Particularly the differences in fine motor skills and neuromotor functioning undoubtedly plays a part in the girls' better motoric control, greater order, and regularity of drawing performance.

On the other hand, the advantages in linguistic skills do not seem to be very obviously connected with drawing performance. The advantages were mostly found in the more mechanical aspects of language use, which have not been found to have any relationship to drawing. No sex differences have been demonstrated in level of conceptual development.

Actually, it would seem more likely to expect a connection between boys' superiority in spatial abilities and drawing development, and such a connection may well exist, although it may not manifest itself very clearly in the drawing of a human figure. The observation (e.g., by Kerschensteiner 1905) that boys are better at the depiction of perspective and the use of space seems probable in light of these findings. Similarly, the better ability to visualize objects could be expected to help boys in the drawing of three-dimensional objects. The drawing of such objects was exactly that area of drawing where boys were found to excel the most. In the drawing of the human figure, perhaps only the drawing of movement may be connected with spatial abilities.

A detailed discussion of the meaning of hemispheric laterality for the two sexes would lead too far, but the differences in the drawing of the Rey-Osterrieth figure are worth noticing. The sexes do seem to apply different patterns of approach, with girls at the younger ages reproducing more details than boys. This pattern may correspond to the tendency for girls to include more body parts in the human figure drawings, a tendency which is also seen most clearly in the younger age-groups. The possible common factor which is hypothesized as lying behind both fine motor development and linguistic skills may thus be responsible for some of the sex differences in drawing performance.

However, it is obvious that only a small part of the total pattern of sex differences is explainable by differences in cognitive function between the sexes.

COMPARISON WITH STUDIES IN SEX DIFFERENCES OF PERSONALITY AND IN SEXUAL IDENTITY FORMATION

Maccoby and Jacklin (1974) have reviewed an extensive number of studies of sex differences from general developmental psychology. They are very cautious and tend to minimize differences between the sexes rather than to exaggerate them. Therefore, when they reach conclusions about the existence of differences, they are thoroughly substantiated.

They have found that studies of sex differences in activity level show a tendency for boys to be more active than girls, although not consistently so for all ages and experimental conditions. During the first year of life, the evidence indicates no sex differences. From this age onward, studies vary greatly as to whether a sex difference is found, but when it is, boys are more active. Very seldom has a greater level of activity among girls been observed. They conclude by saying: "It is clearly possible that there may be a constitutional contribution to the male's tendency to put out more energy or respond with more movement to certain stimulating conditions" (1974, 177). These results lend some support to the observation of more movement in the drawings by boys.

One area in which rather consistent sex differences are found is in the amount of aggression shown by the two sexes. Maccoby and Jacklin conclude that males are consistently found to be more aggressive than females, also in many cross-cultural studies. Studies indicate sex differences not only in quantity, but also in quality. It is sometimes argued that girls are less aggressive because their aggression is less well tolerated, but Maccoby and Jacklin find the studies showing that small boys are punished as much for their aggression as are girls. They also find evidence that boys have more aggressive fantasies than girls, and that they more easily imitate aggression. If girls were more inhibited in showing their aggression openly, it would be likely to come out in play or fantasy, but boys actually play more aggressively than girls also. They conclude by saying: "We would like to urge serious consideration of the possibility that the two sexes are not equal in initial aggressive response tendencies" (1974, 238). And they continue by outlining the reasons why they think that biological sex differences appear to be involved in aggression: "1) Males are more aggressive than females in all human societies for which evidence is available. 2) The sex differences are found early in life, at a time when there is no evidence that differential socialization pressures have been brought to bear by adults to "shape" aggression differently in the two sexes. 3) Similar sex differences are found in man and subhuman primates. 4) Aggression is related to levels of sex hormones" (1974, 243). The greater aggressiveness found in the drawings by boys thus gets ample support from the results of the research, and there is even indication for the assumption that this greater aggressiveness is, at least partly, biologically determined.

It is a well-established fact that boys are more vulnerable physiologically during the first years of life than girls and also that, all the way through childhood, they show a greater number of psychic problems, including, for example, speech and reading problems as well as general behavior problems. They also show a greater incidence of psychiatric illness as, for example, demonstrated by Rutter and Hersov (1977). In light of this, it is not surprising to find that boys' drawings contain more signs of conflict than those of girls.

Traditional research in developmental psychology can be criticized for not taking seriously the results described by psychoanalysts, but the opposite is also found: namely, psychoanalysts neglecting the results from general psychological research. This may be due partly to a lack of knowledge of these results as many psychoanalysts are doctors or psychiatrists and not psychologists. Another reason may be the often-heard argument that psychoanalytic hypotheses cannot be experimentally tested. Very often, however, the same questions are asked from both sides, and at least it can be examined whether the results support or contradict each other. Whatever the reason may be, it is unfortunate. A study of human beings which does not take into account both our rational and irrational sides is certainly defective.

In the following, results from both kinds of research will be drawn into the argumentation, and it will be seen that, although starting from very different points of departure, some of the psychoanalytic and some of the more traditional sexological research are found to support each other nicely.

Machover's (1953, 1960) negative interpretation of drawings is connected with the fact that she relies on the older Freudian theories, which are singularly negative, particularly in the outlook on the development of the girl. It would go beyond the scope of this study to embark on a detailed discussion of these theories, whose basic ideas may also be regarded as well known; but a few aspects of them need to be considered more closely as they fit very poorly with the observations of the drawings. It is generally characteristic of this theory that it has, as expressed by Chassequet-Smirgel (1981) "approached the problems of femininity through the study of male sexuality. . . . Such an approach is detrimental to any understanding of the essence of femininity" (p. 3).

Two assumptions in particular of Freudian theory need reconsideration. One is the hypothesis that the development of the two sexes is identical until the phallic stage, that girls are supposed to have no idea about the existence of their own vagina until puberty, and that they grow up dominated by penis envy to the point of absurdity where the wish for a child is seen as a substitute for the wish for a penis. (This is no attempt to deny the existence of penis envy in general, which has been amply demonstrated; it would lead too far to go into a detailed discussion of this phenomenon, but it can be regarded as playing a different role in the total development of the girl from that described in traditional Freudian theory.)

In the light of this theory, of course, girls can have no pride in their own femininity, and the decoration of the body and face in their drawings must be regarded as only defensive. But the lack of an acceptance of a basic feminine identity fits very poorly with the existence of so many and pervasive sex differences as actually seen in drawings.

Another assumption in Freudian theory that is totally incompatible with the results of the study is the theory about the weaker superego of women than of men, supposedly because girls, who are already "castrated," do not have as strong an incentive to develop a superego as boys who may still fear castration. But the observation of drawings shows those of girls to be more orderly, restricted, and controlled than those of boys, rather demonstrating the existence of a stronger superego.

Other psychoanalytic theories have advanced different viewpoints of the development of the two sexes, particularly of the development of the girl, which correspond better with what can be observed in drawings.

Studies and analyses of even very small children (2–3 years old) have amply demonstrated the existence of a different development of the two sexes already during the earliest stages. Klein (1975) postulates, for example, the existence of an Oedipal conflict already during the oral stage and finds that girls already from this age have fantasies about a penis, not of their own, but of the incorporation of their father's penis as an object of (oral) satisfaction. The important points are both the postulation of the very early sex differences and the theory that the girl enters the Oedipal stage, not indirectly through her masculine tendencies and her penis envy, but directly, as a result of her dominant feminine instinctual components. Mahler, Pine, and Bergman's (1975) observations of normal children's development have affirmed the existence of children's concern with sex differences already during the early separation-individuation stages.

In Klein's view, the pars-pro-toto principle reigns at this early age, which means that the father's penis stands for the whole person. The early introjects make up the earliest forms of the superego, which is thus also formed at a much earlier age than thought by Freud, although in a more archaic and sadistic form in the beginning. As the girl is more subordinated to her introjected father than the boy (because of the lack of her own penis), she is also more influenced by her early superego. This leads to the completely opposite viewpoint to that of Freud regarding the relative strength of the superegos of the two sexes.

The study of drawings cannot, of course, by itself answer these questions about the validity of the different theories, but there is clearly greater correspondence between the observation of the sex differences in drawings and the theories of Klein than with those of Freud, both in regard to the pervasiveness of sex differences and to the differential influence of the superego in the two sexes.

The fact that girls cannot observe their own genitals is, according to many authors, including Klein, a constant source of anxiety. The girl fears that her inside will be damaged or destroyed in retaliation for her own (unavoidable) aggressive impulses; the diffuseness of the girl's experience of her own body is, according to Klein, the main reason why her narcissism extends to her whole body. In contrast, the male narcissism is focused upon the penis. That girls are more narcissistic than boys has repeatedly been found, both by Freud (e.g., 1925) and by later authors, e.g., Grunberger (1981), and the fact that their narcissism extends to the whole body also fits well with what can be observed in drawings.

Klein states even more specifically that there is a direct sublimatory path from the fear of a "bad" and "dangerous" inside to the theme of beauty, and that women's need for a beautiful body and for beauty in general is based on their desire to possess a beautiful interior to their body in which "good" and lovely objects are lodged. According to this theory, the decorative sense, which is found by so many authors to be more developed in girls than in boys, should have its starting point in the girl's experience of her own body and be generalized from that.

Klein states that while the girl's greatest concern and anxiety is bound up with her whole body, the boy displaces his anxiety to the penis, which as an external organ can master things in the environment. This leads the boy to turn his interest away from himself and his own body and toward objects in the outer world, toward the outer reality, as an object to be mastered. Through this mastery he proves to himself his creative potentialities and masters his anxiety. These theories support very well the observation that, in drawings, the center of interest for the girl is on the figure itself, while for the boy the interest is turned away from the figure and toward the environment.

The theory about the existence of very early different sexual identities also gains support from sexological research. Stoller (1968) describes a core sex identity which develops already during the first year of life, and which gives the child a fundamental feeling of belonging to one of the sexes. This does not mean that, for example, the phallic phase is without importance, nor that adjustment and minor changes in attitude cannot take place later, but, in general, it seems as if a change of sex identity is difficult, if not impossible, after 18 months of age. Later changes are reported (e.g., Hampson 1965), but they have taken place in children with ambivalent or hermaphroditic identity, and these results do not necessarily mean that similar changes can be made with children with a less ambiguous sex identity.

Hampson's results were taken as evidence that sexual identity is primarily the result of a learning process and that sex differences are not inborn. It is probably no coincidence that they were reported in the sixties, at a time, when the wish to explain all sex differences as the results of socialization and to diminish the role played by biological factors was more prominent. The conclusions regarding the ease with which sex identity can be changed were criticized by Diamond (1965) who maintained that human beings, first and foremost because of genetic and hormonal influences during the prenatal stage, are absolutely predisposed to either male or female sexual orientation at birth. Beach (1965) reached a similar conclusion and criticized Hampson's results with the argument that some of the hormonal factors that predisposed his patients to ambivalent outer sex characteristics also might have influenced other systems, notably the central nervous system and thus also in this way may have influenced their development of sex identity.

Several works (e.g., Stoller 1968; Money and Pollit 1964; Kvale and Fishman 1965; Benjamin 1964) describe cases where a child with clear outer sex characteristics nonetheless has manifested a behavior typical of the opposite sex and where later biological abnormalities were discovered, which showed the child to be more ambiguous sexually than the outer appearance showed. These works might be taken as evidence that biological factors tend to persist in spite of a socialization in the opposite direction. The question as to the relative role of biological factors versus socialization in the development of sexual identity is certainly not yet finally answered; but it seems safe to conclude that sex differences manifest themselves much earlier than was believed when Freud wrote his works.

CONCLUDING REMARKS

The study of sex differences in the drawing of a human figure has led far into very different areas of child psychology and to comparisons with theories reflecting different basic scientific viewpoints and attitudes. The application of such different theories may lead to a fragmented and incoherent picture, a danger of which the present author is well aware. If, however, the picture that emerges has internal consistency, the combination of several theories is not only legal, but can prove very fruitful. The complications make it understandable, however, why earlier studies of drawings have tended to concentrate on certain aspects of them and to be less comprehensive.

There are two reasons why it has been found necessary to involve so many theoretical frames of reference. One is the fact that no single theory of child development encompasses all aspects of it. Some concentrate on cognitive aspects of it, others on visible behavior, and others again have their focus mostly on unconscious motivation, drives, and the structure of personality.

The second reason is the fact that the apparently very simple process of drawing a human being turns out to be a very complex and complicated act, involving very many aspects of the drawer's total personality. If drawings shall be given due credit, these aspects must all be taken into consideration. Drawing involves rationality and irrationality, cognition and emotion, action and fantasy, consciousness and unconsciousness, perception of the outer world and experience of the inner.

History has given enough frightening examples of the negative effect of false assumptions regarding the "inborn" or "natural" qualities of the two sexes to teach that the question of the determination of sex differences must be approached with great caution. On the other hand, an a priori denial of the existence of basic psychological sex differences seems absurd, if any correspondence is believed to exist between physiology and psychology. Of course, the issue of the origin of psychological sex differences can no more be definitively settled in regard to drawings than in all other cases; but some considerations may be offered on this question.

The apparent progress that has taken place in the drawing development of the girls between the earlier studies and the later ones points convincingly in the direction that cultural factors play a part in the rate of development and in the termination of development, a hypothesis which is also supported by results from cross-cultural studies.

On the other hand, it is striking to see the constancy with which actually all other sex differences have manifested themselves during the 75 years covered by the studies, regardless of the cultural changes that have taken place and of the different nationalities involved. It is interesting that also exactly those aspects of drawings which have most obstinately been described as culturally determined belong here.

The results show that differences in maturational rate and in cognitive abilities may account for some of the sex differences found in drawings, namely the better motoric performance and the faster introduction of major body parts among girls. Conversely, the earlier documented better performances among boys in the representation of space—although not very spectacular in human figure drawings—may be connected with better spatial abilities among boys in general. This factor may perhaps also play a part in their greater preference for depiction of varied positions and of movement, although these traits just as well or perhaps better may be explained by the boys' higher level of physical activity.

The main conclusion of this chapter must be, however, that the pervasive sex differences of the drawings, which quite clearly cannot all be conscious to the drawers themselves, are reflections of equally pervasive and basic experiences of different sexual identities. The fundamental body scheme is differently experienced by members of the two sexes, with girls clearly demonstrating a greater preoccupation with their own body and its beauty than boys, who direct their attention more toward the environment.

To see the decorations of the girls' figures as mere imitations of people in their surroundings falls very short of giving an adequate explanation for their clearly symbolic and unnaturalistic features; and the unnaturalistic features of the boys' drawings may be even more difficult to explain in this way. The value that the girls place on their body seems to be an adequate recognition of its preciousness as the container of future life.

This is not the same as saying—as was done in some of the earlier research—that girls have a more secure sexual identity than boys (due to their better sexual differentiation in their drawing of figures). The boy, who directs his attention away from his own body and toward his surroundings, probably expresses his sexual identity as adequately as the girl who concentrates on her body—but, of course, her more detailed drawing of hair and clothes will make the sexes more easily recognizable.

Whether the girl's wish to decorate her body is an attempt at making it "good enough" and thus still contains a defensive aspect, as suggested by Klein (1975), is difficult to say. It is obvious that girls in their drawings show more control and less aggressiveness than boys, but it is difficult to know whether this is a defensive maneuver or whether it—as suggested by other studies—is a consequence of an actually smaller amount of aggression. At any rate, the girl's sexual identity seems as rooted in a basic feminine identity as that of the boy is rooted in a basic masculine one.

And it seems safe to conclude that the sex differences that manifest themselves in figure drawings reflect fundamental sex differences, anchored in differential and probably early rooted experiences of one's body and its qualities.

NINE

Drawings and Body Experience

In the attempts to trace the factors that are influential in the drawing of a human figure, the question has continually been raised as to what extent perception of the outer world played a part and to what extent the drawer's experience of himself as a person—his body image or self-concept—was influential. Different investigators have placed the weight predominantly, or exclusively, on one or the other of these factors.

That visual perception of the surrounding world plays a part is indisputable. However, from the evidence in the previous chapters, it appears clearly that, for example, the sex differences in figure drawings are, to a great degree, also influenced by the drawer's experience of his own body. In order to clarify further the role played by the body experience, it is necessary to go directly to the research on this topic.

As pointed out earlier, if body image is an isolated phenomenon, unrelated to other personality variables, the possible connection between figure drawings and body image becomes of limited interest. But if body image correlates with other personality measures, and if drawings are expressions of a person's body image, then the information gained from drawings may be of more general value.

The following discussion thus has two purposes:

1. To examine whether the results from the research on body image support or contradict the hypothesis that the body image—or body experience—is influential in the drawing of a human figure.

2. If the first question is answered affirmatively, then to see whether the connection between body experience and other personality variables is of such a kind that drawings—on the basis of their value as expressions of the body experience—can tell us anything about personality variables other than the body image itself.

SOME MAJOR ASPECTS OF THE RESEARCH ON BODY EXPERIENCE

Much experimental work has been done in an attempt to clarify the concept of body image, starting with the work by Schilder (1935) and continued by, among others, Fisher and Cleveland (1958), and Fisher (1970, 1986), whose comprehensive works encompass both the results of earlier research and his own experiments.

Fisher (1970) admits that "a disconcerting range of ideas" exists regarding both the nature of body image and the question of which of its aspects are worthy of study and in which way. Some prefer to study the subject phenomenologically, others through projective techniques, and others again through experiments.

He emphasizes the special importance of body experience for children, suggesting that some of the most important aspects of children's relationships with their parents revolve about the satisfaction, incitement, or inhibition of body feelings. And he continues: "Children construct a model of their relationships with others that is heavily phrased in a body vocabulary. They learn to make judgments in body image terms about such basic issues as what is good and bad, attractive or threatening" (1986, preface). In a way it might be said that some of Machover's (1949) more intuitive statements about body image now begin to get scientific support, although also in a more complicated way. He supports her general notion of the singular importance of the body by saying:

One's body is psychologically closer to oneself than anything else; and, thus the body is a prime target onto which one projects intense feelings. The body seems to be a maze of landmarks and prominences that are charged with meaning. When people scan their own bodies, they encounter an array of stimuli, many of which have powerful, often negative, emotional connotations. (1986, 39)

He further states that

although research in other areas has found fewer and fewer psychological distinctions between women and men, the body image literature reveals quite the opposite. The two sexes have very different modes of perceiving their bodies. They organize their body experiences in unlike ways. They differ with respect not only to the broad stylistic attitudes they adopt toward the somatic self, but also to the meanings they assign to its specific parts. This is true even with respect to parts that have no obvious sex-linked functions. There is fairly good evidence that women and men have contrasting perspectives about the role of the somatic self in their total identity. . . . It has become commonplace in our research to find that, if a particular pattern of body perception typifies one sex, the opposite will prove to be true of the other sex. . . . It puzzles me that most of the standard texts on sex differences (e.g. Maccoby & Jacklin, 1974) have ignored those that lie within the realm of body perception; it is just such differences, linked to one's feeling about one's body, that are basic to sexual identity and probably to identity in its broader sense. (1986, preface)

He lists the following aspects or dimensions of the concept that seem to be more or less universally agreed upon as belonging to it:

1. The degree of awareness of the body as compared to the awareness of other aspects of the total perceptual field. Some have high awareness of their body, while others are only minimally aware of it. This dimension of general body awareness seems to be a long-term attribute of the individual. Not only do people differ in their degree of general body awareness, but there are fairly consistent tendencies for individuals, especially males, to distribute their attention selectively to the various sectors of their body. Individuals consistently focus a good deal of attention on certain body sectors and minimal amounts on others, and these patterns make sense psychologically.
2. The degree of positive or negative feelings with which the individual regards his own body. This dimension was found to show fairly consistent positive correlations with self-concept ratings.
3. The perception of one's body size. Body size estimation may not be a unitary variable. Correlations between the degree of over- and underestimation of the sizes of different body areas have been moderate and in some cases only of a chance order.
4. The existence of a body boundary which derives from the observation that individuals vary in their experience of the demarcation between their bodies and the outer world. This is a very important concept that is connected with many other personality variables and has been the object of a great deal of research.
5. The ability to judge one's position in space. This is also an aspect that is linked with many other personality traits and stylistic variables and that shows great individual variations. The spatial ability is probably part of a broader category related to one's ability to separate what is significant from its context.
6. The degree of anxiety that individuals feel toward their body and the degree of experienced vulnerability. It is not known how body anxiety is related to other kinds of anxiety.

7. The individual's feelings regarding masculinity or femininity. These are difficult to measure reliably because of the high degree of defensiveness associated with these concepts; people do not want to describe themselves as not adequately belonging to their physiological sex. It has also been found that some parts of the body are felt to be more masculine, others more feminine. However, Fisher (1970) concludes that currently we lack an understanding of the simple facts of masculine versus feminine body experience.

Also other dimensions are suggested, which are, however, not relevant in this connection.

These dimensions were found not to correlate highly with each other, but to be relatively independent. It was hypothesized (1970) that they may represent different aspects of a highly complicated, but yet coordinated system.

In the following, I describe some of the main results from this research on body experience which are of relevance for the understanding of figure drawings.

Degree of Awareness of the Body as Compared to Awareness of Other Aspects of the Total Perceptual Field

In his first book, Fisher (1970) described a consistent tendency for women to be more aware of their bodies than men, a finding which was further supported in his second work (1986).

In women, but not in men, body awareness was found to be related to boundary definiteness, which again is related to a clear sense of identity and good individuation. From this perspective it looks as if high body awareness in women is an expression of a high degree of individuation. The women with relatively little body awareness may be seen as lacking individuation. By contrast, in men body awareness was not associated with strength, but rather with a focalized concern about oral stimuli. Harlow (1951) found that men who devote special interest to their bodies through weight lifting tended to be insecure and in considerable conflict about being heterosexually expressive. Korchin and Heath (1961) found that men with high autonomic awareness are described as passive-dependent and ineffectual whereas women with high scores are depicted as active and aggressive, and Mordkoff (1966) noted that a high degree of awareness of autonomic sensations was associated with maladjustment in men, but not in women.

Interest in clothing seems closely connected with body awareness. The psychological importance of clothing has also been studied, as early as in 1898 by Hall, who found that the need to secure approval from others seemed to be a necessary factor in the child's enjoyment of clothing. This was especially true of girls. In a follow-up (Flaccus 1906), it was found that girls felt a greater sense of power and worth when they were well dressed. Cantril and Allport (1933) found that men's general interest in clothes was not related to their values; but women with high interest in clothes had high aesthetic and economic values.

In general, it is found that individuals differ grossly in their relative awareness of their bodies as compared to other objects in their environment. It was suggested that there are probably also cultural differences in the importance ascribed to bodily experience. Sets can be established that either intensify or inhibit one's sensitivity to the sensations emanating from one's body.

Differentiated Feelings toward Various Body Parts

The subject of differentiated feelings toward various body parts has both quantitative and qualitative aspects. The quantitative aspect concerns the amount of attention given to different body parts, while the qualitative aspect has to do with specific meanings attributed to certain parts, e.g., in the form of symbolization. There may, of course, be some connection between these aspects. If a certain body part has acquired a symbolic value, perhaps because it signifies a certain conflict, there is the probability that it will, for the very same reason, receive much attention.

Freud was the first to describe a sequential investment of energy and interest in different body zones and areas (oral, anal, and phallic). Fixations could cause an exaggerated interest in specific body parts lasting into adult life. Ever since, clinical literature has offered very many examples of specific symbolic meanings being attached to specific body parts (nose, eyes, mouth, etc.). The general idea is that when a person is either unusually attuned to or avoidant of a certain body area, this may be an expression of personal conflicts or adjustment strategies. Deutsch (1952), in particular, studied the assignment of symbolic meaning to the body. He concluded that the conversion symptom is only an extreme manifestation of a continual process, which occurs in every person, of assigning values and significance to the various sectors of one's body.

Greenacre (1955, 1958) proposed that an individual's images of his face and genitals are particularly fundamental to his body scheme, and that distortions in these images enhance vulnerability to later disturbances. Hart (1950) also described that certain areas of the body lend themselves particularly well to symbolic roles, e.g., the eyes.

The frequent choice of the nose for plastic alterations has raised the question as to whether it occupies an unusually important role in the body schema. Results from a study of women having had surgery of the nose (Meyer et al. 1960) suggested that the typical woman who wanted surgery had difficulties identifying with her mother and that the nose was a symbol of identification with the father. Alteration often resulted in panic, anxiety, and other negative emotions instead of the positive effect that had been anticipated. It was suggested that the initial effect of surgery is a symbolic change in the body image, with the liberation of affects that had been previously bound.

Jacobson et al. (1960) found that men seeking elective plastic surgery are typically more maladjusted than women who do so. It is suggested that a male patient's wish for surgery is often linked with a conscious wish of dissociating himself from his father—at a deeper level, the rage is often directed toward the mother.

A number of studies were made by Fisher (1970) to determine whether there were consistent individual differences in body experiences and whether such differences were related to style of life and personality defenses. Operationally, the question was conceptualized as requiring the measurement of how the individual distributes his attention to a number of major dimensions of his body and then ascertaining whether the specific distribution was predictive of various attitudes, values, and modes of defense that could be roughly placed under the rubric of "personality." It became evident early that there were distinct sex differences; a pattern of body awareness in men usually had entirely different personality correlates than did the same pattern in women.

An important instrument in Fisher's studies was the Body Focus Questionnaire (BFQ), which presents the subject with a series of verbal references to paired body regions and asks him to indicate which of the two stands out most clearly in his awareness. It contains a total of 108 questions, placed on eight scales: Front-Back, Right-Left, Heart, Stomach, Eyes, Mouth, Head, and Arms.

The most outspoken results for the men were those found in the study of differentiation between back and front of one's body. Many authors have hypothesized that the back of one's body is largely associated with anal functions (e.g., Freud 1908; Abraham 1927; Ferenczi 1911; Fenichel 1945; Schilder 1935).

Fisher tested several hypotheses regarding the correlation between high back awareness and anal character traits. The following traits were found to be connected with high awareness of the back: (1) Avoidance of responses that are not carefully controlled. (Anxiety about loss of impulse control is a prominent difficulty ascribed to the "anal personality.") (2) Sensitivity to stimuli with anal connotations. (3) Negative attitudes toward dirt. (4) Measures of self-control and orderliness. (5) Homosexual anxiety. It was also found that men with high back awareness gave faster associations to anal words and enjoyed anal jokes more than others.

The right side of the body has traditionally often been associated with strength, masculinity, and goodness, the left side with weakness, femininity, and badness. Fisher hypothesized that the relative prominence of the right and left sides in an individual's body scheme would be correlated with indices of sexual adjustment and sexual identification.

The results for the men showed that the more intense a man's focus of attention is upon the right side of his body, the more likely he is to have problems in his heterosexual adjustment. He is more likely to have reduced heterosexual interaction, to become defensive when confronted with sexual references, and to be alarmed by situations which cast doubt upon his sex role. Two possible explanations are given: (1) The response of the right side tends to be slower and more controlled than that of the left. This is true of both eye- and hand-movement. The right side might be associated with control, the left with spontaneity. Those having difficulties in heterosexual expression are also those who "ignore" the more spontaneous side of their bodies and favor the more controlled. (2) The right-handed individual is aware that his right hand is stronger than his left. He might therefore associate his right hand with strength and power which are typically masculine attributes. His left hand would be weaker, i.e., more feminine. If he was doubtful about his masculine role, he might be anxiously aware of his right side, watching it to see if it really will function to provide him with the power he feels he needs to be manly.

Eyes have been associated with oral processes (taking in), hostile intent, wishes to see forbidden sexual scenes, and the genital organ itself. Usually there are some incorporative tendencies associated with them.

Fisher hypothesized that the degree of eye awareness was positively correlated with anxiety about incorporation (via the mouth) and negatively so with indications of free expression of incorporative wishes. This formulation builds on the Freudian hypothesis that the use of a substitute zone for an erogenous purpose is due to anxiety which prevents use of the corresponding real erogenous zone.

It was found that awareness of one's eyes in men is clearly negatively correlated with enjoyment of eating and negatively related to their ability to learn and recall words pertaining to food. Awareness of eyes was negatively correlated with how generous subjects recalled their parents to have been.

Heart awareness has been reported as a sign of repressed sexuality or as unexpressed rage and fear of death. It was here tied to hypotheses about morality and religion. Heart awareness was found to be greatest in those men who were nonaesthetic and nonartistic in their interests and who had a limited amount of certain types of experiences (e.g., imaginative fantasy). It was found to be connected with conformance to what is considered proper and virtuous, with the adoption of a way of life based on religion and the dampening down of experiences that have to do with the aesthetic/artistic.

Mouth and stomach awareness in men were found to be more related to hostility than to oral variables. The greater the mouth and stomach awareness, the more the man was found to be sensitized to and conflicted about anger. Both were positively correlated with a perception of the mouth as angry and aggressive. They were also correlated with various measures of masochism.

Head awareness in men was found to be linked with selective responses to stimuli with anal connotations. These selective attitudes seemed to be the opposite of those associated with back awareness. In most instances they involved a less defensive response to anal themes. Some hypotheses are offered as attempts to explain the correlation between head awareness and anal attitudes. One possibility is that the head is primarily identified with the face which is strongly equated with the front of oneself and therefore in opposition to the back. Another explanation is that the head, because of its position, is particularly well-suited to represent the antithesis of the lower area of one's body, which often has anal significance. Some psychoanalysts (e.g., Fenichel 1945) have proposed that, because thinking and the use of words (e.g., via obsessiveness and intellectualized, self-imposed constraints) seem to play such an important role in the control of anal impulses, the head takes on anal meaning symbolically.

The results for women are different and often opposite in character. Women show less consistency than men in their degree of awareness of specific body parts so that their test-retest reliability is lower.

Back awareness in women was also found to be a function of attitudes concerned with anal functions, however, and a derivative of the kind of defense system which Freud referred to in his discussion of the anal character. The greater the amount of attention given to the back, the more likely the woman was to manifest special sensitivity to dirt and anal stimuli, to be inclined to behave in a negativistic or stubborn fashion, and to be characterized by stingy or frugal attitudes. Women were not found to have special attitudes related to homosexual conflicts or anxiety with reference to possible loss of self-control.

High right awareness was found to correlate with an intraceptive orientation, i.e., by investment in understanding and identifying with others.

Eye awareness in women was generally found to be higher than in men, but had little test-retest reliability and was not found to have any correlation with incorporation as in men.

Heart awareness in women was associated with an orientation to be sociable and to value close, friendly interaction with others. It is suggested that there is some analogy with the religious attitude of the men with high heart awareness.

Mouth and stomach awareness tended to be connected with power variables, but the findings were regarded as tentative.

Head awareness was found to have something to do with heterosexual attitudes. Those who had most head awareness had difficulties coping with that which has heterosexual implications—perhaps as the result of an upward displacement. It was suggested that it is a way of escaping body awareness.

Experienced Size of Body and Body Parts

Jourard and Secord (1954), in a study of individuals' feelings toward various body parts, found that, in men, positive feelings were associated with overestimation of size, i. e., the body parts that were most positively estimated tended to be overestimated. In women, positive estimation was associated with a tendency to underestimate size, except in regard to breasts. They conclude that the results probably are a reflection of social desirability for the two sexes.

Fisher (1970) found that men tend to overestimate their physical size, women to experience themselves as more slender than they are; he concluded that both sexes tend toward an idealization.

Nash (1958) let children label a number of body parts masculine or feminine. He found that the larger a body area, the greater the tendency to estimate it as masculine.

Adams and Caldwell (1963) found that, when children were asked to choose one figure out of ten which they thought to be most like themselves and another one which they would choose to be like, 60% of them chose a larger figure for desired body image than for perceived. This was interpreted as a wish to grow and be "big." Disturbed children chose an even larger figure than normal children.

Gellert and Stern (1964) found boys better at estimating their own height than girls. No clear relationship was found between judgment of own height and of an object, and they therefore concluded that the factors involved in the judgment of own height are only minimally accounted for in terms of the ability to make height judgments in general. The most marked deviation from true proportions was seen in the overestimation of the head, a trait which was especially pronounced for girls. Boys were on the whole more realistic than girls in their body proportion judgments, but not so for the proportions of objects.

Shontz (1969) has particularly studied body size perception and agrees with Gellert and Stern that persons experience the size aspects of their bodies differently from the size attributes of nonbody objects. He found that body distances are usually overestimated, whereas nonbody distances are underestimated, and, also, that there is a significant trend for body estimates to be less accurate than nonbody ones. He also found typical patterns of over- and underestimation applying to specific areas of the body, head width and forearm length being most often overestimated, hand and foot length underestimated.

Later findings by Shontz and McNish (1972) showed that the size perception of other human beings also differs from the perception of nonhuman bodies. Shontz suggests that perhaps it is people's own body experience that affects their perceptions of other people's bodies, and studies are mentioned which show that a person's own height and weight will influence judgment of the height and weight of others (Berkowitz 1980; Fillenbaum 1961; Hinckley and Rethlingshafer 1951) and also that the degree of insecurity of one's own body boundaries affects one's perception of body defects on others (Cormack 1966).

Shaffer (1964) found that children displayed a significant inclination to underestimate their own heights relative to their actual heights and also in relation to the estimated heights of various adult authority figures. Sex differences were prominent, girls underestimating themselves more than boys with reference to all adults. They also overestimated the heights of men in relation to women to a greater degree than boys. Failure did not seem to affect the girls' estimations of height, but produced perceptible decreases in the boys' own height judgment. Shaffer raised the question of whether height might not be a more sensitive area for boys than for girls.

Beller and Turner (1964), in a study of the relationship between degree of dependency and overestimation of height in authority figures in children 3–6 years old, found a tendency for those high in dependency to overestimate the height of authority figures more.

Fisher (1964) found that, among college men, the degree to which they overestimated their height was positively correlated with their commitment to the idea of the superiority of the male over the female and also with their Achievement and Dominance scores in a personality test. He concluded that power aspirations seem to find expression in the subject's body size estimates.

Men tend to overestimate their arm length, women to underestimate it (Humphries 1959). The estimation of arm length is also dependent on position and surroundings, however; arms are estimated as longer when stretched toward an empty space than when stretched toward a wall, and also if they point toward something or carry a tool, their estimated length is increased.

The best validated observation concerning size specificity, according to Fisher (1986), is that head size is consistently overestimated at all age levels. Both Wapner (1960) and Gellert (1975) studied the phenomenon in children, and Wapner found that children overestimate the size of the head to an even greater degree than adults until the age of 9. Some have further noted an unusual overestimation of the head in persons who were intellectually oriented (Cleveland et al. 1962) and (in a group of women) that it correlated with amount of education (Furlong 1977). Nash (1951), in a study of pre- and postpubescent boys, saw the same general tendency to overestimate the size of the head. He explains it in the following way: "It is possible that the highly differentiated nature of the head which places it virtually at the center of one's spatial world, results in feelings of the expansion of the head at the expense of the distant organs of the periphery" (p. 98).

Fisher (1986) concluded that the accumulated data regarding estimation of body size indicates that when an individual judges the size of a part of his body, he is influenced by factors aside from the real magnitude of the part. He seems to be affected not only by the situational context of his body (e.g., the spatial extent of his environment), but also by emotional attitudes toward himself and his body. Illustratively, his perception of his bodily size may reflect his level of self-esteem, his degree of field-independence, or his need to prove his superiority over women. Such factors as mood, failure versus success, state of the body boundaries, amount of attention focused on self, and a number of other factors influence body size judgments. Gross shifts in the individual's adjustment level seem to be translated into alterations in perceived body size. Perception of the size of upper versus lower regions of the body call forth different degrees of over- and underestimation, with a tendency for body parts in the lower part of the body to be underestimated and those in the region of the head to be overestimated.

Size overestimation thus has multiple meanings and can be caused by a variety of factors. Among those of particular interest in this connection is the factor mentioned by Fisher (1986), the attachment of great significance to a body area because of its valued function.

Studies of the Body Boundary

Extensive studies have been made of individuals' body boundaries, i.e., the degree to which they feel their body protected by a solid barrier against the environment, or the degree to which they find this barrier penetrable. Assessment of these variables can be expressed in high versus low barrier and penetration scores. This field of research has led to some interesting findings concerning the connection between the body boundary and other aspects of personality. The boundary definition seems to be a centrally important aspect of the body image. It has been found that when people's identity is threatened by feelings of inferiority or in other ways, boundary definiteness is weakened. So the connection between feelings of self-worth and boundary score is close.

Earlier, it was a widely held view that women had a more unstable body concept than men. One of the reasons for this assumption was the well-known study by Witkin et al. (1954), who found that men were better than women at making use of body cues in rendering spatial judgments and were therefore presumably characterized by a better integrated and more articulated body concept. Women were supposed to be more influenced by factors in the environment and thus to have a less solid body barrier. Their results were later criticized, however, and newer findings consistently show women to have higher boundary and lower penetration scores than men (both for adults and children) (Fisher 1986). Women are thus found to have a more clearly demarcated body boundary than men.

Fisher (1986) has noticed pervasive sex differences also in the process of body image development in children. He concludes that girls more often manifest superiority to boys in their mastery of body image tasks, and that girls already at age 6 structure their body boundaries more articulately than do boys, thus experiencing themselves as possessing more secure body borders. He also reports that boys are more concerned with themes of body destruction, an observation that can arouse no great surprise in a clinical psychological practitioner.

Barrier score has been found positively correlated with many other personality measures, mostly indicating better differentiation and greater ego strength. For example, those with definite boundaries have been found to have a special interest in attainment, a strong intent to preserve independence, and enhanced ability to function adequately under difficult circumstances. Barrier score is positively correlated with achievement drive in both adults and children, with clarity of identity as defined by interviewers, and with effectiveness in coping with stress in laboratory and real-life situations. It is also related to being communicative and sensitive to the needs of others, to frequency of initiating messages to others in a group, to taking the initiative, and to seeking an integrative role. It is associated with receptivity toward the environment and with responsiveness to others, and perhaps also at simpler sensory levels with, for example, the ability to make fine color discrimination. Perceptual events are experienced with greater vividness. Moreover, barrier score is positively correlated to arousal levels in those body areas most directly in contact with the environment, e.g., skin, muscle, and peripheral vasculature, negatively to indices of internal activation, e.g., heart rate. It is presumed that the arousal of "exterior" body layers results in an intensified "tuning in" on what is occurring in one's vicinity. The state of an individual's boundary, with its accompanying exterior versus interior physiological levels of arousal, fosters chronic positive or negative conditions for receiving "outside" information.

Fisher hypothesizes that the relatively greater boundary definiteness exhibited by women represents a clearer articulation of the body concept. He (1970) suggests that the role of a woman is more explicitly identified with her body and its functioning than that of a man. A man's role and status are typically defined in terms of his accomplishments and attainments rather than in terms of his body attributes, but for a woman her role is still largely defined in relation to the attractiveness of her body and her ability to bear children. A woman probably more nearly equates self with body. One of the prime eventual goals of most women involves the conversion of her body into a "container" or protective enclosure for the production of children. It is suggested that the successful conceptualization of one's body as a containing, protective form must mean that it is experienced as having clear and dependable boundaries. Fisher (1970) suggests that women see a more meaningful link between their body and their social role as mothers, while men may be more inclined to associate their body with aggression and therefore with the anxiety-provoking theme of potential body damage.

Fisher (1970) maintains that his results have given rise to the forming of a theory about the way in which the sensory prominence of a body area can influence cognitive processes selectively. He states this theory as follows:

The body scheme, considered as a series of landmarks with differential sensory prominence, may be conceptualized as a representation in body experience terms of attitudes the individual has adopted. These are experiences coded as patterns of body awareness (e.g. involving muscle, stomach). It may be presumed that the patterns of body awareness exist as circuits based on the following sequence: perceptual focus upon a body area because of its utility or significance or activation in relation to a goal; increased physiological and also sensory arousal of the area as a consequence of its special prominence; further feedback from such arousal to the subsystem in the CNS [central nervous system] involved in the original highlighting of the area. Thus, the individual's body scheme contains landmarks which reiterate to him that certain things are important and others are not. Just as a contracting stomach is a signal to seek food, the perceptual prominence of certain muscles maintained at high tonus may be a reminder to attend or not to attend to some class of objects. In this sense, the individual with relatively high awareness of his back would be reminded by this persistent "back" sensory signal to avoid situations which stimulate the kinds of conflicts found in the "anal character." It could function also to inhibit and dampen the central "anal" conflict. (1970, p. 356)

Actually, it has been shown experimentally (Fisher 1986) that sensory stimulation of the various peripheral body parts mentioned here also affects the central attitudes that are related to wishes or conflicts associated with these sites, in either an inhibiting or stimulating way.

He continues by saying that probably one of the essential steps in mastering one's body experientially is discriminating its prime landmarks and assigning them to a cognitive map. Most of the major body regions, aside from their obvious semantic labels and designations pertinent to function, acquire consistent specialized meanings, perhaps best described as symbolic in nature. Each signifies, though rarely within conscious awareness, an interest in or a desire to avoid, certain types of experiences. Each becomes equated with a theme or a conflict. The themes largely concern basic life behaviors: incorporation, elimination, self-control, sexual aims, disposition of hostility, religiosity, exercise of power, definition of the distance between self and others.

Fisher further states (1986) that a number of studies have shown that people ascribe to their body properties that parallel the psychological impact of events they are currently encountering. He cites a number of examples, e.g., Shaffer's (1964) observation that children made to experience failure perceive themselves as relatively shorter. He even suggests that "there is a constant process of feeling that one's body is growing larger or smaller as different life conditions are encountered" (1986, 316). He suggests that one of the apparent potentialities of the body image is to represent in body experience terms what is being perceived and coded at other levels of psychic feeling and attitude.

On the basis of the very extensive research on body image, the main idea of the close connection between body experience and personality factors seems indisputable.

The second question raised at the beginning of the present chapter concerning the relationship between body concept and other aspects of personality can thus clearly be answered affirmatively. This means again that a study of the body concept may be of more general interest than just being a goal in itself. If drawings reflect the body concept, these reflections may then have wider implications for conclusions regarding the personality of the drawer.

THE RELATIONSHIP BETWEEN BODY EXPERIENCE AND HUMAN FIGURE DRAWINGS

The first question raised in the present chapter, regarding the relationship between body concept and human figure drawings, is still awaiting an answer, however. The reported results from the body experience research are, of course, no proof of the existence of such a relationship. But many of the results from this research show such consistent agreement with aspects of figure drawings, which have so far not found a plausible explanation, that the existence of a connection is highly supported. If this connection cannot be accepted as an explanation, at least another and better theory must be set forth.

The complexity of the body image is obvious. It has, therefore, little meaning to describe drawings as reflections of a person's body image in general. Specification is needed as to which aspects of the concept a certain drawing can be said to reflect.

The fact that people are found to vary considerably in their relative awareness of their bodies, as compared to other objects in the environment, may be one of the reasons for the difference in expressiveness found in human figure drawings. Some draw highly differentiated figures, in which clearly much energy is invested, and which seemingly offer the observer a lot of information, while others devote little interest to the task and produce meager drawings. These differences may have many causes, but one of them may be a different attention to and interest in the subject of the human figure itself.

The differential attention to inner versus outer body experiences reminds one of the two types of drawers, the visual and the haptic. The visual drawer was found to direct his attention predominantly toward objects in the outer world by focusing on his (visual) perception, while the haptic drawer was found to concentrate mainly on his inner sensations. These different ways of experiencing the world/expressing oneself pictorially may possibly be related to the phenomena of barrier and penetration score. These relationships are so far only hypothetical, but it should be possible to test them experimentally.

The greater body orientation of women than of men corresponds well with the results found in the present study of sex differences, where the girls were found to center their attention primarily on the figure itself, while the boys to a greater degree turned their attention away from the figure toward the surroundings. It was also found to be characteristic that the girls emphasized the prettiness and aesthetic qualities of the figure, while the boys to a greater degree tended to make ridiculous or comic figures, thus avoiding showing any positive investment in the figure itself. Moreover, the greater interest in clothing and its significance for the self-esteem of girls finds ample support in their drawings.

These findings also seem to support the idea, set forth earlier, that the subject of the human figure is one which favors girls. Their relative superiority in some aspects of figure drawings may be explained—not through their greater interest in human beings as is sometimes suggested —but through their greater attention to and investment in their own body.

What seems important, however, is the fact that these aspects of the body concept are found to be related to other personality measures and that a high awareness of the body in women seems positively linked with a high degree of individuation and ego-strength. If this is true, the girls' concentration on the body, head, and clothing in their drawings should probably generally be regarded as stages in a normal development toward individuation and not be regretted as a defensive maneuver or a mere imitation of adult models. Conversely, if it is true that high awareness of the body in men is not associated with ego-strength, the boys' drawings, with interest turned away from the drawn figure itself, should probably be regarded as equally related to a normal development. This is not to say that these traits cannot—like almost all aspects of normal development—also be used defensively. For example, a figure drawn by a girl, overwhelmed with jewelry and flower patterns, may well be an attempt at covering an underlying insecurity of one's femininity (as in real life).

It can, of course, be argued that the psychic health of adults is related to the cultural norms in the society in which they live, and that the combination of high body awareness and psychic well-functioning in women (and vice versa for men) is simply a consequence of the fact that the women who are occupied by their bodies live up to the expectations of society and therefore are regarded as—and rewarded for being— normal, and therefore in harmony with their surroundings. The fact remains, however, that pregnancy and childbirth are biologically and not culturally determined events (although culturally determined attitudes to them of course can vary). No culture has so far been able to change the different biological function of the bodies of the two sexes, and it would indeed be strange if these biological differences did not have their counterparts in differential psychological experiences of one's body. It is interesting also to note that the sex differences in body image development were outspoken already in children.

The different personality patterns associated with the differential awareness of the various body parts as well as the studies of the symbolic meaning attached to certain body parts are interesting findings, which might very well be thought to be related to differences in drawings. Some relationships can be found, but, unfortunately, the body parts chosen for the study in the body experience research are often not those that are most often shown in drawings (e.g., the heart or the back of the person). However, some of the results are highly convincing.

The results stemming from the studies of plastic surgery of the nose confirm the hypothesis of the symbolic value of this body part, which was also strongly suggested by the findings from the drawings. The studies point in the direction of a sexual symbolism connected with the nose, as do the results from the study of drawings.

The back of the figure is rarely seen in drawings so its relation to the findings of a connection between high back awareness and anal character traits cannot be confirmed. Incidentally, the only drawing in the Danish material which showed a person from the back, was of a person sitting on the toilet, an example which, of course, has only anecdotal value.

That eye awareness is generally higher in women than in men fits with the greater emphasis on eyes reflected in the drawings by the girls.

The connection between mouth awareness and anger is interesting, compared to the drawing of teeth as a sign of anger and hostility, one of the details which was found very probably to be related to aggression. That this relationship was found in men, but not in women, is in harmony with the fact that the drawing of teeth occurred twice as often in the figures by the boys than in those by the girls.

Moreover, some relationships can be found in the experienced size of the body parts. A general tendency was found for body parts in the lower extremities to be underestimated in size, while those in the head region were overestimated; particularly girls overestimated the size of the head. These tendencies are directly reflected in drawings where the head is generally disproportionately large, the legs correspondingly too short (a tendency which can also be seen in the drawings of most adults, if untrained drawers). The fact that the overestimation of the head was greatest among the girls corresponds to the results from the drawings.

That men tend to overestimate their arm length while women underestimate it, also has a clear parallel in the drawings, where boys tend to draw long arms and legs, girls short ones. It was found that the estimation of arm length (and perhaps also of other body parts?) among other things was dependent on their position and use, arms holding something, pointing toward something, or stretched out being estimated as longer than arms not in use. This fits well with the fact that both the drawing of movement and of relatively long arms (and legs) belong in the drawings of boys and supports the hypothesis that the drawing of long limbs is connected with a high activity level. It is very possible that the high activity level of the head is also one of the reasons for the systematic overestimation of its size.

The generally found tendency for men to overestimate their total size and for women to underestimate theirs, may find its expression in the long, outstretched figures of the boys and the more compact, almost compressed figures of the girls. It is probable that the attitude to body size is reflected in these aspects of the figure drawings rather than in the actual sizes of the drawn figures. The present study did find a tendency for boys to draw slightly bigger figures than girls, but this finding is not confirmed by the results from other studies, e.g., Craddick (1963), who found that college women draw larger figures than college men.

The size of the figure seems related to self-esteem. The body image research has clearly demonstrated that inferiority feelings may lead to an underestimation of own size or to a (defensive) overestimation. The clusters of emotional indicators associated with aggression versus inhibition (Koppitz 1968) also suggested that the tendency to draw a small or constricted figure was associated with inhibition and anxiety (and probably low self-esteem) whereas aggression was connected with the drawing of a figure with more expanding qualities (such as long arms and big hands). Aggression was not found related to the big size of a figure, but the connection between aggression and self-esteem is not simple; aggression may probably be connected both with high and low self-esteem.

It may be objected that many of the reported results from the studies on body experience are shown to be valid for adults only and that these results cannot without further studies be applied to children. It is true that the studies that have worked only with adults must be applied tentatively. It has been shown, however, that most of the adult body image mode appears relatively early developmentally (Fisher 1986). As early as by the age of 6 or 7 children are reasonably accurate in estimating their body size. Furthermore, Koff and Kiekhofer (1978) found a striking consistency in the degree of veridicality of judgments of body parts size among children and adults and suggested that body size judgments are perhaps more reflective of cognitive than perceptual processes. The correspondence between the children's and the adults' patterns of errors, coupled with the findings that adults consistently misjudge the sizes of certain body parts, suggests that the tendencies observed among the adults may have been established at an earlier age of development and reflect relatively stable and long-standing cognitive predispositions. Except for the probable overestimation of the role of cognition (as an isolated factor) in the process, the continuity of the pattern from childhood into adulthood is an interesting finding. But even if some of the described relationships were shown not to have validity with children, the general finding of a relationship between body experience and figure drawings is sufficiently supported to justify the conclusion that many aspects of body experience seem to be either directly or symbolically reflected in figure drawings.

An interesting aspect of the research on body experience is the generality of those patterns that were found, a result which is also emphasized by Fisher (1986). There seem to be quite general patterns which characterize, for example, the body experience of the two sexes. There seems also to be generality in the factors that influence body experience, such as the influence of activity on experienced size.

Against this background of generalities, individual patterns can be seen, however, like musical variations over a basic theme. Individuals vary in their attention to the different body parts and certainly in the amount and kind of emotion attached to them. While there may be a general human tendency, for example, to invest the nose with symbolic sexual meaning, there may be worlds of difference between the amount of energy invested in this body part and the amount and kind of emotions associated with it.

Both the general nature of these experiences and the individual variations can be seen to be reflected in drawings. The general trends show themselves in group studies such as the present one, in such aspects as general developmental traits and sex differences. The individual aspects are, of course, best found through the study of individual drawings, where the relationship can be established between traits in the drawing and personality characteristics.

The next question is, of course, how these different patterns are formed, why some persons devote great attention to their whole body or parts of it, while others invest their energy in other aspects of their total field of experience. Knowledge about this is at the present time limited, and it goes beyond the scope of this book to enter into a discussion of it. Probably, biological factors play a part, such as one's physical properties, bodily build, size, muscular strength, etc., as well as one's biological sex. But in all probability, very many cultural and environmental factors also play an important part, such as amount of physical activity, general culturally determined attention to or neglect of certain body parts, as well as individual experiences, for example through learning in the close family environment.

TEN

Conclusions

At this point, I am most understanding of and sympathetic with the authors who in their research on drawings limited themselves to the study of few and selected aspects of them. The combination of the statistical treatment of the very many details and of the broader descriptions of the emerging patterns showed itself to be more time-consuming and more complicated than expected. But much too often the more limited approaches have led to results which must be rejected as being based on incomplete and superficial data. In order to avoid this danger, the comprehensive approach was considered necessary.

As it has turned out, the drawing of a human being is seen as a process that includes very many aspects of the drawer's personality and is related to very different layers of it—from conscious perception of objects in the outer world to probably deeply unconscious aspects of his self-concept.

The Danish study differs from earlier studies in the attempt (1) to obtain a more unified view of drawings, encompassing hitherto separately treated aspects, and (2) to fit this view properly into a theoretical psychological framework.

In order to achieve these goals, the following methodological consequences were found necessary:

1. All the different aspects of drawings—developmental traits, sex differences, and clinical "signs"—were included in the study which, consequently, made it very comprehensive.
2. Although for practical purposes it was necessary to describe developmental items and sex differences separately, they are continuously related to each other and, in principle, considered inseparable.
3. A broader field of psychological theory is applied than usually, and theories are combined which are rarely set in connection with each other, such as general developmental psychology and psychoanalysis.
4. Unity is attempted in the application of theory, with concept development as the major frame of reference, but with concept development understood more widely than in earlier studies on drawings. Particular aspects of concept development, namely the concept of sexual identity and the body concept, are considered to be of special importance.
5. Great emphasis is placed on the description of the connection between empirical findings and theory, to try as far as possible to avoid theoretical speculations not based on observable data.

As mentioned, an attempt was made to combine different theoretical frames of reference such as general developmental psychology and psychoanalysis. The need for such a combination is urgent, in theory as well as in clinical practice. As a matter of fact, most practically working clinicians have to work on the basis of their own more or less private combinations of these different theoretical approaches, and most of us do so without being seriously disturbed by it. Human beings have both their rational and their irrational sides, both conscious and unconscious levels of functioning. Artificially excluding either of these aspects, or overemphasizing one at the expense of the other, may apparently make the world look simpler to everybody, but leads to one-sided and distorted results, as evidenced by much of the earlier research on drawings. This seems to be equally true, no matter which part of the totality is excluded. Thus, passing swiftly over the more basic theoretical problems which are inherent in attempts at combinations of the different theories, I have in no way been discouraged by the results, but rather confirmed in the belief that such a combination is fruitful and necessary. It gives meaning to see some aspects of drawings as determined primarily by the drawer's visual perception of his surroundings and by his attempts at problem solving, and to see other aspects as mainly determined by more or less unconscious processes, and—conversely—it seems impossible to explain them adequately on the basis of only one of the theoretical frames of reference.

GENERALIZATION OF RESULTS

With the limitation in mind that the Danish study did not attempt to establish age norms of development, the overall pattern of development found is very similar to the one described by such authors as Goodenough (1926) and Harris (1963). The development follows a similar pattern and stops at about the same age. The level of development in the Danish study is closer to the results found by Harris than to those of Goodenough, but it is impossible to say whether these differences mainly reflect sampling differences or whether they reflect actual changes in level of drawing performance over time. The same insecurity is found in Harris's own study, and the Danish results cannot help to solve this problem.

This overall similarity is what might be expected, as the general educational level of American and Danish children is probably not very different. In both cultures, small children have early and easy access to drawing and to occupation with pictures and books, and they are generally encouraged in such activities. The weight placed on the development of intellectual abilities and on education in general is not grossly different in the two countries. Outspoken differences in the developmental level of figure drawings seem mainly to appear when societies are compared that are very different in general educational levels.

In the Danish study, it was concluded that no clear dividing line could be drawn between quantitative and qualitative sex differences, as all kinds of gradual transitions between the extremes could be found. But because of the earlier distinction between these categories, it is to a certain degree necessary to return to it in the discussion.

With regard to the so-called quantitative differences, the Danish results are different from those of the early studies, but similar to those of later studies, showing a superiority among girls in some aspects of the drawing of the human figure. They are faster at introducing certain body parts and at obtaining a good motoric control. The qualitative sex differences show almost complete correspondence, apart from the fact that the Danish study gives a more comprehensive overview of a greater number of sex differences than most other studies. It can, therefore, be concluded that sex differences to a high degree can be generalized among contemporary studies and the so-called qualitative differences can also be generalized even from earlier studies.

This does not mean, however, that the understanding of their nature is also in agreement with the earlier attempts at explanation. This is not the case, and it may be convenient to summarize the differences of understanding.

It is still unknown whether the differences between earlier and later studies are real or only apparent, but it seems difficult to deny that, in all probability, there exists some real difference in the performance of particularly girls between early and late studies. This may be due to changes of treatment and expectations of girls over time. But apart from this, the differences seem mainly due to the selection of various subjects for drawing and to the emphasis on different variables in the evaluation of the drawings. It is found that girls would be judged superior in studies in which quantitative aspects of drawings are emphasized, due to their concentration on details of hair and clothing. Boys, on the other hand, might be found superior, if qualitative aspects were emphasized, due to their more frequent use of such aspects as movement and profile drawing.

It was further suggested that the drawing of a human figure may favor girls because of their interest in the depiction of that particular subject, while boys might be more interested in other subjects, for example of a more technical nature.

It must therefore be concluded that, although in the drawing of the human figure girls may be found to score higher than boys (if the drawings are scored according to some specific and commonly used criteria), this does not justify the conclusion that girls generally are ahead of boys in drawing development. And the conclusion that this (apparent) superiority in drawing is the consequence of a correspondingly greater maturity, or faster intellectual development, or of a better development of specific intellectual functions, is in no way supported. Apart from the advantages in motoric function and perhaps also the faster introduction of major body parts, which may be due to slightly earlier maturation of the girls around the beginning of school age or to possible differences in drawing patterns, the greater majority of the sex differences are seen as reflecting differences in the children's experiences of their body concept and sex differences in personality. Their universal occurrence, which is indeed surprising if they are explained as a result of socialization, becomes understandable, if they are seen as expressing basic and universal human experiences.

It was suggested in earlier studies that such traits as shading and correction/erasures probably occur too often in children's drawings to be regarded as signs of conflict. This was also confirmed in the present study. These traits cannot generally and automatically be regarded as danger signals. On the contrary, they were found to increase with age and must, in all probability, be generally regarded as developmental traits. But it is still probable that excessive shading of major body parts, which occurs rarely, may have the function of a conflict indicator. What is important is to take the specific emotional quality into consideration in evaluating each case, which excludes any mechanical sign scoring and once more confirms the necessity of the subjective element in any projective use of drawings. It was also found in the present study that excessive shading of one body part more often than not was accompanied also by shading of other body parts. This might signify a general anxiety rather than anxiety connected with a specific body part. And even if only one body part is shaded, it is difficult to know the exact meaning of that.

THE MEANING OF SEX DIFFERENCES

The sex differences were found to manifest themselves in virtually all aspects of drawings, and to be far more comprehensive than usually described. The differences found are characteristic of groups of boys and girls, but only in varying degrees of individuals. For some traits, the overlapping between the sexes is considerable, for others it is negligible. They represent general tendencies that are expressed more or less clearly by individual children. This is not only characteristic of sex differences in drawings, however, but of most sex differences in general.

It is unnecessary to repeat in detail the description and interpretation of the sex differences, which has already been presented. But it is important to note how the total pattern of sex differences in drawings can be meaningfully related to what is known about sex differences in general.

The clearly unnaturalistic features of sex differences in drawings show them convincingly to be manifestations first and foremost of the children's conceptualizations of some aspects of their body experience. These characteristics cannot possibly be explained as more or less helpless attempts at depiction of persons in their surroundings. They are rather private elaborations on the subject of a human being, determined by inner fantasies and bodily experiences as much as by visual perception.

Many of the sex differences in drawings are clearly not conscious to the drawers themselves, and sometimes the children themselves can be struck by surprise at seeing what they have drawn. More than once I have been asked by children, who suddenly see what they have drawn, why they have drawn it like that, "when people don't look like that in reality." This is no easy question to answer!

It may be important also to emphasize once more the fact that the sex differences in drawings seem connected with a basic sexual identity in both sexes, a fact which sounds self-evident, but which certainly has not always been regarded as such.

The interest in the body and its appearance should not be regarded as a defensive maneuver—not to say vanity—in girls, but as a sign of a normal narcissistic investment in their bodies which are of vital importance, not only for their personal lives, but for the continuation of the human race. This outlook is supported by the evidence that investment in the body by girls is associated with ego-strength and a successful individuation, while in boys it is the opposite.

On the other hand, the legend of a more secure sexual identification of girls—which was based on the observation of the easier recognition of the sexes in the drawings of girls (and a typical example of a quick conclusion drawn from unsatisfactory evidence)—can hopefully be finally abandoned. As shown, both age and sex are more easily recognized in the drawings of girls, due to their greater attention to hair and clothing details. As described, a healthy sexual development in boys is not manifested through attention to the body, rather the opposite. The boy who draws in profile, who draws his figure in movement, and who turns attention toward the surroundings shows in all probability as good a sexual identity as the girl, who concentrates on the body.

In the same way, any inference about sexual identity from first drawn sex or any other single trait in drawings can hopefully be avoided in the future.

In light of the earlier reservations concerning the possibility of objectivity in research on sex differences, the results of the study may perhaps be suspected of being only a confirmation of the author's preconceived standpoints. Other persons may judge to see if they find the conclusions here justified or not, but the results were certainly not known to me beforehand. Whereas the results regarding development admittedly were no great surprise, the coherence of the patterns of sex differences was a new discovery, and their relationship with other aspects of sex differences in children and with aspects of body experience were at the beginning unknown to me.

It is also possible that some will be very little satisfied by the results and see a danger in the picture of sex differences presented here. I am aware that the results might be used in an argumentation for women's "natural role" as primarily mothers and taken as support for a society where men are encouraged to take care of world affairs and women restricted to the narrow sphere of the home. Some would probably have preferred to see the sex differences described more in the way done by Koppitz (1968), as relatively superficial dimensions acquired through a (somewhat unfortunate) socialization. But data in a study take their own course. All you can do is to try to follow them, to see where they lead, and to try to describe as honestly as you can what you see on your way —whether it suits you or not. And if the results conflict with your attitudes, hopefully it is the attitudes that become more differentiated and not the data that are distorted. Besides, you can try to foresee and warn against possible misuses of your results.

It should be emphasized that it is not intended by this to argue for a return to hopefully abandoned ideas about men's and (first and foremost) women's "natural" roles in society. The idea of deep-seated, fundamental sex differences does not necessarily and automatically lead to social repression of one of the sexes.

But if the perception of oneself and of the world is colored in different nuances for members of the two sexes even early in their development, it is of no help to anyone to try to deny it. A differential treatment based on the recognition of existing differences should lead to better results than equal treatment based on a denial of differences.

Besides, it must be emphasized that we are talking of children and not of adults. Of course, children go on developing after the age of 13 where the Danish study leaves them, and what we are discussing here are not the final attitudes of adult men and women, but stages on the way toward them.

What the study may teach us is to be acceptant of the differences as they manifest themselves in children's drawings, not to disregard them as signs of conflict or defense, but to understand them as necessary stages in the development toward a well-developed adult sexual identity. This, again, is of course not the same as seeing every and any manifesta-

tion of them as equally good; a differentiated evaluation of these qualities is as necessary as in any other area of child development.

THE BASIC FUNCTION OF HUMAN FIGURE DRAWINGS

A basic question was raised to what extent children's human figure
drawings reflect their visual perception of the environment and to what
extent they reflect aspects of the drawer's body image or self-concept.
The answer to this question can only be approximate.

Already the results from earlier research on the Goodenough/Harris
test (1963) showed clearly that, although there is a positive relationship
between intellectual level (broadly defined) and drawing performance,
the correspondence is far from complete. And—as earlier stated—the
sex differences in the performance on the test cannot be explained
through referral to cognitive sex differences. It has repeatedly been
shown that any kind of physical or psychic disturbance interferes with
the results of the test to a higher degree than in other intelligence tests.

Therefore, it is obvious that some aspects of the drawer's total personality other than the merely intellectual ones take part in the drawing
performance.

The main problem with the drawing test, as far as can be seen, lies in
a misconception of the generality of the conceptual development which
the drawn figure represents. Drawing development is certainly related to
concept development. But drawing is not related to concept development
and intellectual level in general, but to the development of that particular
concept which is the subject of the drawing. Both Goodenough (1926)
and Harris (1963) seem to have almost totally disregarded the importance of the subjective experience of one's own body and its influence on
the development of the body concept. The human figure is conceived by
them primarily as an object in the outer world that can be examined and
looked at as objectively as a table or a chair.

These considerations lead necessarily to the conclusion that what is
"measured" by the Goodenough/Harris test is a much more specific
aspect of concept development than that which the test was supposed to
measure. It is, of course, possible to find children who have a generally
good concept development, and who also have a well-developed body
concept. But in all the many instances where the body concept is not so
well developed, it is impossible without further information to say whether

it is due to a generally slow concept development, or whether it is caused by much more specific disturbances of body experience. The development of the body concept is naturally related to other aspects of concept development, and the total level of intellectual capacities sets limits on the development of this concept as well as on all others. The general level of conceptual development is a necessary, but not a sufficient condition for the final developmental level of the body concept.

Children's drawings of the human figure show with all clarity that perception of surrounding persons is not the only influential factor. The Danish study demonstrated that particularly the younger children are not at all lifelike in their drawing of, for example, clothes and hair. It is not until relatively late in childhood that the symbolic traits are replaced by more realistic ones. It is known that a child's ability to observe analytically is not developed until late in childhood, and until then—as amply described by Werner (1964)—inner fantasies and symbolic imagery influence drawing performance. The role played by motoric, sensoric, and affective functions is extremely important in concept formation, the more so the younger the child, and any theory that isolates concept formation as a purely cognitive function falls short of understanding it adequately. Werner described the principles of concept development in general, but his principles may, of course, also be applied with advantage to the development of the body concept and the sexual identity.

Body experience influences drawings in various ways. Some aspects of it seem to be almost universal and can be recognized in almost all children's drawings. This is, for example, the case with some very common size distortions such as the overestimation of the size of the head or of limbs in activity. The same can be said about the sex-specific characterizations of the body, which are universal for each sex, respectively. At the other extreme, individuals may invest particular body parts with very private, symbolic meanings, which may show themselves in their drawings in very personal and specific ways. Bizarre ears, feet, trunk, or any other body part may be drawn, or special details emphasized in clothing. In still other cases, body parts seem to have an intermediate position between the general and the specific, tending to invite symbolic investment more or less easily. An example of this is the nose, the symbolic meaning of which has been demonstrated in the drawings. The transformation of bodily experiences into drawings seems thus to lie on a continuum from the very general to the highly personal. As demonstrated by the research of Fisher (1970, 1986), people vary in the amount of attention they give to their body, both in general and toward the various parts of it, and these differences will in all probability manifest themselves in the degree of expressiveness of their drawings.

I recognize that there may be still other sources of children's drawings than their observation of other persons or their own body experience, for example their observations of other pictures, both printed pictures and other children's drawings. The influence of these sources is not evident in the present material, however. The drawings are surprisingly little influenced by cartoon-figures or commercial stereotypes; of the 540 drawings, not one represents an attempt to copy any of the well-known cartoon-figures or other stereotypes. The (very few) drawings that show a distorted or bizarre figure have a definitely private stamp. This is not to say that these sources are never influential, but their influence cannot be traced in the Danish study. It would indeed also be difficult to explain, for example, the sex differences found in drawings as imitations of sex stereotypes in commercial pictures, as they do not show much similarity to them.

The connection between body experience and drawing is complicated and is probably best understood if some of the qualities of analogic language are brought to mind again. Identical experiences may manifest themselves identically, but they may also manifest themselves in different symbols on paper, although possibly physiognomically related. On the other hand, different bodily experiences may manifest themselves in similar ways of expression. The lack of possibility of expressing negation except through the presence of that which is negated and the lack of distinction between past, present, and future adds further to the complications.

There will never be unequivocality between body experiences and their manifestations in drawings. But the fundamental question, namely whether body experience manifests itself in drawings, must be answered in the affirmative.

People vary in the attention given to their own body and to their surroundings, they vary in their receptivity to visual and to internal bodily stimuli, and they vary in the specific symbolic meanings attached to various body parts. This means that different drawings will reflect the drawer's perception of the outer world and of his inner world in quite varying degrees. The question to what degree drawings reflect one or the other must therefore be answered for each individual drawing and can never be answered in general. And not only each drawing, but each single trait in a drawing is a compromise between all these different influences.

This does not mean, however, that drawings are without value in the assessment of personality. A global evaluation that is sensitive to the emotional, physiognomic qualities of the drawings and is particularly attentive to the more personal and nonnaturalistic qualities of them, can certainly be valuable and informative. And the results of the Danish study support the intuitively founded belief that the information contained in drawings can give evidence not only of the drawer's body experience, but also of other important and central aspects of his personality.

References

Abraham, K. (1927). The influence of oral eroticism on character formation. In: Jones, E. (ed.). *Selected papers of Karl Abraham*. London: Hogarth Press.

Adams, N. M., and Caldwell, W. E. (1963). The children's somatic apperception test. *Journal of General Psychology, 68,* 43–57.

Ansbacher, H. L. (1952). The Goodenough Draw-A-Man test and primary mental abilities. *Journal of Consulting Psychology, 16,* 176–180.

Anthony, J. E. (1970). Behavior disorders. In: Mussen, P. H. (ed.). *Carmichael's Manual of Child Psychology*, vol. 2. New York: Wiley.

Apfeldorf, M., and Smith, J. (1965). The representation of the body self in human figure drawings. Presented at annual meeting of Eastern Psychological Association, Atlantic City, N.J. In: Fisher, S. (ed.). (1970). *Body Experience in fantasy and behavior*. New York: Meredith Corp.

Armon, V. (1960). Some personality variables in overt female homosexuality. *Journal of Projective Techniques, 24,* 292–309.

Arnheim, R. (1954). *Art and visual perception*. Berkeley: Univ. of California Press.

Ballard, P. B. (1913). What children like to draw. *Journal of Experimental Pedagogy and Training College Record, 2,* 127–129.

Barker, A. J., Mathis, J. K., and Powers, C. (1953). Drawing characteristics of male homosexuals. *Journal of Clinical Psychology, 9,* 185–189.

Beach, F. A. (1965). Retrospect and prospect. In: Beach, F. A. (ed.). *Sex and behavior*. New York: Wiley.

Beller, E. K., and Turner, J. (1964). Personality correlates of children's perceptions of human size. *Child Development, 35,* 441–449.

Bender, L. (1940). The drawing of a man in chronic encephalitis in children. *Journal of Mental and Nervous Diseases, 41, 277–286.*

———. (1967). Psychological problems of children with organic brain disease. In: Frierson, E. C., and Barbe, W. B. (eds.). *Educating children with learning disabilities.* New York: Appleton-Century-Crofts.

Benjamin, H. (1964). Clinical aspects of transsexualism in the male and female. *American Journal of Psychotherapy, 18, 458–469.*

Bennett, V. (1964). Does size of figure drawing reflect self concept? *Journal of Consulting Psychology, 28, 285–286.*

———. (1966). Combinations of figure drawing characteristics related to drawer's self concept. *Journal of Projective Techniques, 30, 192–196.*

Berkowitz, K. S. (1980). Judgments of body size and body satisfaction. Unpublished doctoral dissertation, Case Western Reserve Univ. In: Fisher, S. (ed.). (1986). *Development and structure of the body image.* Hillsdale, N.J.: Lawrence Erlbaum Ass.

Berman, S., and Laffal, J. (1953). Body type and figure drawing. *Journal of Clinical Psychology, 9, 368–370.*

Berrien, F. K. (1935). A study of the drawings of abnormal children. *Journal of Educational Psychology, 26, 143–150.*

Bodwin, R. R., and Bruch, M. (1960). The adaptation and validation of the Draw-A-Person test as a measure of self concept. *Journal of Clinical Psychology, 16, 427–429.*

Brill, M. A. (1937). A study of instability using the Goodenough Drawing Scale. *Journal of Abnormal and Social Psychology, 32, 288–302.*

Broverman, I. K., Broverman, D. M., Clarkson, F. E., Rosenkrantz, P. S., and Vogel, S. R. (1970). Sex-role stereotypes and clinical judgments of mental health. *Journal of Consulting and Clinical Psychology, 34, 1–7.*

Brown, D. G. (1956). Sex-role preference in young children. *Psychological Monographs, 70, no. 421.*

Brown, D. G., and Tolor, A. (1957). Human figure drawings as indicators of sexual identification and inversion. *Perceptual and Motor Skills, 7, 199–211.*

Buck, J. N. (1948). The H-T-P technique: A quantitative and qualitative scoring manual. *Clinical Psychological Monographs, 5, 1–120.*

Burt, C. (1921). *Mental and scholastic tests.* London: P. S. King.

Caligor, L. (1951). The determination of the individual's unconscious conception of his own masculine-feminine identification. *Journal of Projective Techniques, 15, 494–509.*

Cantril, H., and Allport, C. (1933). Recent applications of the study of values. *Journal of Abnormal and Social Psychology, 28, 259–273.*

Centers, L., and Centers, R. A. (1963). A comparison of the body images of amputee and non-amputee children as revealed in figure drawing. *Journal of Projective Techniques and Personality Assessment, 27, 158–165.*

Chasseguet-Smirgel, J. (ed.). (1981). *Female sexuality.* London: Virago.

Cleveland, S. E., Fisher, S., Reitman, E. E., and Rothaus, P. (1962). Perception of body size in schizophrenia. *Archives of General Psychiatry, 7, 277–285.*

Cohen, D. N. (1933). The Goodenough Drawing Scale applied to thirteen-year-old children. Unpublished master's thesis, Columbia Univ. In: Harris, D. B. (ed.). (1963). *Children's drawings as measures of intellectual maturity*. New York: Harcourt, Brace & World.

Cohen, D., and Wilkie, F. (1979). Sex-related differences in cognition among the elderly. In: Wittig, M. A., and Petersen, A. C. (eds.). *Sex-related differences in cognitive functioning. Developmental issues*. New York: Academic Press.

Cohen, S., Money, J., and Uhlenhuth, E. (1972). A computer study of selected features of self-and-other drawings by 385 children. *Journal of Learning Disabilities, 5(3)*, 145–155.

Colligan, R. C. (1967). Learning inhibitions in children related to their HFDs. *Psychology in the Schools, 4*, 328–330.

Connolly, K., and Stratton, P. (1968). Developmental changes in associated movements. *Developmental Medicine and Child Neurology, 10*, 49–56.

Corah, N. L., and Corah, P. L. (1963). A study of body image in children with cleft palate and cleft lip. *Journal of General Psychology, 103*, 133–137.

Cormack, P. H. (1966). A study of the relationship between body image and perception of physical disability. Unpublished doctoral dissertation, State Univ. of New York at Buffalo. In: Fisher, S. (ed.). (1986). *Development and structure of the body image*. Hillsdale, N.J.: Lawrence Erlbaum Ass.

Craddick, R. A. (1963). The self-image in the DAP Test and self portrait drawings. *Journal of Projective Techniques, 27*, 288–291.

Cutter, F. (1956). Sexual differentiation in figure drawings and overt deviation. *Journal of Clinical Psychology, 12*, 369–372.

Datta, L. E., and Drake, A. K. (1968). Examiner sex and sexual differentiation in preschool children's figure drawings. *Journal of Projective Techniques, 32*, 397–399.

David, R. B. (1975). Sensitivity of body cues and the field dependence-independence continuum. Unpublished doctoral dissertation. Columbia Univ. In: Fisher, S. (ed.). (1986). *Development and structure of the body image*. Hillsdale, N.J.: Lawrence Erlbaum Ass.

de Chiara, E. (1982). A visual arts program for enhancement of the body image. *Journal of Learning Disabilities, 15*, 399–405.

Delatte, J. G., Jr., and Hendrickson, N. J. (1982). Human figure drawing size as a measure of self-esteem. *Journal of Personality Assessment, 46*, 603–606.

Des Lauriers, A., and Halpern, F. (1947). Psychological tests in childhood schizophrenia. *American Journal of Orthopsychiatry, 17*, 57–67.

Desai, K. (1958). Developmental stages in drawing a cow. Unpublished B.A. thesis, Univ. of Baroda, India. In: Harris, D. B. (ed.). (1963). *Children's drawings as measures of intellectual maturity*. New York: Harcourt, Brace & World.

Deutsch, F. (1952). Analytic posturology. *Psychoanalytic Quarterly, 21*, 196–214.

Diamond, M. (1965). A critical evaluation of the ontogeny of human sexual behavior. *Quarterly Review of Biology, 40*, 147–175.

Diamond, S. (1954a). The house and tree in verbal phantasy. I: Age and sex differences in themes and content. *Journal of Projective Techniques, 18,* 316–325.

———. (1954b). The house and tree in verbal phantasy. II: Their different roles. *Journal of Projective Techniques, 18,* 415–417.

Dines, P. J. (1982). The applicability of the body image construct to the drawing of human figures. Unpublished doctoral dissertation. George Washington Univ. In: Fisher, S. (ed.). (1986). *Development and structure of the body image.* Hillsdale, N.J.: Lawrence Erlbaum Ass.

DuBois, P. H. (1939). A test standardized on Pueblo Indian children. *Psychological Bulletin, 36,* 523 (abstract). In: Harris, D. B. (ed.). (1963). *Children's drawings as measures of intellectual maturity.* New York: Harcourt, Brace & World.

Dunn, J. A. (1967). Inter- and intra-rater reliability of the new Harris-Goodenough D-A-M test. *Perceptual and Motor Skills, 24,* 269–270.

Dwyer, C. A. (1979). The role of tests and their construction in producing apparent sex-related differences. In: Wittig, M. A., and Petersen, A. C. (eds.). *Sex-related differences in cognitive functions. Developmental issues.* New York: Academic Press.

Edwards, B. (1979). *Drawing on the right side of the brain.* Los Angeles: J. P. Tarcher.

Eggers, M. M. (1931). Comparison of Army Alpha and Goodenough drawings in delinquent women. Unpublished master's thesis, Columbia Univ. In: Harris, D. B. (ed.). (1963). *Children's drawings as measures of intellectual maturity.* New York: Harcourt, Brace & World.

Fay, H. M. (1923). Une méthode pour le dépistage des arriérés dans les grandes collectivités d'enfants d'âge scolaire. *Bulletin de la ligue d'hygiène mentale.*

Fenichel, O. (1945). *The psychoanalytic theory of neurosis.* New York: Norton.

Ferenczi, S. (1911). Stimulation of the anal erotogenic zone as a precipitating factor in paranoia. In: Ferenczi (1955). *Selected papers of Ferenczi.* New York: Basic Books.

Fillenbaum, S. (1961). How fat is fat? Some consequences of similarity between judge and judged object. *Journal of Psychology, 52,* 133–136.

Fisher, S. (1964). Power orientation and concept of self height in men: Preliminary note. *Perceptual and Motor Skills, 18,* 732.

———. (1970). *Body experience in fantasy and behavior.* New York: Meredith Corp.

———. (1986). *Development and structure of the body image.* Hillsdale, N.J.: Lawrence Erlbaum Ass.

Fisher, S., and Cleveland, S. E. (1958). *Body image and personality.* Princeton, N.J.: Van Nostrand.

Fisk, S. B. (1981). Body image in facially deformed children ages four to seven. Unpublished doctoral dissertation, The Fielding Institute. In: Fisher, S. (ed.). (1986). *Development and structure of the body image.* Hillsdale, N.J.: Lawrence Erlbaum Ass.

Flaccus, L. W. (1906). Remarks on the psychology of clothes. *Pedagogical Seminary, 13,* 61–83.

Fowler, R. D. (1953). The relationship of social acceptance to discrepancies between the IQ scores on the Stanford-Binet Intelligence Scale and the Goodenough Draw-A-Man Test. Unpublished master's thesis, Univ. of Alabama. In: Harris D. B. (ed.). (1963). *Children's drawings as measures of intellectual maturity.* New York: Harcourt, Brace & World.

Freud, S. (1908). Character and anal eroticism. In Freud (1924). *Collected papers,* vol. 2. London: Hogarth Press.

———. (1914). On narcissism, an introduction. In: Freud (1925). *Collected papers,* vol. 4. London: Hogarth Press.

Furlong, A. (1977). The impact of feelings of subjective deformity on configurational body-size perception. Unpublished doctoral dissertation, Univ. of Montreal. In: Fisher, S. (ed.). (1986). *Development and structure of the body image.* Hillsdale, N.J.: Lawrence Erlbaum Ass.

Gellert, E. (1968). Comparisons of children's self-drawings with their drawings of other persons. *Perceptual and Motor Skills, 26,* 123–138.

———. (1975). Children's constructions of their self-images. *Perceptual and Motor Skills, 40,* 307–324.

Gellert, E., and Stern, J. B. (1964). Age and sex differences in children's judgments of their height and body proportions. Presented at annual meeting of American Psychology Ass., Los Angeles. In: Fisher, S. (ed.). (1970). *Body experience in fantasy and behavior.* New York: Meredith Corp.

Gibson, J. J. (1950). *The perception of the visual world.* Boston: Houghton Mifflin.

Goodenough, F. (1926). *Measurement of intelligence by drawings.* New York: Harcourt, Brace & World.

Goodnow, J. (1977). *Children's drawings.* London: Fontana.

Grams, A., and Rinder, L. (1958). Signs of homosexuality in human figure drawings. *Journal of Consulting Psychology, 22,* 394.

Gravitz, M. A. (1966). Normal adult differentiation patterns on the figure drawing test. *Journal of Projective Techniques, 30,* 471–473.

Greenacre, P. (1955). Further considerations regarding fetishism. *Psychoanalytic Study of the Child, 10,* 187–194.

———. (1958). Early physical determinants in the development of the sense of identity. *Journal of the American Psychoanalytic Association, 6,* 612–627.

Grözinger, W. (1971). *Kradseri, tegneri, maleri.* Copenhagen: Clausens forlag.

Grunberger, B. (1981). Outline for a study of narcissism in female sexuality. In: Chasseguet-Smirgel, J. (ed.). (1981). *Female sexuality.* London: Virago.

Guinan, J. F., and Hurley, J. R. (1965). An investigation of the reliability of human figure drawings. *Journal of Projective Techniques, 29,* 300–304.

Hall, G. S. (1898). Some aspects of the early sense of self. *American Journal of Psychology, 9,* 351–395.

Hammer, E. F. (1954). Relationship between diagnosis of psychosexual pathology and the sex of the first drawn person. *Journal of Clinical Psychology, 10,* 168–170.

Hammer, E. F. (1958). *The clinical application of projective drawings.* Springfield, Ill.: Charles C. Thomas.

———. (1959). Critique of Swensen's "Empirical evaluations of human figure drawings." *Journal of Projective Techniques, 23,* 30–32.

Hammer, E. F., and Piotrowsky, Z. A. (1953). Hostility as a factor in the clinician's personality as it affects his interpretation of projective drawings (H-T-P). *Journal of Projective Techniques, 17,* 210–216.

Hammer, M., and Kaplan, A. (1964). The reliability of sex of first figure drawn by children. *Journal of Clinical Psychology, 20,* 251–252.

Hampson, J. L. (1965). Determinants of psychosexual orientation. In: Beach, F. A. (ed.). *Sex and behavior.* New York: Wiley.

Handler, L. (1967). Anxiety indices in the DAP test. A scoring manual. *Journal of Projective Techniques and Personality Assessment, 31,* 46–57.

Handler, L., and Reyher, J. (1965). Figure drawing anxiety indices: a review. *Journal of Projective Techniques, 29,* 305–313.

Hanvik, L. J. (1953). The Goodenough test as a measure of intelligence of child psychiatric patients. *Journal of Clinical Psychology, 9,* 71–72.

Harlow, R. G. (1951). Masculine inadequacy and compensatory development of physique. *Journal of Personality, 19,* 312–323.

Harris, D. B. (1963). *Children's drawings as measures of intellectual maturity.* New York: Harcourt, Brace & World.

Hart, H. H. (1950). The eye in symbol and symptoms. *The Yearbook of Psychoanalysis, 6,* 256–275.

Hartman, R. K. (1972). An investigation of the incremental validity of human figure drawings in the diagnosis of learning disabilities. *Journal of School Psychology, 10,* 9–16.

Havighurst, K. J., and Janke, L. L. (1944). Relations between ability and social status in a midwestern community. I: Ten-year-old children. *Journal of Educational Psychology, 35,* 357–368.

Haworth, M. R., and Normington, C. J. (1961). A sexual differentiation scale for the D-A-P test. *Journal of Projective Techniques, 25,* 441–450.

Heider, F., and Simmel, M. (1944). An experimental study of apparent behavior. *American Journal of Psychology, 57,* 243–259.

Heinrich, P., and Triebe, J. K. (1972). Sex preferences in children's HFDs. *Journal of Personality Assessment, 36,* 263–267.

Hinckley, E. D., and Retlingshafer, D. (1951). Value judgments of heights of men by college students. *Journal of Psychology, 31,* 257–262.

Hinrichs, W. E. (1935). The Goodenough Drawing Test in relation to delinquency and problem behavior. *Archives of Psychology, 175,* 82.

Holtzman, W. H. (1952). The examiner as a variable in the DAP test. *Journal of Consulting Psychology, 16,* 145–148.

Humphries, O. A. (1959). Effect of articulation of fingertip through touch on apparent length of outstretched arm. Unpublished master's thesis, Clark Univ.

In: Fisher, S. (ed.). (1970). *Body experience in fantasy and behavior.* New York: Meredith Corp.

Hunt, R. G., and Feldman, M. J. (1960). Body image and ratings of adjustment on human figure drawings. *Journal of Clinical Psychology, 16,* 35–38.

Jacobson, W. E., Edgerton, M. T., Meyer, E., Canter, A., and Slaughter, R. (1960). Psychiatric evaluation of male patients seeking cosmetic surgery. *Plastic and Reconstructive Surgery and the Transplantation Bulletin, 26,* 356–372.

Johnson, D., and Myklebust, H. (1967). *Learning disabilities.* New York: Grune & Stratton.

Johnson, O. G., and Wawrzaszek, F. (1961). Psychologists' judgments of physical handicap from H-T-P drawings. *Journal of Consulting Psychology, 25,* 284–287.

Jourard, S. M., and Secord, P. F. (1954). Body size and body cathexis. *Journal of Consulting Psychology, 18,* 184.

Kamano, D. K. (1960). An investigation of the meaning of human figure drawing. *Journal of Clinical Psychology, 16,* 429–430.

Kandel, D., and Lesser, G. (1972). *Youth in two worlds: United States and Denmark.* San Francisco: Jossey-Bass.

Kellogg, R. (1959). *What children scribble and why.* 570 Union Str., San Francisco: Author.

Kerschensteiner, G. (1905). *Die Entwickelung der zeichnerischen Begabung.* Munich: Gerber.

Klein, M. (1975). *The psychoanalysis of children.* New York: Dell.

Koff, E., and Kiekhofer, M. (1978). Body-part size estimation in children. *Perceptual and Motor Skills, 47,* 1047–1050.

Koppitz, E. (1968). *Psychological evaluation of children's human figure drawings.* New York: Grune & Stratton.

Korchin, S. J., and Heath, H. A. (1961). Somatic experience in the anxiety state: Some sex and personality correlates of "autonomic feedback." *Journal of Consulting Psychology, 25,* 398–404.

Kotkov, B., and Goodman, M. (1953). The Draw-A-Person Test of obese women. *Journal of Clinical Psychology, 9,* 362–364.

Kramer, J. (1959). *Intelligenztest.* Solothurn: St. Antonius Verlag.

Krauss, R. (1930). Über graphischen Ausdruck. *Zeitschrift für angewandte Psychologie, suppl. 48,* 1–141.

Kurtzberg, R. L., Cavior, N., and Lipton, D. S. (1966). Sex drawn first and sex drawn larger by opiate addict and non-addict inmates on the Draw-A-Person Test. *Journal of Projective Techniques, 30,* 55–58.

Kvale, J. N., and Fishman, J. R. (1965). The psychological aspects of Klinefelter's syndrome. *Journal of the American Medical Association, 193,* 567–572.

Kyng, B. (1973). *Koppitz's tegnetest på 5-års børn.* Århus: Psykologisk Inst.

Laird, J. T. (1962a). A comparison of female normals, psychiatric patients and alcoholics, for sex drawn first. *Journal of Clinical Psychology, 18,* 473.

Laird, J. T. (1962b). A comparison of male normals, psychiatric patients and alcoholics for sex drawn first. *Journal of Clinical Psychology, 18,* 302.

Levinger, L. (1966). Children's drawings as indicators of sexual discrimination. *Dissertation Abstracts, 27,* 2873–2874.

Levy, L. R. (1931). The function of the Goodenough Drawing Scale in the study of high school freshmen. Unpublished master's thesis, Columbia Univ. In: Harris, D. B. (ed.). (1963). *Children's drawings as measures of intellectual maturity.* New York: Harcourt, Brace & World.

Levy, S. (1950). Figure drawing as a projective test. In: Abt, L. E., and Bellak, L. (eds.). *Projective psychology.* New York: Knopf.

Lewis, N. (1928). Graphic art productions in schizophrenia. *Research in Nervous and Mental Diseases, 5,* 344–368.

Litt, A., and Margolies, A. (1966). Sex-change in successive DAP tests. *Journal of Clinical Psychology, 22,* 471.

Lowenfeld, V. (1947). *Creative and mental growth.* New York: Macmillan.

Ludwig, D. J. (1969). Self-perception and the Draw-A-Person Test. *Journal of Projective Techniques and Personality Assessment, 33,* 257–261.

Lukens, H. (1896). A study of children's drawings in the early years. *Pedagogical Seminary, 4,* 79–110.

Lundholm, H. (1921). The affective tone of lines. *Psychological Revue, 28,* 43–60.

Luquet, G. H. (1913). *Les dessins d'un enfant.* Paris: F. Alcan.

Lynn, D. B. (1959). A note on sex differences in the development of masculine and feminine identification. *Psychological Revue, 66,* 126–135.

Maccoby, E. E., and Jacklin, C. N. (1974). *The psychology of sex differences.* Stanford: Stanford Univ. Press.

Machover, K. (1949). *Personality projection in the drawing of the human figure.* Springfield, Ill.: Charles C. Thomas.

———. (1953). Human figure drawings of children. *Journal of Projective Techniques, 17,* 85–91.

———. (1960). Sex differences in the developmental pattern of children as seen in human figure drawings. In: Rabin, A. I., and Haworth, M. R. (eds.). *Projective techniques with children.* New York: Grune & Stratton.

Mahler, M. S., Pine, F., and Bergman, A. (1975). *The psychological birth of the human infant.* New York: Basic Books.

Maitland, L. (1895). What children draw to please themselves. *Inland Educator, 1,* 87.

Matthews, W. H. (1971). An investigation of a perceptual motor and body awareness training program with culturally limited kindergarten age children. Unpublished doctoral dissertation, Univ. of Tennessee. In: Fisher, S. (ed.). (1986). *Development and structure of the body image.* Hillsdale, N.J.: Lawrence Erlbaum Ass.

McAninch, M. (1966). Body image as related to perceptual-cognitive-motor disabilities. In: Hellmuth, J. (ed.). *Learning disorders,* vol. 2. Seattle: Special Child Publ.

McCarthy, D. (1944). A study of the reliability of the Goodenough Drawing Test of intelligence. *Journal of Psychology, 18,* 201–206.

McCarthy, H. (1973). Use of the Draw-A-Person Test to evaluate a dance therapy program. *Journal of Music Therapy, 10,* 141–155.

McElwee, E. W. (1932). The reliability of the Goodenough Intelligence Test used with sub-normal children fourteen years of age. *Journal of Applied Psychology, 16,* 217–218.

McHugh, A. (1963). Sexual identification, size, and age associations in children's figure drawings. *Journal of Clinical Psychology, 19,* 381–382.

———. (1965). Age associations in children's figure drawings. *Journal of Clinical Psychology, 21,* 429–431.

Meyer, E., Jacobson, W. E., Edgerton, M. T., and Canter, A. (1960). Motivational patterns in patients seeking elective plastic surgery. *Psychosomatic Medicine, 22,* 194–203.

Money, J., and Ehrhardt, A. E. (1973). *Man and woman, boy and girl.* Baltimore: Johns Hopkins Univ. Press.

Money, J., and Pollit, E. (1964). Cytogenetic and psychosexual ambiguity. *Archives of General Psychiatry, 11,* 589–595.

Money, J., and Wang, C. (1966). Human figure drawing. I: Sex of first choice in gender-identity anormalities, Klinefelter's syndrome and precocious puberty. *Journal of Mental and Nervous Diseases, 143,* 157–162.

Moore, J. E. (1940). A further study of sex differences in speed of reading. *Peabody Journal of Education, 17,* 359–362.

Mordkoff, A. M. (1966). Some sex differences in personality correlates of "Autonomic Feedback." *Psychological Reports, 18,* 511–518.

Mortensen, K. V. (1984). *Children's human figure drawings.* Copenhagen: Dansk psykologisk forlag.

Moustgård, I. K. (1962). Børns tegninger—perceptionspsykologisk belyst. *Formning,* 154–166.

———. (1964). Konstansfænomenernes betydning for børns billedsprog. *Formning,* 160–167.

Muchow, M. (1926). *Beiträge zur psychologischen Charakteristik des Kindergarten- und Grundschulalters.* Berlin: Herbig.

Müller, R. (1970). Eine kritische empirische Untersuchung des "Draw-a-man test" und der "coloured progressive matrices." *Diagnostica, 16,* 138–147.

Murray, D. C., and Deabler, H. L. (1958). Drawings, diagnoses, and the clinician's learning curve. *Journal of Projective Techniques, 22,* 415–420.

Nash, H. (1951). The estimation of body size in relation to actual body size. Personal ethos and developmental status. Unpublished doctoral dissertation, Univ. of California. In: Fisher, S. (ed.). (1970). *Body experience in fantasy and behavior.* New York: Meredith Corp.

———. (1958). Assignment of gender to body regions. *Journal of General Psychology, 92,* 113–115.

Nathan, S. (1973). Body image in chronically obese children as reflected in figure drawings. *Journal of Personality Assessment, 37,* 456–463.

Nebes, R. (1974). Hemispheric specialization in commisurotomized man. *Psychological Bulletin, 81,* 1–14.

Nichols, R. C., and Strümpfer, D. J. (1962). A factor analysis of DAP test scores. *Journal of Consulting Psychology, 26,* 156–161.

Nielsen, H. H. (1961). Human figure drawings by normal and physically handicapped children. *Scandinavian Journal of Psychology, 2,* 129–138.

Oetzel, R. (1962). Selected bibliography on sex differences. Mimeogr. report, Stanford Univ. In: Nash, J. (ed.). (1970). *Developmental psychology.* Englewood Cliffs, N.J.: Prentice-Hall.

Palmer, H. R. (1953). The relationship of differences between Stanford-Binet and Goodenough IQ's to personal adjustment as indicated by the California Test of Personality. Unpublished master's thesis, Univ. of Alabama. In: Harris, D. B. (ed.). (1963). *Children's drawings as measures of intellectual maturity.* New York: Harcourt, Brace & World.

Partridge, L. (1902). Children's drawings of men and women. In: Barnes, E. (ed.). *Studies in education.* Philadelphia: n.p.

Pechoux, R., Kohler, M., and Girard, V. (1947). Réflexions sur l'évaluation de l'intelligence chez les enfants irréguliers. *Journal de médecine de Lyon, 28,* 337–343.

Peretti, P. O. (1969). Cross-sex and cross-educational level performance in a color-word interference task. *Psychonomic Science, 79,* 67–70.

Petersen, A. C., and Wittig, M. A. (1979). Sex-related differences in cognitive functioning: an overview. In: Wittig, M. A. and Petersen, A. C. (eds.). *Sex-related differences in cognitive functioning. Developmental issues.* New York: Academic Press.

Peterson, E. G., and Williams, J. M. (1930). Intelligence of deaf children as measured by drawings. *American Annals of the Deaf, 75,* 273–290.

Phatak, P. (1959). A study of the revised Goodenough Scale with reference to artistic and non-artistic drawings. Unpubl. mimeogr. author, Univ. of Baroda, India. In: Harris, D. B. (ed.). (1963). *Children's drawings as measures of intellectual maturity.* New York: Harcourt, Brace & World.

Piaget, J. (1951). Die Psychologie der frühen Kindheit. In: Katz, D. (ed.): *Handbuch der Psychologie.* Bâle: n.p.

Pikulski, J. (1972). A comparison of figure drawings and Wisc IQs among disabled readers. *Journal of Learning Disabilities, 5,* 156–159.

Pollit, E., Hirsch, S., and Money, J. (1961). Priapism, impotence and human figure drawing. *Journal of Mental and Nervous Diseases, 139,* 161–168.

Potts, N. H. (1970). Effect of sensory-motor training on the body image concept of preschool children. Unpublished doctoral dissertation, Texas Women's Univ. In: Fisher, S. (ed.). (1986). *Development and structure of the body image.* Hillsdale, N.J.: Lawrence Erlbaum Ass.

Reichenberg-Hackett, W. (1953). Changes in Goodenough drawings after a gratifying experience. *American Journal of Orthopsychiatry, 23,* 501–517.

Rey, A. (1946). Epreuves de dessin témoins du développement mental. I. *Archives de psychologie, Genève, 31,* 369–380.

Ricci, C. (1887). *L'arte dei bambini*. Bologna: Zanchelli.

Richey, M. H. (1965). Qualitative superiority of the "Self" figure in children's drawings. *Journal of Clinical Psychology, 21,* 59–61.

Roback, H. B. (1968). Human figure drawings: their utility in the clinical psychologist's armamentarium for personality assessment. *Psychological Bulletin, 70,* 1–19.

Roberts, J. (1972). Intellectual development of children by demographic and socioeconomic factors. *Department of Health, Education and Welfare Publication No. (HSM) 72-1012, Series 11, no. 110.* Washington, D.C.: U.S. Government Printing Office.

Rottersman, L. (1950). A comparison of the IQ scores on the new revised Stanford-Binet, Form L, the Wechsler Intelligence Scale for Children, and the Goodenough Draw-a-man test at the six year level. Unpublished master's thesis, Univ. of Nebraska. In: Harris, D. B. (ed.). (1963). *Children's drawings as measures of intellectual maturity.* New York: Harcourt, Brace & World.

Rouma, G. (1913). *Le langage graphique de l'enfant.* Brussels: Misch et Thron.

Rutter, M., and Hersov, L. (1977). *Child psychiatry. Modern approaches.* Oxford: Blackwell Scientific publ.

Schaefer, C. E., and Sternfield, M. (1971). Comparative validity of the Harris Quality and Point Scale. *Perceptual and Motor Skills, 33,* 997–998.

Schilder, P. (1935). *The image and appearance of the human body.* London: Kegan, Paul, Trench, Trubner.

Schmidt, L. D., and McGowan, J. F. (1959). The differentiation of human figure drawings. *Journal of Consulting Psychology, 23,* 129–133.

Schubert, D. (1969). Decrease of rated adjustment on repeat DAP tests apparently due to lower motivation. *Journal of Projective Techniques and Personality Assessment, 33,* 34.

Secord, P. F., and Jourard, S. (1953). The appraisal of body-cathexis: Body cathexis and the self. *Journal of Consulting and Clinical Psychology, 17,* 343–347.

Shaffer, J. P. (1964). Social and personality correlates of children's estimates of height. *Genetic Psychology Monographs, 70,* 97–134.

Sherman, L. J. (1958a). Sexual differentiation or artistic ability? *Journal of Clinical Psychology, 14,* 170–171.

———. (1958b). The influence of artistic quality on judgments of patient and non-patient status from human figure drawings. *Journal of Projective Techniques, 22,* 338–340.

Shirley, M., and Goodenough, F. (1932). A survey of the intelligence of deaf children in Minnesota Schools. *American Annals of the Deaf, 77,* 238–247.

Shontz, F. C. (1969). *Perceptual and cognitive aspects of body experience.* New York: Academic Press.

Shontz, F. C., and McNish, R. D. (1972). The human body as stimulus object: Estimates of distances between body landmarks. *Journal of Experimental Psychology, 95,* 20–24.

Silverstein, A. B., and Robinson, H. A. (1956). The representation of orthopedic disability in children's figure drawings. *Journal of Consulting Psychology, 20*, 333–341.

Silverstein, A. B., and Robinson, H. A. (1961). The representation of physique in children's figure drawings. *Journal of Consulting Psychology, 25*, 146–148.

Sims, N. (1951). Analysis of the human figure drawings of orthopedic and nonorthopedic children. Unpublished master's thesis, Univ. of Nebraska. In: Fisher, S. (ed.). (1986). *Development and structure of the body image*. Hillsdale, N.J.: Lawrence Erlbaum Ass.

Smith, F. O. (1937). What the Goodenough Intelligence Test measures. *Psychological Bulletin, 34*, 760–761.

Springer, N. N. (1938). A comparative study of the intelligence of deaf and hearing children. *American Annals of the Deaf, 83*, 138–152.

———. (1941). A study of drawings of maladjusted and adjusted children. *Journal of General Psychology, 58*, 131–138.

Starr, S., and Marcuse, F. L. (1959). Reliability in the DAP Test. *Journal of Projective Techniques, 23*, 83–86.

Stoller, R. J. (1968). *Sex and gender*. New York: Science House.

Strauch, A. B. (1976). The development of sex differences in spatial and verbal abilities. *American Psychologist*.

Sunal, C. S. (1976). A study of the effects of a perceptual-motor curriculum in body image, and space and directionality, for kindergarteners identified as having potential learning disabilities. Unpublished doctoral dissertation, Univ. of Maryland. In: Fisher, S. (ed.). (1986). *Development and structure of the body image*. Hillsdale, N.J.: Lawrence Erlbaum Ass.

Swensen, C. H. (1955). Sexual differentiation on the DAP Test. *Journal of Clinical Psychology, 11*, 37–41.

———. (1957). Empirical evaluations of human figure drawings. *Psychological Bulletin, 54*, 431–466.

———. (1968). Empirical evaluations of human figure drawings. *Psychological Bulletin, 70*, 20–44.

Swensen, C. H., and Newton, K. R. (1955). The development of sexual differentiation on the DAP test. *Journal of Clinical Psychology, 11*, 417–419.

Swensen, C. H., and Sipprelle, C. N. (1956). Some relationships among sexual characteristics of human figure drawings. *Journal of Projective Techniques, 20*, 224–226.

Vandenberg, S. G., and Kuse, A. R. (1979). Spatial ability: a critical review of the sex-linked major gene hypothesis. In: Wittig, M. A., and Petersen, A. C. (eds.). *Sex-related differences in cognitive functioning. Developmental issues*. New York: Academic Press.

Vane, J. R. (1967). An evaluation of the Harris revision of the Goodenough D-A-M Test. *Journal of Clinical Psychology, 23*, 375–377.

Vane, J. R., and Kessler, R. T. (1964). The Goodenough Draw-a-Man Test: Long term reliability and validity. *Journal of Clinical Psychology, 20*, 487–488.

Von Fieandt, K., and Moustgård, I. K. (1977). *The perceptual world*. London: Academic Press.

Waber, D. P. (1979). Cognitive abilities and sex-related variations. In: Wittig, M. A., & Petersen, C. C. (eds.). *Sex-related differences in cognitive functioning. Developmental issues*. New York: Academic Press.

Wapner, S. (1960). An experimental and theoretical approach to body image. Presented at Sixteenth International Congress of Psychology, Bonn. In: Fisher, S. (ed.). (1970). *Body experience in fantasy and behavior*. New York: Meredith Corp.

Watzlawick, P., Beavin, J., and Jackson, D. (1967). *Pragmatics of human communication*. New York: Norton.

Weider, A., and Noller, P. A. (1950). Objective studies of children's drawings of human figures. I: Sex awareness and socio-economic level. *Journal of Clinical Psychology, 6*, 319–325.

———. (1953). Objective studies of children's drawings of human figures. II: Sex, age, intelligence. *Journal of Clinical Psychology, 9*, 20–23.

Weininger, O., Rotenberg, G., and Henry, A. (1972). Body image of handicapped children. *Journal of Personality Assessment, 36*, 248–253.

Werner, H. (1964). *Comparative psychology of mental development*. New York: International Univ. Press.

Werner, H., and Kaplan, B. (1964). *Symbol formation*. New York: Wiley.

Whitaker, L. (1961). The use of an extended Draw-a-Person Test to identify homosexual and effeminate men. *Journal of Consulting Psychology, 25*, 482–485.

White, T. H. (1979). Correlations among the Wisc-R, PIAT and DAM. *Psychology in the Schools, 16*, 497–501.

Whitmyre, J. W. (1953). The significance of artistic excellence in the judgment of adjustment inferred from human figure drawings. *Journal of Consulting Psychology, 17*, 421–422.

Williams, J. H. (1935). Validity and reliability of the Goodenough Intelligence Test. *School and Society, 41*, 653–656.

Wisotsky, M. (1959). A note on the order of figure drawing among incarcerated alcoholics. *Journal of Clinical Psychology, 15*, 65.

Witkin, H. A., Lewis, H. B., Hirzman, M., Machover, K., Meisner, P. B., and Wapner, S. (1954). *Personality through perception*. New York: Harper.

Wittig, M. A., and Petersen, A. C. (1979). *Sex-related differences in cognitive functioning. Developmental issues*. New York: Academic Press.

Yater, A. C., Barclay, A. G., and McGilligan, R. (1969). Interrater-reliability of scoring Goodenough-Harris drawings by disadvantaged preschool children. *Perceptual and Motor Skills, 28*, 281–282.

Yepsen, L. N. (1929). The reliability of the Goodenough drawing test with feeble-minded subjects. *Journal of Educational Psychology, 20*, 448–451.

Index

Abraham, K., 243
Accessory objects. *See* Surrounding objects
Activity or action. *See* Movement represented in drawings
Adams, N. M., 246
Adolescents, 36, 42; and drawing development, 126, 210, 218; and expressions of sexual interest, 126; and sexual differences in drawing, 89. *See also* Older children; Puberty
Affectivity, 50, 205, 207, 210, 214, 218, 266
Age differentiation in drawn figures, 59, 184; and drawing development, 130–31; sex differences in, 87, 94–95, 130–31, 173–75
Age norms, 12, 25–27. *See also* Chronological age; Mental age
Aggression, 124, 127, 214; and body experience, 250, 254, 255–56; and projective drawing tests, 51, 55; and sex differences in drawing, 82, 83, 189, 190, 198, 229–30, 236; and words or names included in drawings, 120
Allport, C., 241
Anal character traits, 243, 244–45, 254
Analogic language, 6, 214–17, 219, 267

Ansbacher, H. L., 43
Anthony, J. E., 222
Anxiety, 135, 151, 262; and body experience, 239, 240, 243, 244; and drawings of clouds, 124; interpreting signs of, 63, 64, 65, 214; and line quality, 190
Apfeldorf, M., 58
Archetypal patterns, 14, 28
Armon, V., 88
Arms, 113, 114, 149, 209; cut off from body, 177; omission of, 157, 158; position of, 167–69; sex differences in drawing of, 73, 74, 112, 113, 157, 158, 165–69, 182, 183, 195
Arnheim, R., 29, 30–31, 209
Art education. *See* Learning, influence of
Artistic abilities, 26, 27, 45, 66
Art therapy, 70
Asymmetries, 112, 116. *See also* Symmetry

Babbling, 211
Back awareness, 243, 245, 251, 254
Balance, 14. *See also* Symmetry
Ballard, P. B., 11
Barclay, A. G., 39

About the Author

KAREN VIBEKE MORTENSEN is the head of the Child and Family Guidance Center of Copenhagen County and is author or coauthor of several books on children's drawings and adolescent psychiatry.